The World Almanac™
5,001
Incredible Facts for Kids on America's Past, Present, and Future

World Almanac for Kids™

WORLD ALMANAC BOOKS

Photographs copyright © Getty Images and Shuttterstock except pages 4 (White House/Pete Souza); 5 (Lyndon B. Johnson Presidential Library); 14-15 (Library of Congress); 18-19 (National Archives and Records Administration); 21, 25, 29 (Library of Congress); 30 (Metropolitan Museum of Art); 32, 40 (Library of Congress); 41 (National Archives and Records Administration); 43, 46-47 (U.S. Dept. of Defense); 51 (Library of Congress); 63 (U.S. Navy); 69 (National Portrait Gallery); 81, 158, 259-60 (Library of Congress).

World Almanac books may be purchased in bulk at special discounts for sales promotion, corporate gifts, fund-raising, or educational purposes. Special editions can also be created to specifications. For details, contact the Special Sales Department, World Almanac, 307 West 36th Street, 11th Floor, New York, NY 10018 or info@skyhorsepublishing.com.

Published by World Almanac, an imprint of Skyhorse Publishing, Inc., 307 West 36th Street, 11th Floor, New York, NY 10018.

www.skyhorsepublishing.com

10 9 8 7 6 5 4 3 2 1

Cover design by Brian Peterson
Cover photo credit: Getty Images and Shutterstock
Interior design by Bobi NYC

Library of Congress Cataloging-in-Publication Data is available on file.

Print ISBN: 978-1-5107-6716-4
Ebook ISBN: 978-1-5107-6717-1

Printed in China

contents

Entertainment

Geography

Living Things

Business and Science

Places

Transportation

535 Incredible Final Facts

Sports

Index

U.S. HISTORY

100 POWERFUL FACTS ABOUT THE PRESIDENTS

#	Name	Political Party	Dates Served
1	George Washington	Federalist	1789–1797
2	John Adams	Federalist	1797–1801
3	Thomas Jefferson	Democratic-Republican	1801–1809
4	James Madison	Democratic-Republican	1809–1817
5	James Monroe	Democratic-Republican	1817–1825
6	John Quincy Adams	National Republican	1825–1829
7	Andrew Jackson	Democrat	1829–1837
8	Martin Van Buren	Democrat	1837–1841
9	William Henry Harrison	Whig	1841
10	John Tyler	Whig	1841–1845
11	James K. Polk	Democrat	1845–1849
12	Zachary Taylor	Whig	1849–1850
13	Millard Fillmore	Whig	1850–1853
14	Franklin Pierce	Democrat	1853–1857
15	James Buchanan	Democrat	1857–1861
16	Abraham Lincoln	Republican	1861–1865
17	Andrew Johnson	Democrat	1865–1869
18	Ulysses S. Grant	Republican	1869–1877
19	Rutherford B. Hayes	Republican	1877–1881
20	James Garfield	Republican	1881
21	Chester A. Arthur	Republican	1881–1885
22	Grover Cleveland	Democrat	1885–1889
23	Benjamin Harrison	Republican	1889–1893
24	Grover Cleveland	Democrat	1893–1897
25	William McKinley	Republican	1897–1901
26	Theodore Roosevelt	Republican	1901–1909

#	Name	Political Party	Dates Served
27	William Howard Taft	Republican	1909–1913
28	Woodrow Wilson	Democrat	1913–1921
29	Warren G. Harding	Republican	1921–1923
30	Calvin Coolidge	Republican	1923–1928
31	Herbert Hoover	Republican	1929–1933
32	Franklin D. Roosevelt	Democrat	1933–1945
33	Harry S. Truman	Democrat	1945–1953
34	Dwight D. Eisenhower	Republican	1953–1961
35	John F. Kennedy	Democrat	1961–1963
36	Lyndon B. Johnson	Democrat	1963–1969
37	Richard M. Nixon	Republican	1969–1974
38	Gerald R. Ford	Republican	1974–1977
39	James E. Carter	Democrat	1977–1981
40	Ronald Reagan	Republican	1981–1989
41	George H.W. Bush	Republican	1989–1993
42	William J. Clinton	Democrat	1993–2001
43	George W. Bush	Republican	2001–2009
44	Barack Obama	Democrat	2009–2017
45	Donald J. Trump	Republican	2017–2021
46	Joseph R. Biden	Democrat	2021–

47. John Adams was the first president to live in the White House.

48. James Madison was the shortest president, at just 5 feet, 4 inches (1.63 m) tall.

49. Abraham Lincoln was the tallest president. He was 6 feet, 4 inches (1.9 m) tall.

50. John Tyler had 15 children.

51. George Washington wore false teeth made of ivory, gold, and elephant and walrus tusks.

52. James Buchanan was the only president who was never married.

53. Rutherford B. Hayes was the first president to have a telephone installed in the White House.

54. The first White House phone number was "1."

55. Benjamin Harrison was the first person to have electricity installed in the White House.

56. However, Benjamin Harrison was too afraid of getting an electric shock to touch the light switches himself.

57. James Garfield could write Latin with one hand and Greek with the other hand at the same time.

58. Grover Cleveland was the only president to be married in the White House.

59. Cleveland is also the only president to serve two nonconsecutive terms.

60. After his presidency, William Howard Taft served as the U.S. Supreme Court Chief Justice and swore in Presidents Calvin Coolidge and Herbert Hoover.

61. Theodore Roosevelt and Franklin D. Roosevelt were fifth cousins.

62. There have been two father-and-son presidential pairs: John Adams and John Quincy Adams and George H.W. Bush and George W. Bush.

63. There have been four presidential assassinations: Lincoln, Garfield, McKinley, and Kennedy.

64. James Madison was Princeton University's first graduate student.

65. Monrovia, the capital of Liberia, was named after James Monroe.

66. John Quincy Adams enjoyed skinny-dipping in the Potomac River.

67. Andrew Jackson participated in more than 100 duels.

68. Though he was president on the eve of the Civil War, James Buchanan called the conflict over slavery and states' rights "happily, a matter of but little practical importance" in his inaugural address.

69. Richard Nixon is the only president to resign from office.

70. Gerald Ford, who replaced Nixon, was appointed vice president in 1973 and assumed the presidency before ever appearing on a presidential ballot.

71. Ronald Reagan was a successful movie actor before becoming president.

72. While he was president, Grover Cleveland had a secret surgery to remove a cancerous tumor from his mouth.

73. Theodore Roosevelt was shot while giving a speech. He continued speaking for 90 minutes after the attempted assassination.

74. William Taft, the heaviest president, weighed 340 pounds (154 kg).

75. James Madison was the lightest president. He weighed about 100 pounds (45 kg).

76. Franklin Roosevelt was the only president to serve four terms.

77. Martin Van Buren was the first president born in the United States.

78. William Henry Harrison was only president for a month before dying of pneumonia.

79. Millard Fillmore and his wife established the first White House library.

80. The middle initial "S" in Ulysses S. Grant's and Harry S. Truman's names doesn't stand for anything.

81. Rutherford B. Hayes held the first Easter Egg Roll on the White House lawn in 1878.

82. Woodrow Wilson was the first president to have a speech heard on the radio.

83. Herbert Hoover was the first president born west of the Mississippi River.

84. Lyndon Johnson is the only president to be sworn in on an airplane.

85. Theodore Roosevelt, Woodrow Wilson, Jimmy Carter, and Barack Obama have all won the Nobel Peace Prize.

86. Donald Trump was the first president who did not have a background in politics or the military.

87. Eight presidents were left-handed: James Garfield, Herbert Hoover, Harry Truman, Gerald Ford, Ronald Reagan, George H.W. Bush, Bill Clinton, and Barack Obama.

88. Only five presidents have worn beards. All served as president during the 19th century.

89. Five presidents did not have biological children. They were George Washington, James Madison, Andrew Jackson, James Polk, and James Buchanan.

90. Five presidents were elected without winning the popular vote: John Quincy Adams, Rutherford B. Hayes, Benjamin Harrison, George W. Bush, and Donald Trump.

91. Jimmy Carter became the longest living president in March 2019, at age 94 years, 172 days.

PRESIDENTIAL PETS

92. Herbert Hoover's son had two pet alligators and an opossum living in the White House.

93. Calvin Coolidge and first lady Grace Coolidge had a pet raccoon named Rebecca that walked on a leash.

94. Theodore Roosevelt and his children had many unusual pets, including a pig, several bears, a badger, a snake named Emily Spinach, and a one-legged rooster.

95. Andrew Jackson had a parrot named Polly who liked to swear. She learned the curse words from Jackson himself.

96. During World War I, Woodrow Wilson had a herd of sheep grazing on the front lawn of the White House.

97. John F. Kennedy's dog, Pushinka, was a gift from the Soviet Union. Security officials checked her for implanted listening devices before she moved into the White House.

98. Pushinka's mother had flown in outer space on one of the *Sputnik* missions.

99. Bill Clinton's cat, Socks, was the first presidential pet to have a website.

100. Although several presidential pets have been rescues, Joe Biden's dog, Major, was the first dog adopted from an animal shelter to live in the White House.

25

MAGNIFICENT MARTIN LUTHER KING, JR. FACTS

1. King's birth name was Michael King, Jr. His father renamed himself and his son after the Protestant German religious leader Martin Luther.

2. King grew up in Atlanta, Georgia, and was the son of a Baptist minister.

3. King skipped two grades and enrolled in college at age 15.

4. He won a public-speaking contest when he was a teenager.

5. King was arrested 29 times.

6. One of King's most famous essays, "Letter from a Birmingham Jail," was written after he was arrested for leading a protest march in Birmingham, Alabama.

7. In 1956, King's house was bombed while his wife and daughter were inside. Neither were hurt.

8. King was almost assassinated ten years before his death. In 1958, a woman stabbed him with a letter opener while he was autographing books in a store.

9. King was awarded the Nobel Peace Prize when he was 35 years old. At the time, he was the youngest person to win.

10. Between 1957 and 1968, King traveled more than six million miles and made more than 2,500 speeches.

11. He traveled all over the world, including visits to England, Ghana, and India.

12. King was married to Coretta Scott King and had four children: two sons and two daughters.

13. In the 1950s, King was the pastor of the Dexter Avenue Baptist Church in Montgomery, Alabama.

14. He helped lead the successful Montgomery bus boycott in 1955–1956.

15. He wrote his first public political speech in less than an hour.

16. King wrote six books.

17. On August 28, 1963, King delivered his famous "I Have a Dream" speech before 250,000 people in front of the Washington Monument.

18. He made up parts of that speech on the spot.

19. King was named *Time* magazine's Man of the Year in 1963.

20. In 1965, King was present when President Lyndon Johnson signed the Civil Rights Act into law.

21. On April 4, 1968, King was assassinated as he stood on the balcony at the Lorraine Motel in Memphis, Tennessee.

22. King was awarded the Presidential Medal of Freedom in 1977.

23. He is the only non-president to have a national holiday in his name.

24. Martin Luther King Jr. Day was first celebrated in 1986.

25. King is also the only non-president honored with his own memorial on Washington, D.C.'s National Mall.

30 FAR-TRAVELING FACTS ABOUT THE PIONEERS

1. In the Louisiana Purchase of 1803, the United States claimed a massive amount of territory west of the Mississippi River from France.

2. Hundreds of thousands of people moved west after gold was discovered in California in 1848.

3. The Homestead Act of 1862 promised 160 acres of land in certain territories to anyone who lived on it.

4. There were few trees to use for lumber in the midwestern prairies, so settlers there dug houses into the sod, or ground. These houses were called "soddies."

5. The westward movement had a devastating effect on many Native American populations, who were killed or forced to move off their land as others moved west.

6. The first overland migrants to Oregon were a group of 70 pioneers in 1841.

7. The first group bound for Oregon traveled a fur traders' route from Missouri over the Rocky Mountains and northwest to the Columbia River.

8. The route from Missouri to Oregon soon became known as the Oregon Trail.

9. The Oregon Trail was about 2,000 miles (3,219 km) long.

10. The Oregon Trail traveled from Missouri through present-day Kansas, Nebraska, Wyoming (where it crossed the Rocky Mountains), Idaho, and Oregon.

11. Traveling the full length of the Oregon Trail took four to six months.

12. In 1843, 1,000 people headed west on the Oregon Trail. Most were farmers and their families.

13. The 1843 Oregon Trail group included more than 100 wagons and 5,000 head of cattle.

14. Missionary Marcus Whitman, who had traveled west with his wife a few years earlier, led the 1843 trip.

15. By the early 1850s, up to 50,000 people a year traveled the Oregon Trail.

16. So many wagons traveled west that you can still see the ruts their wheels made in the ground in many places in the western U.S.

17. Other important western trails included the California Trail and the Mormon Trail.

18. Pioneers carried everything they could in their covered wagons, including bedding, furniture, household supplies, tools, guns, and food.

19. Covered wagons were called "prairie schooners," because they looked like ships sailing over the grass.

20. A typical wagon was just six feet (2 m) wide and 12 feet (4 m) long.

21. Many household goods were abandoned along the way to lighten the load as travelers faced rushing rivers and steep mountain trails.

22. Travelers had to leave in April or May to finish the journey to Oregon before heavy winter snows made the trip impossible.

23. To rest at night, pioneers often drew their wagons into a protective circle. Horses were kept in the middle of the circle.

24. On a good day, a wagon could travel up to 20 miles (32 km) on the trail. But mud and bad weather often slowed travel.

25. It's estimated that about 20,000 people died along the Oregon Trail.

26. The most common causes of death on the Oregon Trail were disease and accidents.

27. Travelers burned buffalo poop (called buffalo chips) for fuel.

28. Independence Rock in Wyoming marked the halfway point of the Oregon Trail journey. Thousands of settlers carved their names on this rock.

29. The completion of the transcontinental railroad in 1869 was the beginning of the end for covered-wagon journeys, as a train could cross the country in as little as one week.

30. In 1890, the U.S. government said the frontier no longer existed because so many people had moved to the West.

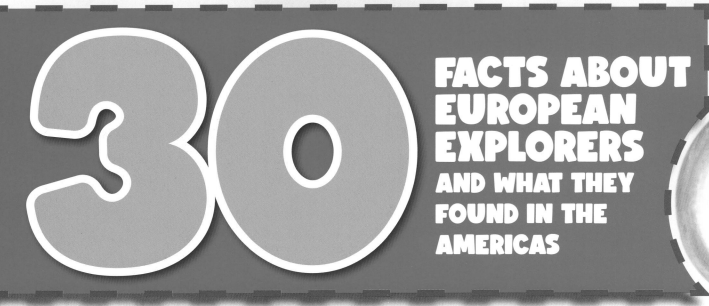

30 FACTS ABOUT EUROPEAN EXPLORERS AND WHAT THEY FOUND IN THE AMERICAS

1. Juan Ponce de León led the first European expedition to Florida in 1513. He was searching for the mythical "Fountain of Youth."

2. Hernando de Soto landed in Florida and headed west between 1539 and 1542. He is believed to be the first European to cross the Mississippi River.

3. Francisco Vásquez de Coronado, the first European to explore the American Southwest, traveled through modern-day Arizona, New Mexico, Texas, and western Kansas.

4. Juan Batista de Anza was the first person of European descent to establish an overland trail from Mexico to the northern Pacific coast of California.

5. De Anza's path led through the Sonoran Desert and brought hundreds of settlers to California during the mid-1700s.

6. De Anza also founded the cities of San Francisco and San Jose.

7. Spanish explorer Álvar Núñez Cabeza de Vaca arrived in Florida in 1527. Then he traveled from Florida to Texas on a raft and walked from Texas to Mexico City.

8. Cabeza de Vaca and his fellow travelers were the first Europeans to see the bison.

9. "Cabeza de Vaca" means "head of a cow."

10. Historians aren't sure if Juan Rodríguez Cabrillo was Spanish or Portuguese, but they do believe he was the first European to explore the Californian coast.

11. In 1542, Cabrillo sailed from Acapulco to southern California and claimed California for King Charles I of Spain. He also named San Diego Bay and Santa Barbara.

12. French explorer and soldier Antoine Laumet de la Mothe de Cadillac founded the city of Detroit in 1701.

13. One of the earliest descriptions of North America was written by Pierre François-Xavier de Charlevoix, a French Jesuit priest, explorer, and writer.

14. Juan de Fuca was a Greek navigator who sailed for Spain under a Spanish name. His original name was Apostolos Valerianos.

15. De Fuca may have been the first European to see the northwestern coast of the United States. He sailed from Mexico to Vancouver Island in 1592.

16. Most people didn't believe de Fuca's story about the strait he discovered. He didn't get credit until Charles William Barkley charted it nearly 200 years later.

17. The Strait of Juan de Fuca, which connects the Pacific Ocean to Puget Sound, was named after him in 1787.

18. French explorer René-Robert Cavelier, sieur de La Salle was sent by the French king to explore North America in 1682. He was the first European to travel the length of the Mississippi River.

19. La Salle named the entire Mississippi basin Louisiana, in honor of the French King, and claimed it for France on April 9, 1682.

20. La Salle also explored Lake Michigan, Lake Huron, Lake Erie, and Lake Ontario.

21. Marcus de Niza was a Spanish priest who explored what is now western New Mexico in 1539 in search of the legendary "Seven Cities of Gold."

22. De Niza and his companion, an enslaved Moroccan explorer named Estevanico, reported they did discover the golden cities, but they turned out to be Zuni Indian pueblos.

23. Estevanico, who had previously explored Texas, died during the expedition with de Niza.

24. The first Europeans in Texas were probably Alonso Álvarez de Pineda and his crew. They arrived there in 1519.

25. De Pineda named Corpus Christi Bay because he explored the area on the Catholic feast day of Corpus Christi.

26. Gaspar de Portolá, a Spanish soldier, leader, and explorer, traveled up the California coast in 1768. Portolá led a large group of settlers, missionaries, and soldiers to San Diego and Monterey in order to establish new Franciscan missions.

27. Giovanni da Verrazzano was an Italian explorer sailing for France when he landed at Cape Fear in 1524, then sailed north, to New York and up to Maine and Canada.

28. Verrazzano was the first European to explore present-day New York. The Verrazzano Narrows Bridge in New York City is named after him.

29. In 1728, sailing for Russia, Vitus Bering and Aleksei Chirikov traveled through the area now called the Bering Strait.

30. In 1741, Bering and Chirikov arrived in the Aleutian Islands and mainland Alaska, both of which they claimed for Russia.

30 FACTS ABOUT NATIVE AMERICAN CULTURE BEFORE COLONIZATION

1. The first peoples in North America hiked over a land bridge from Asia to what is now Alaska about 12,000 years ago.

2. About 10 million people lived in what is now the United States before Europeans arrived.

3. Historians divide pre-colonial North America—excluding present-day Mexico—into 10 culture areas: the Arctic, the Subarctic, the Northeast, the Southeast, the Plains, the Southwest, the Great Basin, California, the Northwest Coast, and the Plateau.

4. The Arctic area extends into Alaska and included the Inuit and the Aleut.

5. The Inuit, who lived in the northern part of the region, were nomadic. They hunted seals, polar bears, and other animals.

6. The Aleut lived in fishing villages along the southern shore.

7. The Subarctic area covered Alaska and western Canada and was home to few people. Native groups in the Subarctic mostly either spoke Athabaskan or Algonquian.

8. Iroquoian and Algonquian were the two main language groups in the Northeast culture area, which covered the Atlantic coast as far south as North Carolina and inland to the Mississippi River valley.

9. Iroquoian speakers included the Cayuga, Oneida, Erie, Onondaga, Seneca, and Tuscarora. Most lived in villages near rivers and lakes.

10. Algonquian speakers included the Pequot, Meskwaki, Shawnee, Wampanoag, Lenape, and Menominee. They farmed and fished in villages along the ocean.

11. Farming tribes such as the Cherokee, Chickasaw, Choctaw, Creek, and Seminole made up the Southeast cultural area.

12. Tribes such as the Sioux lived in the Great Plains. They were once settled hunters and farmers, but the Great Plains tribes became more nomadic after horses were introduced in the 1700s.

13. Southwestern tribes lived in the desert. Some, like the Hopi, Zuni, Yaqui, and Quechan, were settled farmers.

14. Other Southwestern tribes were nomads. These groups included the Navajo and the Apache.

15. The people of the Great Basin included the Ute and Paiute. They were mostly nomadic hunters and gatherers.

16. Before colonization, the California area had more people living there than any other part of the U.S. About 300,000 people called this area home.

17. California groups included more than 100 different tribes that spoke more than 200 different languages.

18. The Northwest Coast provided plenty of food. Native people, such as the Tlingit, Coos, Chinook, and Salish, lived in villages.

19. The Plateau area covered present-day Idaho, Montana, and eastern Oregon and Washington. Most people of the Plateau fished, hunted, and gathered berries and nuts for food.

20. Plateau tribes included the Klamath, Klikitat, Modoc, Nez Perce, Walla Walla, and Yakima.

21. Native homes varied by location. Some tribes in the Northeast lived in large permanent structures called longhouses.

22. Many tribes in the Southwest lived in stone and dried mud houses called pueblos. These structures had thick walls to keep cool air in and hot air out.

23. Nomadic tribes such as the Ute and Paiute built wikiups out of branches and leaves. These structures were light and easy to move.

24. The Navajo built houses called hogans out of packed mud and bark.

25. Native Americans used many different tools and weapons made of stone, animal bones, and wood.

26. Some tribes carved boats out of trees and wove nets and baskets.

27. Others used clay to make bowls and other types of pottery.

28. Native Americans domesticated dogs, llamas, and alpacas.

29. Crops included corn, beans, squash, and potatoes.

30. The largest Native American city in what is now the U.S. was Cahokia in southwestern Illinois. It had a population of 10,000 to 20,000 people.

30 ESSENTIAL FACTS ABOUT NATIVE AMERICAN HISTORY AFTER COLONIZATION

1. European exploration and colonization spelled disaster for Native American cultures throughout the United States.

2. Many Native Americans died of diseases brought by the settlers. They had no immunity to European diseases such as smallpox and measles.

3. By the 1890s, the Native American population had dropped to an estimated 250,000.

4. Colonial wars in the Northeast forced many Native tribes to take sides against each other.

5. Between 1814 and 1824, President Andrew Jackson negotiated treaties to take land from Native American tribes.

6. These treaties gave the United States control of three-quarters of Alabama and Florida, as well as parts of Georgia, Tennessee, Mississippi, Kentucky, and North Carolina.

7. In 1830, the federal government passed the Indian Removal Act to force the relocation of Southeastern tribes so that European Americans could have their land.

8. Between 1830 and 1838, the government forced nearly 100,000 Native Americans out of the southern states and into "Indian Territory" (later the state of Oklahoma).

9. This series of forced migrations is known as the Trail of Tears. Thousands of others died on their forced marches west.

10. The people of the Great Plains relied on bison for food, clothing, and many other needs. However, white settlers and hunters had killed almost all of the bison by the end of the 19th century.

11. Without food and with others moving onto their lands, Plains tribes were forced onto government reservations.

12. Spanish colonists and missionaries enslaved or killed many of the Pueblo Indians.

13. During the second half of the 19th century, the federal government resettled most of the Southwest Native peoples onto reservations.

14. Native Americans in California were also treated harshly by Spanish colonizers and missionaries. In the San Diego area, forced labor and disease almost wiped out this area's Native population.

15. In 1860, the first Native American boarding school was established on the Yakima Reservation in Washington state.

16. The goal of these schools was to use education to force Native Americans to replace their cultural traditions and language and assimilate.

17. All but one of the boarding schools were in the western part of the country. The lone eastern Native American boarding school was the Carlisle Indian School in Carlisle, Pennsylvania.

18. The Carlisle School was run by Richard Henry Pratt, a former Army officer. His motto was "Kill the Indian, save the man."

19. In 1978, the Indian Child Welfare Act finally gave Native American parents the legal right to deny their children's placement in school outside the reservation.

20. In 1924, the Indian Citizenship Act was passed, granting U.S. citizenship to Native Americans.

21. Charles Curtis became the first Native American to serve as vice president when he was elected in 1928. Curtis grew up on a Kaw reservation.

22. Curtis was also the first Native American to serve in the House of Representatives (1893–1907) and the Senate (1906–1929).

23. In 1934, the Indian Reorganization Act gave more control to tribal governments and helped reverse some policies that forced Native Americans to assimilate.

24. Wounded Knee, on the Pine Ridge Indian Reservation in southwestern South Dakota, has been the site of two major conflicts between Native Americans and the U.S. government.

25. In 1890, U.S. Army forces at Wounded Knee killed nearly 300 Native Americans. At least half of the dead were women and children.

26. The massacre occurred as federal soldiers attempted to disarm a tribal encampment.

27. In 1973, members of the American Indian Movement, a militant civil rights group, occupied Wounded Knee for 71 days to protest conditions on the reservation.

28. In 2009, President Barack Obama signed the Native American Apology Resolution. This document apologized for the mistreatment and violence against Native Americans throughout history.

29. One in four Native Americans lives below the poverty line.

30. According to the U.S. Census Bureau, the current total population of Native Americans in the United States is 6.79 million, or just over 2 percent of the population.

25 WONDERFUL WOMEN'S SUFFRAGE FACTS

1. The 19th amendment to the U.S. Constitution, granting women the right to vote, was passed in 1920. But many nonwhite women were still prevented from voting.

2. Many of the first women's suffrage activists got their start in the abolition, or antislavery, movement before the Civil War.

3. Lucretia Mott and Elizabeth Cady Stanton organized the first U.S. women's rights convention in Seneca Falls, New York, on July 19–20, 1848.

4. Mott and Stanton originally met at an antislavery event in London, England.

5. Only women could attend the first day of the Seneca Falls Convention, but everyone was welcome on the second day.

6. Elizabeth Cady Stanton declared the convention was a "protest against a form of government, existing without the consent of the governed— to declare our right to be free as man is free."

7. The convention also saw the reading of the "Declaration of Sentiments," which was modeled after the Declaration of Independence.

8. For two decades, there were two major women's suffrage groups. One group wanted to include women in the passage of the 14th and 15th amendments, which granted Black men equal protection under the law and the right to vote.

9. The other group feared adding women meant the amendments would not pass.

PRESIDENT WILSON IS DECEIVING THE WORLD WHEN HE APPEARS AS THE PROPHET OF DEMOCRACY
PRESIDENT WILSON HAS OPPOSED THOSE WHO DEMAND DEMOCRACY FOR THIS COUNTRY
HE IS RESPONSIBLE FOR THE DISFRANCHISEMENT OF MILLIONS OF AMERICANS
WE IN AMERICA KNOW THIS THE WORLD WILL FIND HIM OUT.

10. In 1890, the two groups merged to form the National American Women's Suffrage Association.

11. Women's suffrage leader Susan B. Anthony and 15 other women voted illegally in the 1872 presidential election.

12. All 16 women who voted in the 1872 election with Anthony were arrested. Anthony was convicted and fined $100, which she refused to pay.

13. Victoria Woodhull ran for president in 1872, representing the Equal Rights Party.

14. The text that would become the 19th Amendment in 1920 was first proposed in Congress in 1878.

15. The official colors of the women's suffrage movement were gold, white, and violet. The colors stood for "Give Women the Vote."

16. National suffrage organizations printed flyers in many different languages besides English in order to reach immigrant populations.

17. Alice Paul wanted the suffrage movement to be more militant. In 1913, she helped form the Congressional Union for Woman Suffrage.

18. Paul's group demonstrated outside the White House in 1917. Their protests ended in violence when guards attacked many of the women.

19. Alice Paul was jailed for her activities and sent to a psychiatric ward in the prison when she went on a hunger strike.

20. In January 1918, President Woodrow Wilson announced his support for the 19th Amendment.

21. Many states granted women the right to vote in local elections before the federal government passed the 19th amendment.

22. These states included Wyoming, Utah, Colorado, Idaho, Washington, California, Oregon, Montana, Arizona, Kansas, Alaska, Illinois, North Dakota, Indiana, Nebraska, Michigan, Arkansas, New York, South Dakota, and Oklahoma.

23. Wisconsin, Illinois, and Michigan were the first states to ratify the 19th Amendment. They all ratified it on June 10, 1919, six days after it was approved by Congress.

24. Tennessee was the 36th state to ratify the 19th Amendment. Ratification by 36 states was required under the U.S. Constitution to make the amendment law.

25. Mississippi didn't ratify the 19th Amendment until 1984.

50 CRUCIAL FACTS ABOUT THE CIVIL RIGHTS MOVEMENT

25 DATES TO KNOW

1. **1948:** President Harry S. Truman signs an order aimed at desegregating the armed forces and military bases.

2. **1954:** The U.S. Supreme Court decision, *Brown v. Board of Education of Topeka*, says that segregated schools are unconstitutional.

3. **1955:** Black 14-year-old Emmett Till is murdered in Mississippi, for allegedly flirting with a white woman. His mother insists on an open coffin so the world can see what happened to her son, and a photo of Till in his coffin spreads widely.

4. **1955:** Black seamstress and civil rights activist Rosa Parks is arrested after she refuses to give up her seat on a bus for a white passenger, setting off the Montgomery bus boycott.

5. **1956:** After more than a year, the Montgomery bus boycott ends when the Supreme Court declares Alabama's laws on segregated public transportation were unconstitutional.

6. **1957:** Martin Luther King Jr. becomes a founding member and leader of the Southern Christian Leadership Conference (SCLC), which uses nonviolent actions to fight against racism.

7. **1957:** Nine Black students integrate the all-white high school in Little Rock, Arkansas. The teens become known as the Little Rock Nine.

8. **1960:** Four Black college students stage a sit-in at a Woolworth's lunch counter in Greensboro, North Carolina. The sit-in movement spreads all over the South, eventually leading to the desegregation of lunch counters and restaurants.

9. **1960:** The Student Nonviolent Coordinating Committee is formed to provide young African Americans a voice in the civil rights movement.

10. **1960:** Armed guards escort six-year-old Ruby Bridges to an all-white school in New Orleans. She has to sit alone in a classroom with her teacher, but becomes a powerful symbol of equal rights.

11. **1961:** The Freedom Rides begin. This movement sent Black and white young people to ride buses together throughout the South to challenge ongoing segregation on buses. Riders faced violent attacks.

12. **1962:** James Meredith becomes the first Black student enrolled at the University of Mississippi.

13. **1963:** Photos and TV news footage showing violence against civil rights demonstrators in Birmingham, Alabama, makes the nation more aware of racist conditions and sways public sympathy toward the marchers, many of whom are children and teenagers.

14. **1963:** In June, President John F. Kennedy introduces a civil rights bill to Congress.

15. **1963:** On August 28, about 250,000 people gather peacefully on the National Mall in the March on Washington for Jobs and Freedom. Martin Luther King, Jr., delivers his famous "I Have a Dream" speech.

16. **1963:** Four Black girls are killed when a bomb explodes at Birmingham's 16th Street Baptist Church on September 15. The church was targeted as a meeting place for civil rights organizers.

17. **1964:** During Freedom Summer, groups of Black and white activists traveled throughout Mississippi to increase the number of registered Black voters. Three of these activists—two white men from the north and one Black man from the south—were murdered.

18. **1964:** President Lyndon B. Johnson signs the Civil Rights Act, aimed at ending employment discrimination and segregation in public facilities, into law.

19. **1965:** On February 21, African American leader Malcolm X is assassinated while speaking in New York City.

20. **1965:** In March, Martin Luther King, Jr., makes several attempts to lead voting rights marchers from Selma to Montgomery, Alabama. Footage of marchers being attacked by state troopers airs nationally on TV.

21. **1965:** The Voting Rights Act passes, outlawing discriminatory practices against African Americans registering to vote.

22. **1966:** Huey Newton and Bobby Seale found the Black Panthers, a group that takes a more radical approach to ending racial discrimination and police brutality.

23. **1967:** The Supreme Court decision *Loving v. Virginia* makes interracial marriage legal in all states.

24. **1968:** Martin Luther King, Jr., is assassinated on April 4.

25. **1968:** President Lyndon B. Johnson signs the Fair Housing Act, aimed at preventing racial discrimination in housing, into law.

25 CIVIL RIGHTS FIGURES TO KNOW

1. **Martin Luther King, Jr.:** The most prominent figure in the civil rights movement, King focused on nonviolent means to achieve equality.

2. **Malcolm X:** A member of the Nation of Islam until 1964, Malcolm X encouraged Black people to defend themselves "by any means necessary" and initially rejected integration.

3. **Rosa Parks:** Called "the mother of the civil rights movement," Parks's refusal to give up her seat on a bus sparked the Montgomery bus boycott.

4. **Claudette Colvin:** Nine months before Rosa Parks refused to move to the back of the bus, 15-year-old Claudette Colvin was arrested for this very same act of defiance. As one of four women plaintiffs in *Browder v. Gayle*, she was part of the court case that successfully overturned bus segregation laws in Alabama.

5. **John Lewis:** As a young man, Lewis organized and took part in marches and sit-ins and was targeted and injured by police. He went on to become a U.S. congressman.

6. **Bayard Rustin:** An adviser to Martin Luther King, Jr., Rustin played a major role in organizing the Montgomery bus boycott and the March on Washington.

7. **James Farmer:** The leader of the Congress of Racial Equality (CORE), Farmer organized the 1961 Freedom Rides.

8. **Medgar Evers:** A civil rights activist in Mississippi, Evers was assassinated in front of his home in 1963.

9. **Myrlie Ivers-Williams:** Medgar Evers's widow was also an activist and served as chairman of the board of the National Association for the Advancement of Colored People (NAACP).

10. **Ella Baker:** Longtime civil rights activist Baker created the Student Nonviolent Coordinating Committee (SNCC) because she felt young people were the key to advancing civil rights. She believed voting rights were the key to freedom.

11. **Thurgood Marshall:** Before he became the first Black U.S. Supreme Court Justice in 1967, Marshall worked as a civil rights attorney and took part in many important cases, including *Brown v. Board of Education of Topeka*.

12. **Asa Philip Randolph:** Founder of the first African American labor union in 1925, Randolph went on to become a major figure behind 1963's March on Washington.

13. **Roy Wilkins:** The executive secretary and later, executive director, of the NAACP was a key organizer of the March on Washington and the Selma-Montgomery marches.

14. **Whitney Young:** An adviser to Presidents John F. Kennedy, Lyndon Johnson, and Richard Nixon, Young led the National Urban League into a major force for increasing employment for Black workers.

15. **Linda Brown:** Brown was just seven years old when she tried to integrate her local school in Topeka, Kansas, in a case that eventually led to the Supreme Court ruling "separate but equal" schools were unconstitutional.

16. **Oliver L. Brown:** Linda's father, Brown became the lead plaintiff when the NAACP took the Topeka Board of Education to court to force school integration.

17. **Elizabeth Eckford:** One of the Little Rock Nine who integrated a high school in Little Rock, Arkansas, Eckford became famous in a photograph taken as she tried to enter the school passing a crowd of jeering, spitting white students and adults.

18. **Ernest Green:** One of the Little Rock Nine, Green became the first African American graduate of Little Rock High School in 1958.

19. **Septima Poinsette Clark:** After she lost her teaching job for being a member of the NAACP, Clark founded Citizenship Schools in South Carolina to teach African Americans how to read and write, as well as how to organize and gain political power.

20. **Fred Shuttlesworth:** A major civil rights leader, Shuttlesworth was one of the founders of SCLC and helped organize the Selma-Montgomery marches.

21. **Dorothy Height:** Height was the president of the National Council of Negro Women, which she led from 1957 until 1997.

22. **Pauli Murray:** A lawyer and activist, Murray wrote *States' Laws on Race and Color*, a key reference book for civil rights lawyers.

23. **Fannie Lou Hamer:** After being arrested and savagely beaten for her role in a protest march, Hamer became one of the most outspoken civil rights activists of the 1960s.

24. **Shirley Chisholm:** Chisholm became the first Black woman elected to the U.S. House of Representatives. In 1972, she became the first Black woman to run for president when she tried to win the Democratic nomination.

25. **Daisy Bates:** A journalist and NAACP leader in Arkansas, Bates worked to spread news of the Little Rock Nine and other desegregation efforts in the media.

40 HARD-WORKING FACTS ABOUT THE LABOR MOVEMENT

1. The goal of the labor movement is to protect the rights and safety of workers.

2. Labor groups focused on better pay, safer working conditions, and reasonable hours.

3. The earliest recorded strike occurred in 1768 when tailors in New York organized to protest a cut in pay.

4. The first major trade union in the U.S. was the Federal Society of Journeymen Cordwainers (shoemakers), which formed in Philadelphia in 1794.

5. Local craft unions became common in cities through the 1800s.

6. In 1852, the International Typographical Union became the first national union to bring together local unions.

7. In the 19th century, unions mostly represented skilled trade workers, not factory workers.

8. Almost all early union members were white males. There were few unions for African Americans or women until much later.

9. The girls and women of the Lowell textile mills became an exception in the mostly male early labor movement when they went on strike in 1834.

10. The first national labor union was the aptly named National Labor Union. It operated between 1866 and 1873.

11. The NLU's goal was to organize skilled and unskilled laborers, farmers, and reformers into a group that would push Congress to limit the workday to eight hours.

12. The National Labor Union may have had as many as 500,000 members during its short life.

13. The NLU opposed strikes and focused on political action.

14. Black caulkers in the shipbuilding industry held a strike at the Washington Navy Yard in 1835.

15. Women tailors, shoe binders, mill workers, and laundresses formed their own unions.

16. In 1867, the National Union for Cigar Makers was the first union to welcome women and African Americans.

17. In 1912, the International Brotherhood of Electrical Workers began accepting female telephone operators.

18. In 1925, Asa Philip Randolph founded the first labor union that was mostly made up of African Americans, the Brotherhood of Sleeping Car Porters.

19. Randolph was finally able to gain recognition for the Brotherhood of Sleeping Car Porters by the Pullman Car Company, the American Federation of Labor (AFL), and the U.S. government in 1937.

20. Owners fought back against labor demands by firing workers. Often, they would pit one ethnic group against another when hiring new workers.

21. When Irish workers won raises in pay from the railroads, owners replaced them with lower-paid Chinese workers.

22. In 1867, more than 2,000 Chinese workers on the transcontinental railroad walked off their jobs to protest low pay compared with white workers. Their strike failed after the railroad owner cut off their food and supplies.

23. The U.S. government often sent troops to break up strikes.

24. The Federation of Organized Trades and Labor Unions was formed in 1881.

25. Five years later, the American Federation of Labor (AFL) formed.

26. In 1913, Congress created the Department of Labor.

27. The Clayton Antitrust Act of 1914 made it legal for employees to strike and boycott their employers.

28. The federal government passed the Fair Labor Standards Acts of 1938, which called for minimum wage, overtime pay, and basic child labor laws.

29. Union membership grew quickly during the Great Depression of the 1930s.

30. The Congress of Industrial Organizations (CIO) organized large numbers of Black workers into labor unions for the first time.

31. There were more than 200,000 African Americans in the CIO in 1940.

32. After World War II, unions used collective bargaining agreements to work out new and improved contracts with employers.

33. In 1955, the AFL and CIO merged to form the AFL-CIO.

34. Support from the AFL-CIO helped pass civil rights laws in the 1960s.

35. César Chávez and Dolores Huerta formed the National Farm Workers Association in the 1960s to protect the rights of migrant workers, who were mostly Mexican-American. The NFWA later changed its name to the United Farm Workers (UFW).

36. In the late 1960s and early 1970s, Chávez and Huerta helped organize a national grape boycott to improve conditions for farm workers. The boycott received support from consumers all over the U.S.

37. In 1979, 21 million Americans were members of labor unions, the highest number in history.

38. Union membership declined sharply during the 1980s. By the end of the decade, less than 17 percent of American workers belonged to unions.

39. Government employees, including police, firefighters, and teachers, are more likely to be in unions than workers for corporations or small businesses.

40. In recent years, the biggest gains in union membership have been among workers younger than 35.

60

MOVING FACTS ABOUT IMMIGRATION

1. The United States was built on immigration. Some 2 million Europeans migrated to the United States before 1840.

2. Most early immigrants were British.

3. The Puritans, who landed in what is now Massachusetts in 1620, were among the first immigrants. They were looking for freedom to practice their religion.

4. Immigration was relatively free and open during the 18th and early 19th centuries.

5. Between 1846 and 1851, almost one million people emigrated from Ireland to escape starvation during the Irish Potato Famine.

6. About 4.5 million Irish emigrated to the United States between 1820 and 1930.

7. About five million Germans emigrated to the U.S. during the 19th century.

8. Many immigrants traveled to the Midwest and became farmers.

9. Many German immigrants settled in cities such as Milwaukee, St. Louis, and Cincinnati, which still have large German populations.

10. In the late 1800s, more immigrants arrived from Poland, Russia, and Italy.

11. Jewish immigrants came to America to escape religious persecution in Europe and Russia.

12. Many immigrants believed the United States was a land of plenty. A common expression said the streets were paved with gold.

13. In reality, life in the U.S. could be very difficult.

14. Many immigrants lived in cities such as New York, Philadelphia, and Chicago where major industries demanded waves of inexpensive labor, but many immigrants lived in poverty.

15. Immigrants gathered with others from their home countries in ethnic neighborhoods where familiar languages and traditions could be maintained.

16. Many immigrants lived in crowded tenement buildings. Diseases such as tuberculosis were common.

17. Some immigrants worked for very low wages in sweatshops that operated out of the same overcrowded tenements.

18. Jacob Riis published a book called *How the Other Half Lives*. His descriptions and photos exposed the harsh life in the tenements to middle- and upper-class Americans.

19. The government did little to help immigrants. Instead, religious organizations and neighborhood charities set up schools and provided food and medical care.

20. Nearly 12 million immigrants arrived in the United States between 1870 and 1900.

21. Between 1849 and 1882, a large number of Asian immigrants settled in the western United States.

22. About 25,000 Chinese immigrants came to California during the Gold Rush in the late 1840s and early 1850s.

23. The influx of Asians caused racist or anti-immigrant sentiment among certain parts of America's white population.

24. Many Chinese immigrants worked on the transcontinental railroad.

25. In 1882, the federal government stopped immigration from China by passing the Chinese Exclusion Act.

26. The Chinese Exclusion Act was the first U.S. law to block immigrants based on their race or nation of origin.

27. Before 1892, states regulated immigration.

28. The federal government wanted to control immigration, so it opened a processing center at Ellis Island in 1892.

29. Most European immigrants were processed at Ellis Island in New York harbor.

30. Many immigrants from Asia were processed at Angel Island in California.

31. More than 70 percent of immigrants came through New York City.

32. Before Ellis Island was built in 1892, most European immigrants arrived in New York through Castle Garden in lower Manhattan.

33. From the 17th to 19th centuries, hundreds of thousands of Africans were brought to America against their will to be enslaved labor.

34. Between 1921 and 1965, immigrants were accepted into the United States through a quota system. This system favored European immigrants.

35. Today, the majority of the country's immigrants—about 80 percent—come from Asia and Latin America.

36. In 2019 immigrants made up about 14 percent of the U.S. population.

37. The U.S. foreign-born population reached a record 45.8 million in 2019.

38. Immigrants today account for 13.7 percent of the U.S. population.

11164-U.S. Inspectors examining eyes of immigrants, Ellis Island, New York Harbor. Copyright Underwood & Underwood.

39. About 77 percent of immigrants are in the United States legally.

40. About one million people are granted "lawful permanent resident" status in the U.S. each year.

41. In 2018, the top country of origin for new immigrants coming into the U.S. was China, with 149,000 people.

42. India (129,000), Mexico (120,000), and the Philippines (46,000) complete the top four countries for new U.S. immigrants in 2018.

43. Asians are projected to become the largest immigrant group in the U.S. by 2055.

44. A program called Deferred Action for Childhood Arrivals (DACA) grants temporary protection from deportation and permission to work for undocumented individuals who were brought to the U.S. as children.

45. More than 643,500 people were protected by DACA in 2020. Most of these people were from Mexico.

TOP 15 FACTS ABOUT ELLIS ISLAND

1. Ellis Island opened in 1892.

2. The first immigrant recorded there was Annie Moore, a 15-year-old girl from Ireland.

3. Today, there is a statue of Annie Moore at Ellis Island.

4. Because the waters surrounding Ellis Island were too shallow for large ships to navigate, most docked and unloaded their passengers in Manhattan.

5. American citizens and first- and second-class passengers were allowed to enter the country after only a brief inspection in Manhattan.

6. Passengers in steerage (where tickets were the cheapest) were herded onto ferries and shuttled to Ellis Island for further processing.

7. Arrivals waited in long lines in the Great Hall until they were called to have their paperwork checked.

8. Immigrants also faced physical and mental health examinations before they could leave the island.

9. Immigrants suspected of being sick were marked with chalk letters and sent for further questioning and examination.

10. Of the 12 million people who passed through its doors between 1892 and 1954, around 2 percent were deemed unfit.

11. Ellis Island included a hospital, dormitories, a cafeteria, a power plant, and other buildings.

12. After 1924, immigrants were inspected when they got on boats in Europe, and Ellis Island inspectors just checked their papers.

13. Ellis Island closed as an immigration station in 1954.

14. Ellis Island was abandoned for many years. The Great Hall was restored and opened to the public as a museum in 1990.

15. The Ellis Island website includes lists of passengers and other documents people can use to find family records.

50 AMAZING AMERICAN REVOLUTION FACTS

1. The American Revolution is also called the Revolutionary War in the U.S. and the American War for Independence in the United Kingdom.

2. The war was fought between Great Britain and its American colonies.

3. After the French and Indian War, Great Britain had a lot of debts. It placed new taxes on the American colonies to bring in money.

4. Some of these taxes came from British laws such as the Sugar Act, the Townshend Acts, the Tea Act, and the Stamp Act.

5. Many Americans were angry about these new taxes. They said that Parliament could make laws, but only representatives elected by Americans could tax them.

6. The English disagreed and said Parliament had supreme authority over the colonies.

7. A popular slogan was "No taxation without representation."

8. In September 1774, George Washington, John Adams, Samuel Adams, Patrick Henry, John Jay, and other leaders met in Philadelphia. This group was called the First Continental Congress.

9. The First Continental Congress issued a declaration of the rights due every citizen. These rights included life, liberty, property, assembly and trial by jury.

10. On April 19, 1775, colonial militiamen fought British soldiers at the Battles of Lexington and Concord in Massachusetts.

11. The Second Continental Congress voted to form a Continental Army, with Washington as its commander in chief.

12. Washington had much less military experience than British generals.

13. The Battle of Bunker Hill, fought on June 17, 1775, was the Revolution's first major battle.

14. This battle was actually fought mostly on Breed's Hill in Boston.

15. The British won the battle but suffered heavy losses. This encouraged the colonists to keep fighting.

16. Colonists who rebelled against Great Britain were called patriots, revolutionaries, continentals, colonials, rebels, Yankees, or Whigs.

17. Colonists who remained loyal to the British were called loyalists, Royalists, King's Men, or Tories.

18. British soldiers were called lobster backs or redcoats because of their brightly colored uniforms.

19. The Battle of Saratoga, in 1777, was a major victory for the United States.

20. Because of the success at Saratoga, the French officially entered the war in support of the colonies against Great Britain.

21. France had been secretly sending supplies to the colonists since 1776.

22. The British held New York City throughout most of the war.

23. A network of Americans called the Culper Spy Ring operated in New York City and discovered many secrets about British troop movements and other plans.

24. Women provided important support for the Continental Army. Several also fought in battles.

25. General Benedict Arnold was an American hero who helped win the Battle of Fort Ticonderoga in 1775.

26. Later, Arnold felt disrespected by American leaders. He defected to the British and his name became another word for "traitor."

27. While most major battles were fought in the north during the early years of the war, later battles were fought in the south.

28. The British occupied Georgia in early 1779 and captured Charleston, South Carolina, in May 1780.

29. By the fall of 1781, American soldiers forced British General Charles Cornwallis and his men to withdraw to Virginia's Yorktown peninsula.

30. With help from the French army, General Washington sent 14,000 soldiers against the British, and Cornwallis surrendered on October 19.

31. While the Battle of Yorktown effectively ended the war, the British did not remove their troops from Charleston and Savannah until late 1782.

32. Fighting also occurred outside the colonies. On March 3, 1776, the Continental Navy captured New Providence Island, in the Bahamas.

33. American warships and privateers also raided British merchant ships and warships in the Atlantic Ocean.

34. The Treaty of Paris officially ended the war on September 3, 1783.

35. About 231,000 men served in the American army during the war.

KEY BATTLES IN THE AMERICAN REVOLUTION

#	Name	Date	Where Fought
1	Battles of Lexington & Concord	April 1775	Massachusetts
2	Siege of Fort Ticonderoga	May 1775	New York
3	Battle of Bunker Hill	June 1775	Massachusetts
4	Battle of Brooklyn	August 1776	New York
5	Battle of Trenton	December 1776	New Jersey
6	Battle of Princeton	January 1777	New Jersey
7	Battle of Brandywine	February 1777	Pennsylvania
8	Battle of Germantown	October 1777	Pennsylvania
9	Battle of Saratoga	October 1777	New York
10	Battle of Monmouth	June 1778	New Jersey
11	The Capture of Savannah	December 1778	Georgia
12	The Battle of Camden	March 1780	South Carolina
13	The Battle of Cowpens	August 1780	South Carolina
14	Battle of Guildford Courthouse	March 1781	North Carolina
15	Battle of Yorktown	October 1783	Virginia

40 FIERY FACTS ABOUT THE WAR OF 1812

1. The War of 1812 was fought between June 1812 and February 1815.

2. It is sometimes called "the Second War of Independence."

3. This was the first time the U.S. Congress declared war on another nation.

4. Great Britain angered America by impressing, or kidnapping, American sailors to serve in the British navy.

5. Great Britain also blocked American trade with France.

6. Many people called the conflict "Mr. Madison's War" after then-President James Madison.

7. The War of 1812 was fought in the United States, Canada, and at sea.

8. There were battles in Alabama, Louisiana, Georgia, Mississippi, Ohio, Illinois, Indiana, Michigan, Wisconsin, coastal Maine, and Chesapeake Bay.

9. Early in the war, the U.S. invaded Canada. The invasion did not go well.

10. Many battles were fought in rivers, lakes, and on the ocean.

11. The British blockaded many American ports along the Atlantic Ocean, especially in the south.

12. Naval battles were common in Chesapeake Bay.

13. The U.S. won several important naval battles in the Great Lakes.

14. Pirate-style raids were carried out against trade ships throughout the Atlantic.

15. There were many naval battles on Lake Erie and Lake Ontario.

16. Native Americans played a major role in the War of 1812.

17. Native Americans fought on both sides, although most fought on the side of the British against the United States.

18. Native Americans fought battles on the frontier, along the Gulf Coast, and in Canada.

19. Tecumseh was a Shawnee leader who organized a confederation of Native American tribes, known as Tecumseh's Confederacy.

20. Most Native Americans were driven to fight to try to keep American settlers from moving onto their lands.

29. First lady Dolley Madison and some staff members escaped before the British arrived.

30. Dolley Madison was able to save important papers and a large painting of George Washington before she fled.

31. British soldiers reportedly sat down to eat leftover food from the White House kitchen, using White House dishes and silver. Then they trashed the presidential mansion and set it on fire.

32. Troops also set fire to the U.S. Capitol.

33. The fires were put out by a huge thunderstorm less than a day later. The British left the city after holding it for just 26 hours.

34. This attack was the only time a foreign enemy has captured Washington, D.C.

35. Francis Scott Key wrote the words to "The Star-Spangled Banner" during a naval battle at Fort McHenry in Baltimore in September 1814.

36. Key watched the battle from a ship located about eight miles away. When the British retreated with the American flag still flying over the fort, Key wrote the poem to capture the moment.

37. Future presidents Andrew Jackson and William Henry Harrison became famous as war heroes.

38. Both the U.S. and Great Britain were eager to end the expensive war.

39. The Treaty of Ghent was signed on December 24, 1814, to end the war.

40. News of the peace deal didn't reach 5,000 British troops gathered outside New Orleans from Europe in time. They attacked the city on January 8, 1815, but were easily beaten by 4,000 defenders led by Major General Andrew Jackson.

21. Tecumseh was killed at the Battle of the Thames and his Confederacy fell apart.

22. The well-known Sauk leader, Black Hawk, also fought on the side of the British during the war.

23. African Americans were not officially allowed to join the U.S. Army during the War of 1812, but many served in the U.S. Navy.

24. Approximately one-quarter of the U.S. sailors at the Battle of Lake Erie were Black, and about 350 men of the "Battalion of Free Men of Color" fought at the Battle of New Orleans.

25. British Vice Admiral Alexander Cochrane issued a proclamation in April 1814 promising freedom to any enslaved Americans who served with the King's forces in the war.

26. On August 24, 1814, British troops entered Washington, D.C., and burned the White House.

27. This attack was revenge for an American attack on the city of York in Ontario, Canada, in June 1813.

28. President James Madison was not at the White House when the British arrived. He had left to review troops in Maryland.

60 FASCINATING FACTS ABOUT THE CIVIL WAR

1. The Civil War was fought between the United States of America and the Confederate States of America between 1861 and 1865.

2. The main reason for the war was whether slavery should be legal or illegal.

3. The Confederate States were made up of 11 Southern states that seceded, or left, the United States, or the Union.

4. The 11 states that made up the Confederacy were South Carolina, Mississippi, Florida, Alabama, Georgia, Louisiana, Texas, Virginia, Arkansas, Tennessee, and North Carolina.

5. The first battle of the war occurred early on April 12, 1861, when Confederate rebels opened fire on Fort Sumter in Charleston harbor, South Carolina.

6. No one was killed in the battle of Fort Sumter.

7. After a 34-hour battle, Major Robert Anderson surrendered the fort to Confederate troops led by P.G.T. Beauregard.

8. The North had the advantage in the war because it had more men to fight and more war materials and industry than the South.

9. At the start of the war, the value of all manufactured goods produced in all the Confederate states added up to less than one-fourth of those produced in New York State alone.

10. The Confederacy had some advantages. Its soldiers were fighting to defend territory they knew well.

11. The size of the Confederacy was also an advantage. Northern armies had to capture and hold huge areas of land across the south.

12. The Confederacy also had many important ports, including New Orleans, Charleston, Mobile, Norfolk, and Wilmington.

13. One-third of the soldiers in the Union Army were immigrants.

14. One in ten Union soldiers were African American.

15. Black men were permitted to join the Union Army in 1863.

16. Black soldiers were paid much less than white soldiers at first. The highest paid Black soldier earned about half of the lowest paid white soldier.

17. In September 1864, Congress finally began to pay Black and white soldiers the same.

18. More than three million men fought in the war.

19. Between 620,000 and 850,000 men, or at least 2 percent of the population, died.

20. More men died in the Civil War than in any other American conflict, including World War I and World War II.

21. Disease was the chief killer during the war. Two-thirds of the dead perished from disease, not battle wounds.

22. The Battle of Gettysburg was the bloodiest battle of the Civil War.

23. The Civil War divided families, with some members fighting for the North and others for the South.

24. Senator John J. Crittenden of Kentucky had two sons who became major generals during the Civil War—one for the North and one for the South.

25. Missouri sent 39 regiments to fight in the siege of Vicksburg—17 to the Confederacy and 22 to the Union. In both the North and South, men were offered awards, or "bounties," for enlisting.

26. New York offered bounties of as much as $677.

27. Bounty jumping soon became popular. Men would sign up, desert, then enlist again.

28. One man repeated the bounty-jumping process 32 times before being caught.

29. Congress passed a draft law on March 3, 1863, that required all men aged 20–45 to register for the draft.

30. Men could get out of being drafted by paying $300, or by finding a substitute draftee. This led to draft riots in New York City.

31. The war devastated the material resources of Confederate states.

32. In an effort to gather fresh supplies for the Confederate forces, Confederate General Robert E. Lee launched an invasion of the North in the summer of 1863.

33. Lee was defeated by Union General George G. Meade at the Battle of Gettysburg in Pennsylvania.

34. Soon afterward, Vicksburg, Mississippi, fell to Union troops on July 4, 1863.

35. Many historians mark the two Union victories at Gettysburg and Vicksburg as the "turning point" in the Civil War.

36. Some newspapers called Union General Ulysses S. Grant a "butcher" for the huge losses of life during the spring of 1864.

37. However, Robert E. Lee's army lost the most men in proportion to the army's size.

38. Unlike modern wars, many top officers, including generals, led their troops into battle.

39. For this reason, generals were 50 percent more likely to die in combat than privates.

40. Andersonville Prison in southwest Georgia was built to hold 10,000 Union prisoners of war in 1864.

41. Andersonville Prison quickly became the fifth-largest city in the Confederacy by population, holding 33,000 prisoners in unsafe conditions. More than 10,000 prisoners died.

42. After four years of conflict, the major Confederate armies surrendered to the United States in April of 1865.

43. Lee's army surrendered to Grant at Appomattox Court House in Virginia.

44. Private John J. Williams of Indiana is generally recognized as the last man killed in the Civil War, in a battle at Palmito Ranch, Texas, on May 13, 1865, a month after Lee's surrender.

45. The war bankrupted much of the South and left its roads, farms, and factories in ruins.

46. After the war, smaller numbers of Union soldiers remained in southern states to restore agriculture, rebuild roads and towns, maintain order, and distribute food and other aid. Many southerners were unhappy with the continued occupation.

47. The Confederate states were slowly re-admitted to the United States over the next twenty years in a period known as Reconstruction.

48. The Union took over General Robert E. Lee's wife's Virginia estate during the war and eventually turned it into a cemetery for soldiers who died in the war.

49. Today Arlington National Cemetery is the burial place of about 400,000 people, including 250,000 service members.

50. President John F. Kennedy, President William Howard Taft, and other notable Americans are also buried at Arlington National Cemetery.

10 BLOODIEST BATTLES IN THE U.S. CIVIL WAR

Name of Battle	Location	Year Fought	Casualties (dead and injured)
Gettysburg	Pennsylvania	1863	23,049 Union/25,000 Confederate
Spottsylvania Courthouse	Virginia	1864	18,399 Union/12,687 Confederate
Chickamauga	Georgia	1863	16,170 Union/18,454 Confederate
Battle of the Wilderness	Virginia	1864	17,666 Union/11,033 Confederate
Antietam	Maryland	1862	12,410 Union/10,316 Confederate
Shiloh	Tennessee	1862	13,047 Union/10,699 Confederate
Chancellorsville	Virginia	1863	17,287 Union/13,303 Confederate
Second Battle of Bull Run	Virginia	1862	14,462 Union/11,739 Confederate
Stone's River	Tennessee	1863	12,906 Union/11,739 Confederate
Fredericksburg	Virginia	1862	12,653 Union/4,201 Confederate

40 FIGHTING FACTS ABOUT WORLD WAR I

1. World War I began in 1914, but the United States didn't join the war until 1917.

2. President Woodrow Wilson tried to keep the U.S. out of the war, but German submarine warfare on American merchant ships forced Congress to declare war on Germany on April 6, 1917.

3. Another factor that pushed the U.S. to declare war was the Zimmerman telegram, a secret telegram sent from German Foreign Secretary Arthur Zimmerman to the German ambassador in Mexico that the British intercepted in January 1917.

4. Zimmerman proposed that Mexico ally with Germany against the United States and promised Mexico the territories of Texas, New Mexico, and Arizona in return. Wilson and the American public were furious when they learned about this.

5. 82 out of 88 senators voted to enter the war on April 4, 1917. Two days later, the United States declared war on Germany.

6. The U.S. joined the Allies (Britain, France, Russia, Italy, and Japan), who were at war with the Central Powers (Germany, Austria-Hungary, and Turkey).

7. The United States didn't become an official member of the Allies. Instead, it called itself an "associated power."

8. The entry of the U.S. into the war made it possible for the Allies to defeat the Central Powers, because the U.S. provided so many men and supplies to replenish the nations that had been fighting longer.

9. 4,734,991 U.S. armed service members fought in World War I.

10. 116,516 U.S. service members died during the war.

11. More U.S. military personnel died of disease (63,114) than in battle (53,402).

12. Most of the deaths from disease were because of the influenza pandemic of 1918.

13. On June 26, 1917, the United States sent 14,000 troops to France to prepare for combat.

14. There were 85,000 U.S. troops in France in March 1918.

15. There were more than two million U.S. troops in Europe at the end of the war.

16. General John J. Pershing was the commander of U.S. troops in Europe.

17. The U.S. Navy was the second largest in the world when America entered the war in 1917.

18. The U.S. Navy focused on building destroyers and submarine chasers to protect Allied shipping from German submarine attacks.

19. By the end of the war, more than 380 U.S. ships were stationed overseas.

20. The U.S. Navy played a major role in helping to blockade Germany, keeping out supplies and hurting Germany economically.

21. The U.S. forces that were sent to Europe during World War I were called the American Expeditionary Forces (AEF).

22. U.S. soldiers were nicknamed "doughboys" during the war.

23. No one is really sure where the "doughboy" nickname came from.

24. America's last surviving World War I veteran was Frank Buckles, who died in 2011 at the age of 110.

25. Buckles enlisted in the Army at age 16 in August 1917 and drove military vehicles in France.

26. Women and children were also part of the war effort.

27. Women took jobs in factories producing supplies needed for the war effort and on the homefront.

28. Women also served in ambulance corps and the American Red Cross at home and abroad.

29. Children sold war bonds to raise money for the war effort.

30. Women and children at home planted "victory gardens" to help feed their families and free up more food to send for the troops.

31. U.S. troops had never seen a war like World War I. Unlike earlier wars, much of the fighting took place in trenches and in the air.

32. World War I also featured new technologies such as tanks, airplanes, and poison gas.

33. After suffering huge losses, Germany surrendered at 11:11 on the morning of November 11, 1918, which became known as Armistice Day.

34. After Armistice Day, the United States, Great Britain, and France met to create the Treaty of Versailles.

35. Germany was not invited to the treaty discussions and was shocked at its demands.

36. Germany had to take full responsibility for starting the war.

37. Germany had to give some territory to France.

38. Germany also had to pay a huge amount of money in war damages.

39. The Treaty of Versailles was signed on June 28, 1919.

40. Germany's unhappiness with the Treaty of Versailles and its obligations under the terms of the treaty helped set the stage for World War II.

50 CRUCIAL FACTS ABOUT WORLD WAR II

1. World War II began on September 1, 1939, when Germany invaded Poland.

2. In response, Great Britain and France declared war on Germany on September 3.

3. Although the United States was not part of the war, President Franklin D. Roosevelt wanted to help the nations fighting Germany, especially Great Britain, which desperately needed supplies.

4. Through a program called Lend-Lease, the United States "lent" supplies to the British. The British did not have to pay back the United States until after the war.

5. The U.S. also signed Lend-Lease agreements with 30 other countries.

6. The Lend-Lease program allowed the U.S. to fight against Nazi Germany without entering the war.

7. Japan was an ally of Germany. On December 7, 1941, the Japan planes bombed the U.S. naval base at Pearl Harbor in Hawaii.

8. The Americans were taken completely by surprise by the Japanese attack.

9. All eight battleships in the harbor were hit, along with many other vessels and more than 180 aircraft.

10. More than 2,330 troops were killed and over 1,140 were wounded at Pearl Harbor.

11. On December 8, Congress declared war on Japan. Three days later, Congress declared war on Germany and Italy.

12. Only one person, Montana Representative Jeannette Rankin, voted against the war.

13. Germany and Italy declared war on the United States on December 11, 1941.

14. The U.S. joined the Allies (Britain, France, and the Soviet Union) to fight the Axis Powers (Germany, Italy, and Japan). Many other nations were also involved in the conflict.

15. The U.S. entry into the war boosted the nation's economy and helped end the Great Depression.

16. 17 million new jobs were created during the war.

17. Many women went to work in factories and other workplaces where they often couldn't get jobs before the war.

18. Women took jobs in aircraft manufacturing plants, munitions plants, military uniform production factories, and more.

19. Because steel and other resources were needed to build weapons and equipment, Americans took part in recycling and scrap metal drives.

20. Americans also supported the war effort by purchasing Liberty bonds, which were sold by the U.S. government to raise money for the war.

21. During the war, fuel and many foods were rationed and could only be bought by giving the cashier payment along with special stamps given to each family in ration books.

22. Fearing that Japan might invade the West Coast of the United States, the government forced 110,000 Japanese Americans to leave their homes and businesses there and confined them to internment camps.

23. Japan had almost total control of the Pacific islands in the early years of the war.

24. The U.S. Pacific Fleet's victory at the Battle of Midway in June 1942 was a turning point in the war.

25. American troops also won victories in island battles, including Guadalcanal and Iwo Jima, in 1942 and 1943.

26. This "island-hopping" strategy took many lives, but was successful in turning back the Japanese.

27. British and American forces won control of North Africa by 1943.

28. After an Allied invasion of Sicily and southern Italy, the Italian government fell in 1943.

29. Fighting in Italy was especially difficult because of mountainous terrain and bad weather.

30. Italy surrendered and joined the Allies to fight against Germany.

31. More than one million Black soldiers fought in World War II, but the U.S. armed forces were still segregated by race.

32. The "D-Day" landing of Allied troops in Normandy, France, in 1944 helped turn the tide of war against Germany.

33. The Germans surrendered on May 7, 1945.

34. Between July 17 and August 2, 1945, U.S., British, and Soviet leaders decided to divide Germany into four occupation zones, to be controlled by the Soviet Union, Britain, the United States, and France.

35. War continued in the Pacific, and the United States planned an invasion of Japan which could have killed up to one million troops.

36. Instead of a ground invasion, the U.S. dropped the first atomic bomb on Hiroshima, Japan, on August 6, 1945, killing at least 80,000 people, including many civilians.

37. Three days later, it dropped a second atomic bomb on Nagasaki, Japan, killing at least 40,000 people.

38. Japan surrendered on August 15.

39. World War II officially ended on September 2, 1945, when U.S. General Douglas MacArthur accepted Japan's formal surrender aboard a battleship in Tokyo Bay.

40. More than 407,000 U.S. armed service members were killed in World War II.

UNITED we are strong

UNITED we will win

TOP 10 FACTS
ABOUT D-DAY

1. More than 156,000 forces from the United States, Canada, and Great Britain landed on Normandy Beach in France on June 6, 1944.

2. The invasion date was called "D-Day" and the operation was called Operation Overlord.

3. "D-Day" is a U.S. Army term for the start date of a military operation.

4. Operation Overlord was the largest amphibious operation in military history.

5. The invasion was led by U.S. General Dwight D. Eisenhower, the Supreme Allied Commander in Europe.

6. The operation combined 156,115 U.S., British, and Canadian troops; 6,939 ships and landing vessels; 2,395 aircraft; and 867 gliders that delivered airborne troops.

7. The Allies used fake radio transmissions and tanks and airplanes made of wood and balloons to fool the Germans into thinking the invasion would take place in a different part of France.

8. Storms delayed the invasion until General Eisenhower decided to move forward during a break in the weather.

9. During the invasion, Comanche "code-talkers" relayed critical messages in code based on their Native American language to keep their messages secret.

10. The D-Day invasion was successful, but more than 4,400 Allied soldiers died.

45 HARD FACTS ABOUT THE VIETNAM WAR

1. The end of World War II saw a briefly independent Democratic Republic of Vietnam under leader Ho Chi Minh.

2. Allied nations wanted Vietnam to return to its prewar status as a colony of France. At the same time, Chinese and Soviet Communist governments sent advisers and equipment to guerilla fighters in North Vietnam.

3. After the French lost a battle at Dien Bien Phu in 1954, they left and Vietnam was split into two nations.

4. The U.S. first sent military advisers to Vietnam in 1954. Their goal then was to keep South Vietnam from falling to the Communist-controlled North Vietnam.

5. In 1955 President Dwight D. Eisenhower pledged his support to South Vietnam and its leader Ngô Dình Diem.

6. Following the "domino theory," which said that if one Southeast Asian country fell to Communism, others would follow, President John F. Kennedy increased U.S. aid to South Vietnam.

7. By 1962, there were about 9,000 U.S. troops in Vietnam, compared to fewer than 800 during the 1950s.

8. By 1963, there were 16,000 U.S. troops and advisers in South Vietnam.

9. South Vietnam's president Ngô Dình Diem was assassinated on November 2, 1963.

10. President John F. Kennedy wanted to remove U.S. advisers from Vietnam but was assassinated just 20 days after Diem.

11. The U.S. Congress passed the Gulf of Tonkin resolution in August 1964, allowing President Lyndon B. Johnson to send ground troops to fight against North Vietnam.

12. U.S. planes began heavy bombing of North Vietnam in 1965.

13. They also bombed Vietnam's neighbor, Laos, even though the country was neutral.

14. Laos was bombed to stop supplies from crossing the border into North Vietnam.

15. By June 1965, 82,000 combat troops were stationed in Vietnam.

16. At that time, most Americans supported the war in Vietnam, but that would soon change.

17. South Korea, Thailand, Australia, and New Zealand also sent troops to Vietnam, although nowhere near as many as the U.S. did.

18. Large areas of South Vietnam were heavily bombed by the U.S. to attack North Vietnamese soldiers.

19. People who lived in bombed or other war-torn areas were forced to flee to refugee camps.

20. By November 1967, the number of American troops in Vietnam had grown to 500,000.

21. More than 15,000 U.S. troops were killed and more than 109,500 were wounded by November 1967.

22. As the war stretched on, some troops began to mistrust the government's reasons for keeping them there.

23. Many Americans did not believe U.S. claims that they were winning the war.

24. Between July 1966 and December 1973, there were more than 503,000 "incidents of desertion" by U.S. military personnel, meaning someone left their service assignment without permission for at least 30 days.

25. Images of the war were shown on U.S. television news shows, which turned many Americans against the war.

26. In October 1967, about 35,000 demonstrators staged a massive Vietnam War protest outside the Pentagon in Washington, D.C.

27. Opponents of the war argued that most victims of the war were civilians, not enemy soldiers, and that the United States was supporting a corrupt dictatorship in Saigon.

28. 88.4 percent of troops deployed to Vietnam were white, 10.6 percent were Black, and 1 percent were of other races.

29. Between 1961 and 1966, Black troops made up almost 20 percent of all combat-related deaths.

30. Most of the American troops had at least a high school education.

31. Some young men enrolled in college to get out of being drafted and sent to Vietnam.

32. Others left the country to avoid the draft.

33. More than three-quarters of the Americans who fought in Vietnam volunteered to join the military. But some may have done so knowing they would otherwise be drafted.

34. U.S. soldiers slaughtered more than 400 unarmed civilians in the village of My Lai in March 1968. It was covered up for more than a year before the incident became public, angering Americans who were already turning away from supporting the war.

35. In 1968, with more Americans coming out against his support for the Vietnam War, President Lyndon Johnson announced he would not run for re-election.

36. The new president, Richard Nixon, conducted peace talks with North Vietnam, but continued bombing campaigns.

37. Nixon also oversaw the invasion and bombing of neighboring countries Laos and Cambodia.

38. In January 1973, the United States and North Vietnam concluded a final peace agreement.

39. However, war between North and South Vietnam continued until April 30, 1975, when North Vietnamese forces captured the southern capital, Saigon, and renamed it Ho Chi Minh City.

40. As North Vietnamese forces entered Saigon, American helicopters rescued members of its embassy and flew some South Vietnamese to safety.

41. North and South Vietnam were reunified as the Socialist Republic of Vietnam in 1976.

42. The U.S. spent more than $120 billion on the conflict in Vietnam from 1965–73.

43. 58,200 U.S. troops were killed in the Vietnam War. Another 300,000 were wounded.

44. A survey by the U.S. Veterans Administration found that about 500,000 of the three million troops who fought in Vietnam suffered from post-traumatic stress disorder (PTSD).

45. In 1982, the Vietnam Veterans Memorial was unveiled in Washington, D.C., ultimately becoming one of the most popular and powerful monuments on the National Mall.

40 FACTS ABOUT U.S. WARS IN IRAQ AND AFGHANISTAN

1. On August 2, 1990, Iraqi dictator Saddam Hussein seized control of the oil fields in the neighboring country of Kuwait.

2. On August 7, President George H.W. Bush announced the U.S. was joining 38 other countries in an international effort to protect Kuwait.

3. This military operation was called Desert Shield.

4. Bush ordered a huge increase in U.S. troops and resources in the Persian Gulf.

5. About 600,000 troops were sent to the area by members of the coalition.

6. 470,000 of those troops were sent by the U.S.

7. On November 29, 1990, the United Nations Security Council demanded Iraq leave Kuwait by January 16, 1991.

8. When Iraq did not leave, Congress authorized President Bush to use American troops to fight against Iraq.

9. That operation, known as Desert Storm, began on January 17.

10. Desert Storm was led by U.S. General Norman Schwarzkopf.

11. The operation began with heavy bombing of Hussein's armies in Iraq and Kuwait.

12. During Desert Storm, the U.S. used "smart bombs" to destroy buildings and minimize civilian casualties.

13. Hussein targeted civilians with SCUD missiles launched into Saudi Arabia and Israel.

14. U.S. Patriot missiles attempted to destroy SCUD missiles in flight.

15. After intense bombing of Iraq's capital, Baghdad, the U.S.-led coalition marched into Kuwait and across the Iraq border.

16. General Schwarzkopf declared a cease-fire on February 28.

17. Iraq officially surrendered on March 3, 1991.

18. Desert Storm lasted only 43 days.

19. The land war was called the "100-Hour Ground War."

20. During Desert Storm, the U.S. partnered with Saudi Arabia's Prince Khaled bin Sultan to co-command the allied forces.

21. U.S. land forces gathered in Saudi Arabia during the build-up to Desert Storm.

22. 147 U.S. soldiers were killed in action in Desert Storm.

23. On September 11, 2001, a terrorist group called Al-Qaeda attacked the World Trade Center in New York City and the Pentagon in Washington, D.C.

24. Al-Qaeda operated in Afghanistan and had the support of that nation's Taliban government.

25. Soon after the September 11 attacks, the U.S. and a coalition of other nations sent troops to Afghanistan to defeat the Taliban and destroy Al-Qaeda.

26. The U.S. partnered with anti-Taliban groups in Afghanistan to do much of the fighting.

27. The Taliban government was removed from power, but Al-Qaeda and its leader, Osama bin Laden, remained.

28. By spring 2010, more than 1,000 U.S. troops had been killed in Afghanistan.

29. Troops were still in Afghanistan as of early 2021.

30. On March 19, 2003, the U.S., Great Britain, and other countries launched a war on Iraq.

31. The goal of the Iraq War was to overthrow Saddam Hussein's regime.

32. President George W. Bush also based his case for war on the idea that Iraq was developing "weapons of mass destruction."

33. Iraq's government forces were defeated quickly, with a new interim government established by 2004, but insurgents in Iraq belonging to various factions waged years of intense guerilla war against U.S.-led coalition forces.

34. Saddam Hussein went into hiding but was captured by American soldiers on December 13, 2003.

35. U.S. forces declared an end to the Iraq War in December 2011. No weapons of mass destruction were found in Iraq.

36. Despite the end of the war, U.S. troops were still in Iraq.

37. On May 2, 2011, U.S. forces killed Osama bin Laden in Pakistan.

38. Many injuries and deaths in Iraq were caused by IEDs (improvised explosive devices).

39. As of February 2021, the United States had lost 7,036 soldiers in the Iraq and Afghanistan conflicts combined. Many thousands more were wounded.

40. In 2013, the U.S. military lifted its ban on women serving in direct ground combat units.

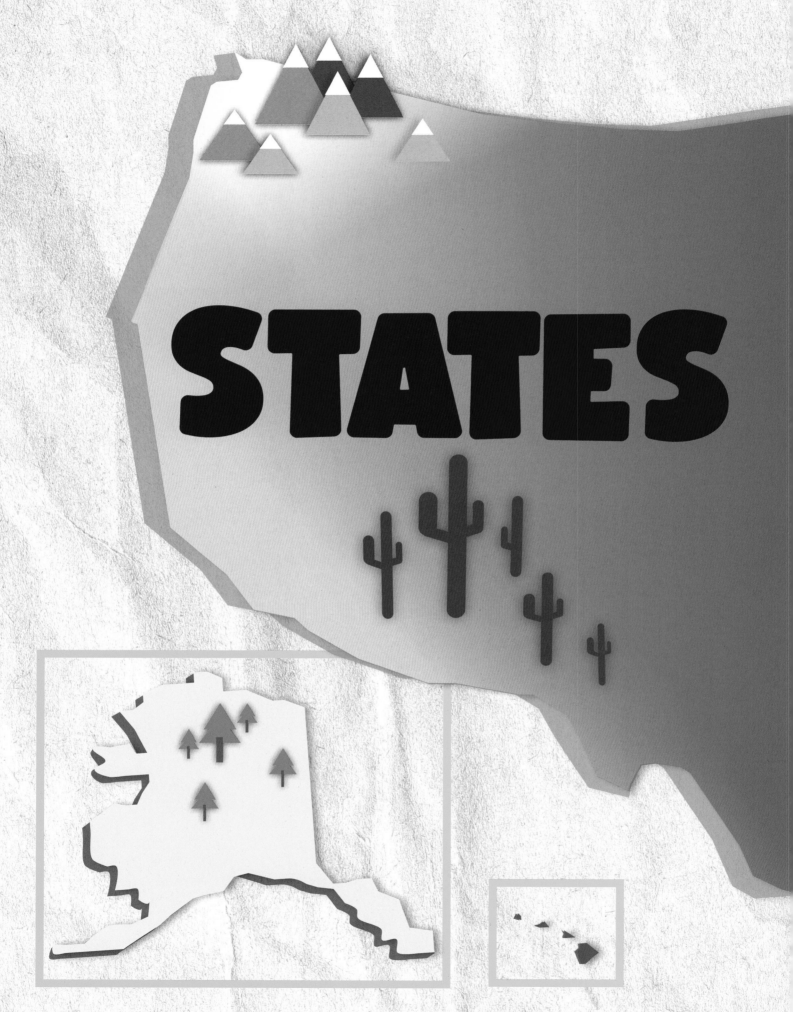

STATES

AND TERRITORIES

30 STATE FACTS ABOUT ALABAMA

15 Fast Facts

#	Fact
1	Abbreviation: AL
2	Date of Statehood: December 14, 1819
3	Nicknames: Heart of Dixie (unofficial)
4	Population: 5,024,279
5	Total Area: 52,420 square miles (135,767 sq km)
6	Area Rank: 30
7	Capital: Montgomery
8	Largest City: Birmingham
9	Motto: "We Dare Defend Our Rights"
10	Bird: Yellowhammer
11	Mammal: Black bear
12	Insect: Monarch butterfly
13	Flower: Camellia
14	Tree: Longleaf pine
15	Fruit: Blackberry

5 Famous People From Alabama

1. Hank Aaron, baseball player
2. George Washington Carver, scientist
3. Helen Keller, activist and author
4. Coretta Scott King, civil rights activist
5. Harper Lee, author

ET 320-3

1. Cheaha Mountain is the highest point in Alabama, at 2,413 feet (735 m) above sea level.

2. "Alabama" means "tribal town" in the Creek language.

3. Booker T. Washington founded the Tuskegee Institute, now Tuskegee University, in 1881.

4. The famous Black aviators known as the Tuskegee Airmen flew 15,000 missions during World War II.

5. Alabama was the first state to have an alcoholic beverage as its official drink.

6. Montgomery had one of the world's first electric streetcar systems. The "Lightning Route" opened in 1886.

7. In 1836, Alabama was the first state to declare Christmas a legal holiday.

8. It's technically illegal to play cards or dominoes in Alabama on Sundays.

9. Workers in Huntsville built the rocket that carried astronauts to the moon.

10. Enterprise, Alabama, is home to the Boll Weevil Monument. The statue celebrates the destructive insect that helped convince farmers to grow crops other than cotton.

30

STATE FACTS ABOUT
ALASKA

15 Fast Facts

1	Abbreviation: AK
2	Date of Statehood: January 3, 1959
3	Nickname: The Last Frontier (unofficial)
4	Population: 733,391
5	Total Area: 665,384 square miles (1,723,337 sq km)
6	Area Rank: 1
7	Capital: Juneau
8	Largest City: Anchorage
9	Motto: "North to the Future"
10	Bird: Willow Ptarmigan
11	Mammal: Moose
12	Fish: King salmon
13	Insect: Skimmer dragonfly
14	Flower: Forget-me-not
15	Tree: Sitka spruce

5 Famous People
From Alaska

1. Carlos Boozer, basketball player
2. Susan Butcher, sled dog racer
3. Jewel Kilcher, musician
4. Sarah Palin, politician
5. Curt Schilling, baseball player

1. Alaska was the 49th state to join the United States.

2. The word "Alaska" comes from the Aleut word "Alyeska," which means "great land."

3. Alaska is home to many Native people, including the Aleut, Inuit, Tlingit, and Yupik.

4. Denali is the tallest mountain in North America.

5. Russia is believed to have been the first European nation to send explorers to Alaska.

6. The U.S. bought Alaska from Russia in 1867 for two cents an acre.

7. Gold was discovered in Alaska in 1872.

8. One of the strongest earthquakes ever recorded struck Alaska on March 27, 1964.

9. Alaska's state fossil is the woolly mammoth.

10. The state flag was designed by a 13-year-old boy in 1927.

30 STATE FACTS ABOUT ARIZONA

15 Fast Facts

1	Abbreviation: AZ
2	Date of Statehood: February 14, 1912
3	Nickname: Grand Canyon State
4	Population: 7,151,502
5	Total Area: 113,990 square miles (295,233 sq km)
6	Area Rank: 6
7	Capital: Phoenix
8	Largest City: Phoenix
9	Motto: "God Enriches"
10	Bird: Cactus wren
11	Mammal: Ringtail
12	Reptile: Arizona ridge-nosed rattlesnake
13	Fish: Apache trout
14	Flower: Saguaro cactus blossom
15	Tree: Palo verde

1. The Arizona Tree Frog was designated the state amphibian of Arizona in 1986.

2. Petrified wood is the state fossil.

3. Arizona has an official neckware: the bolo tie.

4. People lived in the area now known as Arizona at least 20,000 years ago.

5. Arizona was part of Mexico until 1848.

6. Many former mining towns in Arizona are now ghost towns.

7. The original London Bridge was shipped stone-by-stone and reconstructed around a concrete base in Lake Havasu City.

8. Arizona is on Mountain Standard Time all year long, except within the boundaries of the Navajo Nation, which observes the daylight saving time change.

9. The blue in the Arizona state flag is the same shade as the blue in the U.S. flag.

10. Almost six million people visit the Grand Canyon every year.

30 STATE FACTS ABOUT ARKANSAS

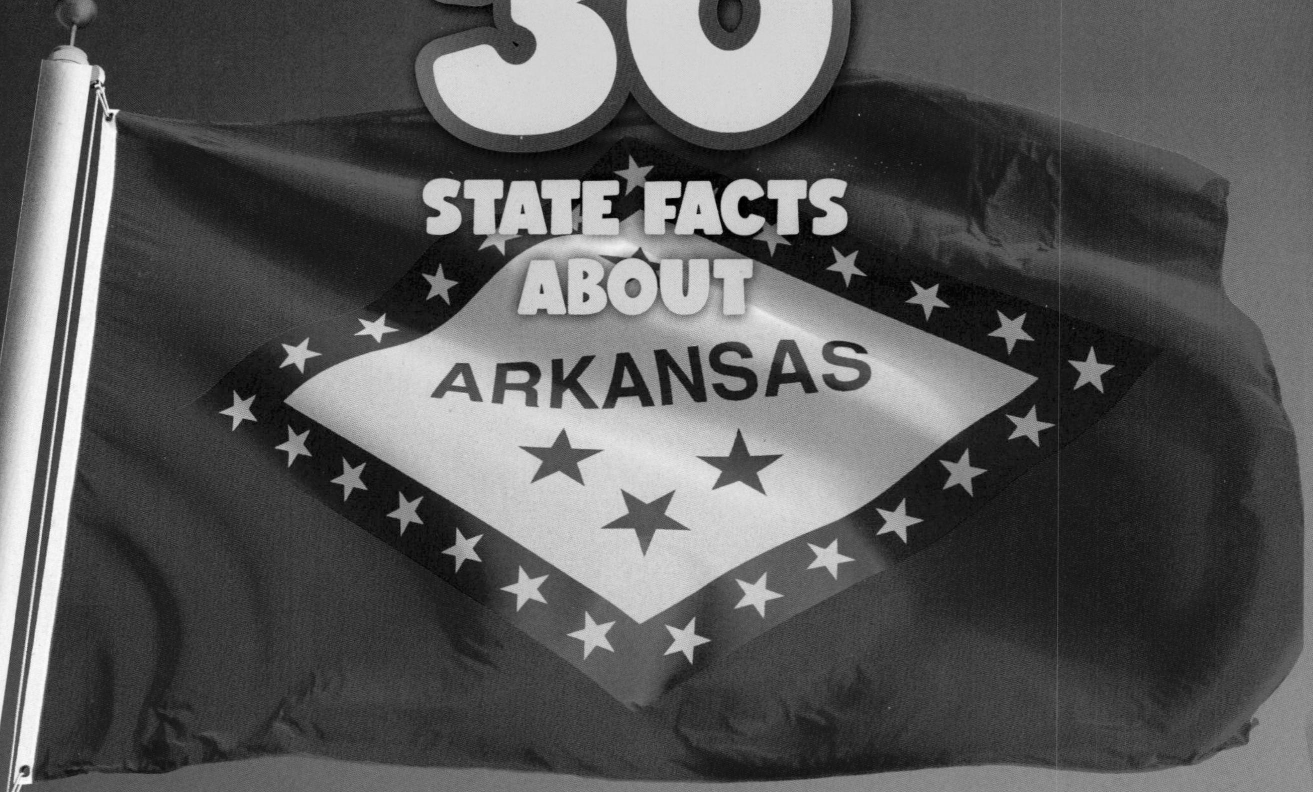

15 Fast Facts

1 Abbreviation: AR

2 Date of Statehood: June 15, 1836

3 Nickname: Natural State

4 Population: 3,011,524

5 Total Area: 53,179 square miles (137,733 sq km)

6 Area Rank: 29

7 Capital: Little Rock

8 Largest City: Little Rock

9 Motto: "The People Rule"

10 Bird: Mockingbird

11 Mammal: White-tailed deer

12 Insect: Honeybee

13 Fruit and Vegetable: Pink tomato

14 Flower: Apple Blossom

15 Tree: Pine tree

5 Famous People From Arkansas

1. Johnny Cash, musician

2. Bill Clinton, U.S. president

3. John Grisham, author

4. General Douglas MacArthur, military leader

5. Scottie Pippen, basketball player

1. People from Arkansas are called Arkansans.

2. Arkansas's name came from the Algonquin name for Quapaw Indians.

3. Walmart was founded in Bentonville, Arkansas.

4. Milk is the official state beverage.

5. Arkansas is the only U.S. state with naturally occurring diamonds.

6. The state flag has 25 stars to symbolize Arkansas becoming the 25th state.

7. Hattie Ophelia Caraway, the first woman elected to the U.S. Senate, was from Arkansas.

8. In 1881, the state's General Assembly passed a resolution that the state's name should be spelled "Arkansas" but pronounced "Arkansaw."

9. In 1947, the Arkansas legislature made it illegal to mispronounce the state's name.

10. Arkansas has four different official state songs in different musical styles.

30 STATE FACTS ABOUT CALIFORNIA

15 Fast Facts

1	Abbreviation: CA
2	Date of Statehood: September 9, 1850
3	Nickname: Golden State
4	Population: 39,538,223
5	Total Area: 163,695 square miles (423,968 sq km)
6	Area Rank: 3
7	Capital: Sacramento
8	Largest City: Los Angeles
9	Motto: "Eureka!"
10	Bird: California valley quail
11	Mammal: Grizzly bear
12	Insect: California dogface butterfly
13	Fruit: Avocado
14	Flower: California poppy
15	Tree: California redwood

BADWATER BASIN
282 FEET/85.5 METERS
BELOW SEA LEVEL

1. California grows 80 percent of the almonds in the world, 99 percent of the walnuts in the U.S. (and 75 percent of the world's supply), and 98 percent of the pistachios in the U.S.

2. California became a U.S. territory in 1848, at the end of the Mexican-American War.

3. In 1849, gold was discovered at Sutter's Mill in California. More than 100,000 people rushed to California, getting the nickname "49ers."

4. The state's motto is Greek for "I have found it" and has to do with the discovery of gold.

5. The highest and lowest places in the continental U.S. are both in California.

6. California's Mount Whitney is the highest peak in the lower 48 states. It rises 14,505 feet (4,421 m) above sea level.

7. Badwater Basin in Death Valley is the lowest point in the U.S. at 282 feet (86 m) below sea level.

8. California is ranked #1 in U.S. population.

9. California has the largest state economy in the U.S., with big contributions from agriculture, entertainment, and technology industries.

10. San Francisco outlawed burials in 1900 and, in 1912, began to move and rebury its dead in nearby Colma.

5 Famous People From California

1. Kamala Harris, politician
2. Kendrick Lamar, musician
3. George Lucas, filmmaker
4. Sally Ride, astronaut
5. Serena Williams, tennis player

30 STATE FACTS ABOUT COLORADO

15 Fast Facts

1	Abbreviation: CO
2	Date of Statehood: August 1, 1876
3	Nickname: Centennial State
4	Population: 5,773,714
5	Total Area: 104,094 square miles (269,602 sq km)
6	Area Rank: 8
7	Capital: Denver
8	Largest City: Denver
9	Motto: "Nothing Without Providence"
10	Bird: Large bunting
11	Mammal: Rocky Mountain bighorn sheep
12	Reptile: Western painted turtle
13	Insect: Colorado hairstreak butterfly
14	Flower: Rocky Mountain columbine
15	Tree: Colorado blue spruce

5 Famous People From Colorado

1. Tim Allen, actor
2. Scott Carpenter, astronaut
3. Melissa Benoist, actress
4. Kristen Schaal, actress and comedian
5. Trey Parker, actor and writer

1. The first Stegosaurus fossils were found in Morrison, Colorado, in the 1870s.

2. Stegosaurus is Colorado's official state fossil.

3. Colorado's Picketwire Canyon is home to one of the largest preserved sets of dinosaur tracks in the world.

4. The 1976 Winter Olympics were supposed to be held in Denver, but the state's voters turned down the idea.

5. "Colorado" means "colored red" in Spanish.

6. The U.S. government owns more than one-third of the land in Colorado.

7. The 13th step of the state capitol building in Denver is exactly one mile above sea level.

8. Katharine Lee Bates was inspired to write "America the Beautiful" after climbing Pikes Peak.

9. The Royal Gorge Bridge spans the Arkansas River at a height of 1,053 feet (321 m), making it the highest suspension bridge in the U.S.

10. Blanca Peak, just southeast of Colorado's Great Sand Dunes, is one of the sacred mountains of the Navajo people. It is also known as "Sisnaajiní."

30
STATE FACTS ABOUT
CONNECTICUT

1	Abbreviation: CT
2	Date of Statehood: January 9, 1788
3	Nickname: Constitution State
4	Population: 3,605,944
5	Total Area: 5,543 square miles (14,356 sq km)
6	Area Rank: 48
7	Capital: Hartford
8	Largest City: Bridgeport
9	Motto: "He Who Transplanted Still Sustains"
10	Bird: American robin
11	Mammal: Sperm whale
12	Shellfish: Eastern oyster
13	Insect: Praying mantis
14	Flower: Mountain laurel
15	Tree: Charter Oak

1. The Charter Oak, Connecticut's state tree, referred to a real tree. Tradition says the colony's charter was hidden in the tree to protect it from the British.

2. The Charter Oak fell in a storm in 1856, when it was more than 200 years old.

3. Connecticut's first European settlement was created by the Dutch in 1633. The first British settlers arrived in 1636.

4. The first lighthouse in Connecticut was built in 1760. The state is home to about 20 lighthouses today.

5. The USS *Nautilus*, the world's first nuclear-powered submarine, was built in Groton in 1954.

6. The word "Connecticut" comes from the Algonquian word "quinnitukqut" which means "at the long tidal river."

7. Connecticut is also called "the Nutmeg State."

8. Founded in 1764, the *Hartford Courant* is the country's oldest continuously published newspaper.

9. The first Frisbee was developed in Connecticut from a pie tin.

10. In 1901, Connecticut set the first speed limit laws for cars. It was illegal to drive faster than 12 miles an hour.

5 Famous People From Connecticut

1. George W. Bush, U.S. president

2. Suzanne Collins, author

3. Nathan Hale, Revolutionary War hero

4. Anika Noni Rose, actress

5. Noah Webster, lexicographer

30 STATE FACTS ABOUT DELAWARE

15 Fast Facts

1 Abbreviation: DE

2 Date of Statehood: December 7, 1787

3 Nickname: First State

4 Population: 989,948

5 Total Area: 2,489 square miles (6,446 sq km)

6 Area Rank: 49

7 Capital: Dover

8 Largest City: Wilmington

9 Motto: "Liberty and Independence"

10 Bird: Blue hen chicken

11 Mammal: Grey fox

12 Insect: Ladybug

13 Fruit: Strawberry

14 Flower: Peach blossom

15 Tree: American holly

1. Delaware is considered the lowest state, with an average altitude of 60 feet (18 m) above sea level.

2. Delaware was the first of the thirteen original colonies to ratify the Constitution.

3. Dover International Speedway has hosted at least one Nascar race every year since 1969.

4. The DuPont family founded one of the world's largest chemical companies in Delaware.

5. In 1974, a second-grade class successfully petitioned to have the ladybug named the state insect.

6. A 2015 study discovered Delaware has the fastest internet speeds in the U.S.

7. Delaware has no state sales tax.

8. Delaware has only three counties.

9. In 1619, explorer Samuel Argall named the Delaware River and Bay after the governor of Virginia, Lord De La Warr. The state took its name from the river.

10. The first known inhabitants of Delaware were the Nanticoke and Lenni Lenape tribes.

5 Famous People
From Delaware

1. Joe Biden, U.S. president

2. Annie Jump Cannon, astronomer

3. Éleuthère Irénée du Pont, industrialist

4. Raúl Esparza, actor

5. Aubrey Plaza, actress

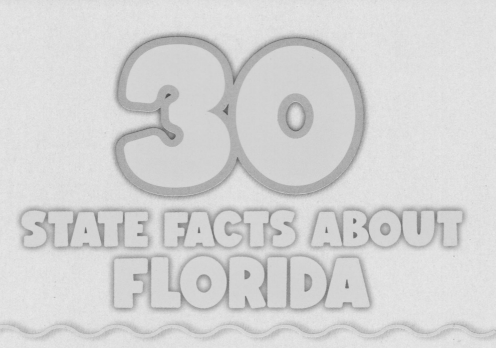

30

STATE FACTS ABOUT FLORIDA

15 Fast Facts

1	Abbreviation: FL
2	Date of Statehood: March 3, 1835
3	Nickname: Sunshine State
4	Population: 21,538,187
5	Total Area: 65,758 square miles (170,312 sq km)
6	Area Rank: 22
7	Capital: Tallahassee
8	Largest City: Jacksonville
9	Motto: "In God We Trust"
10	Bird: Northern mockingbird
11	Mammal: Florida panther
12	Reptile: American alligator
13	Butterfly: Zebra longwing
14	Flower: Orange blossom
15	Tree: Sabal palmetto palm

1. Florida has both a state marine mammal (the manatee) and a state saltwater mammal (the dolphin).

2. Florida has the longest shoreline—8,436 miles (13,576 km)—in the lower 48 states.

3. You're never more than 60 miles (97 km) from a salt water coast no matter where you are in Florida.

4. Key West is the southernmost city in the continental United States.

5. NASA's Mercury, Gemini, Apollo, and space shuttle missions all launched into space from Cape Canaveral.

6. Orlando has more theme-park visitors than anywhere else in the world.

7. Walt Disney World Resort is the biggest and most visited recreational resort.

8. Florida produces more than 70 percent of the nation's oranges.

9. Spanish explorers founded St. Augustine in 1565, making it the oldest city in the U.S.

10. South Florida is the only place on Earth where both alligators and crocodiles live in the wild.

5 Famous People From Florida

1. Antonio Brown, football player
2. Ariana Grande, singer
3. Zora Neale Hurston, author
4. A. Philip Randolph, labor leader
5. Bob Ross, painter

YOU NOW KNOW MORE THAN 1,000 NEW FACTS.

30 STATE FACTS ABOUT GEORGIA

15 Fast Facts

1	Abbreviation: GA
2	Date of Statehood: January 2, 1788
3	Nickname: Peach State
4	Population: 10,711,908
5	Total Area: 59,425 square miles (153,910 sq km)
6	Area Rank: 24
7	Capital: Atlanta
8	Largest City: Atlanta
9	Motto: "Wisdom, Justice, and Moderation"
10	Bird: Brown thrasher
11	Mammal: White-tailed deer
12	Reptile: Gopher tortoise
13	Insect: Honeybee
14	Flower: Cherokee rose
15	Tree: Southern live oak

5 Famous People From Georgia

1. Jimmy Carter, U.S. president
2. Ciara, singer
3. Martin Luther King, Jr., civil rights activist
4. Julia Roberts, actress
5. Jackie Robinson, baseball player

1. Georgia was named after King George II of England.

2. Georgia was founded in 1732 by James Oglethorpe, a British Parliament member and prison reformer. He wanted to find a place where prisoners who could not pay their debts could have a second chance.

3. Peach trees were introduced to Georgia in the 1700s. Peaches are still a major fruit crop in the state.

4. The state also produces more pecans, peanuts, and Vidalia onions than any other state.

5. Georgia is the largest state east of the Mississippi River.

6. The first newspaper in a Native American language was published in New Echota starting in 1828, using Sequoyah's Cherokee syllabary.

7. In 1946–1947, Georgia had three governors at the same time.

8. The world's largest bas-relief (etched) stone sculpture is located on the face of Stone Mountain. It is a memorial to Confederate leaders.

9. The Center for Civil and Human Rights opened in Atlanta in 2014. It includes galleries featuring the original writings of Martin Luther King, Jr.

10. The Masters Golf Tournament takes place in Augusta every year.

30 STATE FACTS ABOUT HAWAII

15 Fast Facts

1	Abbreviation: HI
2	Date of Statehood: August 21, 1959
3	Nickname: Aloha State
4	Population: 1,455,271
5	Total Area: 10,932 square miles (28,314 sq km)
6	Area Rank: 43
7	Capital: Honolulu
8	Largest City: Honolulu
9	Motto: "The Life of the Land is Perpetuated in Righteousness"
10	Bird: Nene (Hawaiian goose)
11	Mammal: Hawaiian monk seal
12	Reptile: Gold dust day gecko
13	Insect: Kamehameha butterfly
14	Flower: Yellow hibiscus
15	Tree: Kukui (candlenut)

5 Famous People From Hawaii

1. Lois Lowry, author
2. Bruno Mars, musician
3. Jason Momoa, actor
4. Barack Obama, U.S. president
5. Michelle Wie, golfer

1. Hawaii is the only U.S. state not attached to North America.

2. Eight main islands and many smaller atolls and islets across some 1,500 miles (2,400 km) make up the state.

3. Hawaii is the only state that grows coffee as a major crop.

4. More than one-third of the world's pineapples are grown in Hawaii.

5. During the 1800s, workers came from many Asian countries to work on sugar cane plantations.

6. Hawaii was ruled by a monarchy for many years.

7. Queen Liliuokalani was overthrown in 1893 by a group of men from the United States, Germany, and Britain who had interests in the pineapple and sugar industries.

8. The action was backed by the U.S. military, and the U.S. government took over the island in 1900.

9. Kilauea is the world's most active volcano.

10. Hawaii has its own time zone.

30 STATE FACTS ABOUT IDAHO

15 Fast Facts

1	Abbreviation: ID
2	Date of Statehood: July 3, 1890
3	Nickname: Gem State
4	Population: 1,839,106
5	Total Area: 83,569 square miles (216,443 sq km)
6	Area Rank: 14
7	Capital: Boise
8	Largest City: Boise
9	Motto: "It Is Perpetual"
10	Bird: Mountain bluebird
11	Horse: Appaloosa
12	Insect: Monarch butterfly
13	Vegetable: Potato
14	Flower: Syringa
15	Tree: White pine

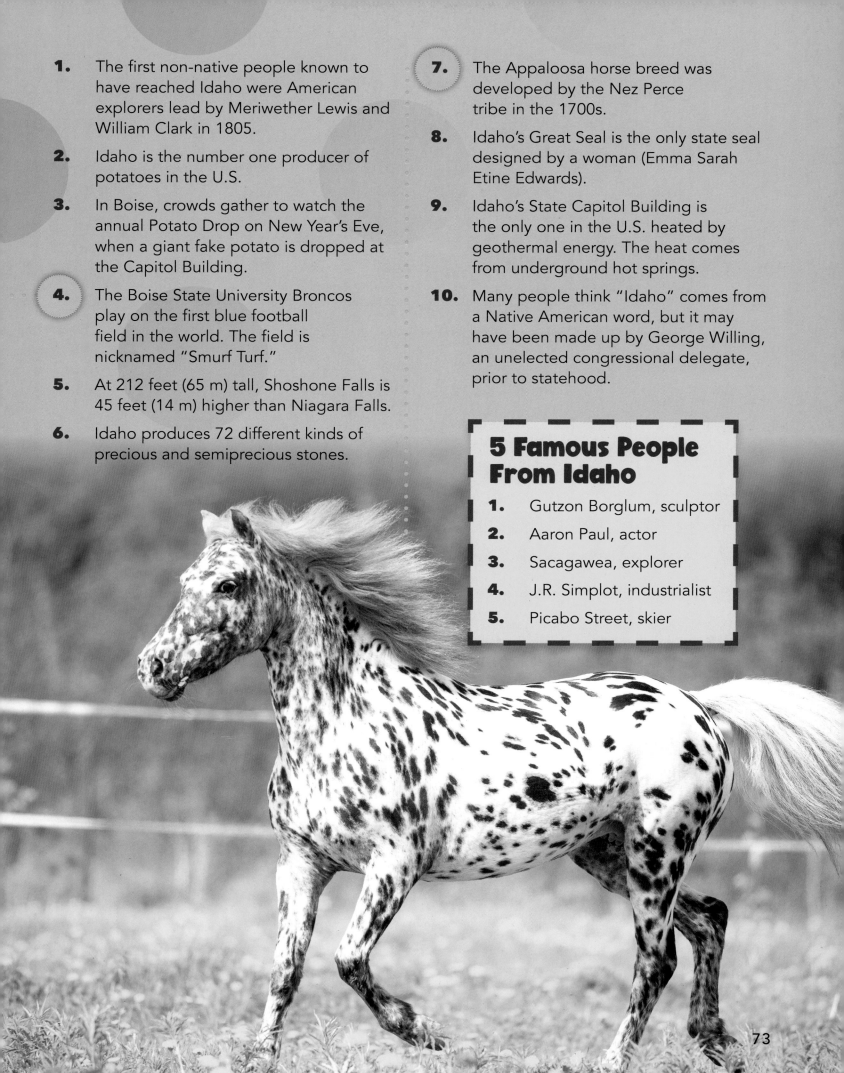

1. The first non-native people known to have reached Idaho were American explorers lead by Meriwether Lewis and William Clark in 1805.

2. Idaho is the number one producer of potatoes in the U.S.

3. In Boise, crowds gather to watch the annual Potato Drop on New Year's Eve, when a giant fake potato is dropped at the Capitol Building.

4. The Boise State University Broncos play on the first blue football field in the world. The field is nicknamed "Smurf Turf."

5. At 212 feet (65 m) tall, Shoshone Falls is 45 feet (14 m) higher than Niagara Falls.

6. Idaho produces 72 different kinds of precious and semiprecious stones.

7. The Appaloosa horse breed was developed by the Nez Perce tribe in the 1700s.

8. Idaho's Great Seal is the only state seal designed by a woman (Emma Sarah Etine Edwards).

9. Idaho's State Capitol Building is the only one in the U.S. heated by geothermal energy. The heat comes from underground hot springs.

10. Many people think "Idaho" comes from a Native American word, but it may have been made up by George Willing, an unelected congressional delegate, prior to statehood.

5 Famous People From Idaho

1. Gutzon Borglum, sculptor
2. Aaron Paul, actor
3. Sacagawea, explorer
4. J.R. Simplot, industrialist
5. Picabo Street, skier

30 STATE FACTS ABOUT ILLINOIS

15 Fast Facts

1. Abbreviation: IL
2. Date of Statehood: December 3, 1818
3. Nickname: Prairie State
4. Population: 12,812,508
5. Total Area: 57,914 square miles (149,997 sq km)
6. Area Rank: 25
7. Capital: Springfield
8. Largest City: Chicago
9. Motto: "State Sovereignty, National Union"
10. Bird: Northern cardinal
11. Mammal: White-tailed deer
12. Reptile: Painted turtle
13. Insect: Monarch butterfly
14. Flower: Violet
15. Tree: White oak

5 Famous People From Illinois

1. Hillary Clinton, first lady and secretary of state
2. Walt Disney, animator and theme park entrepreneur
3. Melissa McCarthy, actress
4. Michelle Obama, first lady
5. Ronald Reagan, U.S. president

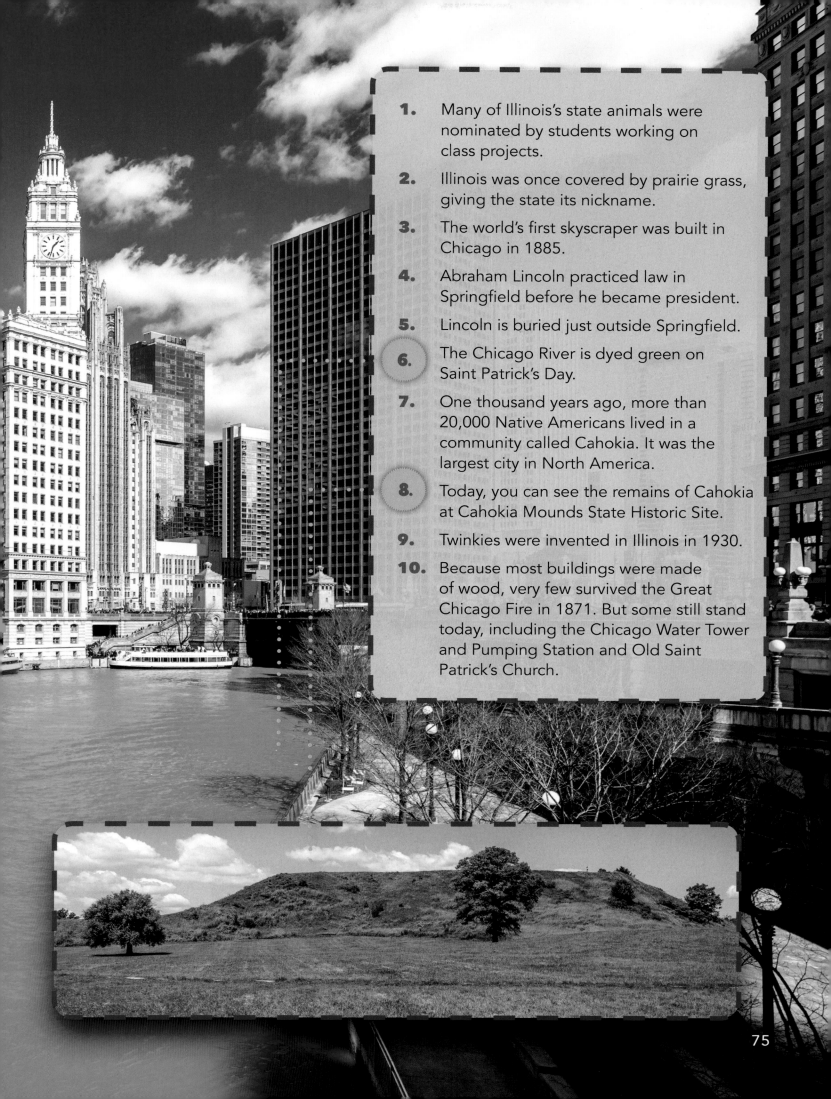

1. Many of Illinois's state animals were nominated by students working on class projects.

2. Illinois was once covered by prairie grass, giving the state its nickname.

3. The world's first skyscraper was built in Chicago in 1885.

4. Abraham Lincoln practiced law in Springfield before he became president.

5. Lincoln is buried just outside Springfield.

6. The Chicago River is dyed green on Saint Patrick's Day.

7. One thousand years ago, more than 20,000 Native Americans lived in a community called Cahokia. It was the largest city in North America.

8. Today, you can see the remains of Cahokia at Cahokia Mounds State Historic Site.

9. Twinkies were invented in Illinois in 1930.

10. Because most buildings were made of wood, very few survived the Great Chicago Fire in 1871. But some still stand today, including the Chicago Water Tower and Pumping Station and Old Saint Patrick's Church.

30 STATE FACTS ABOUT INDIANA

15 Fast Facts

1 Abbreviation: IN

2 Date of Statehood: December 11, 1816

3 Nickname: Hoosier State

4 Population: 6,785,528

5 Total Area: 36,420 square miles (94,327 sq km)

6 Area Rank: 38

7 Capital: Indianapolis

8 Largest City: Indianapolis

9 Motto: "Crossroads of America"

10 Bird: Northern cardinal

11 Mammal: none

12 Insect: Say's firefly

13 Flower: Peony

14 Tree: Tulip tree

15 Stone: Salem limestone

5 Famous People From Indiana

1. Larry Bird, basketball player

2. Jim Davis, cartoonist

3. Benjamin Harrison, U.S. president

4. Janet Jackson, singer

5. Wilbur Wright, aviation pioneer

1. No one knows exactly what "Hoosier" means or where it came from, but the word has been used to identify Indiana residents since the early 19th century.

2. "Indiana" means "land of the Indians."

3. Fewer than 8,000 Native Americans live in Indiana today.

4. Indiana was once called "Mother of Vice Presidents" because in 10 of the 13 elections between 1868 and 1916, there was a man from Indiana on the ballot.

5. About 20 percent of the nation's popcorn is grown in Indiana.

6. John Chapman, better known as Johnny Appleseed, is buried near Fort Wayne.

7. The Indianapolis Motor Speedway opened in 1909. It's home to the Indy 500, the largest single-day sporting event in the world.

8. Wabash was the first city in the United States to install electric street lights, in 1880.

9. Corydon was the first state capital (1816–1825).

10. Indiana is home to almost 100 historic covered bridges.

30 STATE FACTS ABOUT IOWA

15 Fast Facts

1	Abbreviation: IA
2	Date of Statehood: December 28, 1846
3	Nickname: Hawkeye State
4	Population: 3,190,369
5	Total Area: 56,273 square miles (145,746 sq km)
6	Area Rank: 26
7	Capital: Des Moines
8	Largest City: Des Moines
9	Motto: "Our Liberties We Prize and Our Rights We Will Maintain"
10	Bird: Eastern goldfinch
11	Mammal: none
12z	Insect: none
13	Flower: Wild rose
14	Tree: Oak
15	Stone: Geode

5 Famous People From Iowa

1. Mamie Eisenhower, first lady
2. Danai Gurira, actress and writer
3. Herbert Hoover, U.S. president
4. Elijah Wood, actor
5. Grant Wood, painter

1. The name Iowa comes from the Iowa River, which was named for a Sioux tribe called the Ioways.

2. "Hawkeye State" is a tribute to Black Hawk, leader of the Native American Sauk tribe.

3. Iowa is also called the Corn State.

4. 90 percent of the land in Iowa is devoted to agriculture.

5. The United States acquired Iowa as part of the Louisiana Purchase.

6. The Iowa caucuses have launched every U.S. presidential race since 1972. During the caucuses, people choose delegates who will vote for their chosen candidates for the presidential nomination.

7. Iowa is the only state whose name starts with two vowels.

8. Many woolly mammoth bones have been found in Iowa.

9. Iowa and Missouri almost went to war in the 1830s over a surveying mistake.

10. Iowan Arabella Mansfield became the first woman lawyer in the U.S. in 1869.

30 STATE FACTS ABOUT KANSAS

15 Fast Facts

1	Abbreviation: KS
2	Date of Statehood: January 29, 1861
3	Nickname: Sunflower State
4	Population: 2,937,880
5	Total Area: 82,278 square miles (213,099 sq km)
6	Area Rank: 15
7	Capital: Topeka
8	Largest City: Wichita
9	Motto: "To the Stars Through Difficulties"
10	Bird: Western meadowlark
11	Mammal: American buffalo
12	Reptile: Ornate box turtle
13	Insect: Honeybee
14	Flower: Sunflower
15	Tree: Cottonwood

5 Famous People From Kansas

1. Bob Dole, U.S. senator
2. Amelia Earhart, aviator
3. Dwight Eisenhower, U.S. president
4. Janelle Monáe, singer and actress
5. Gordon Parks, photographer

1. In 1854, the Kansas-Nebraska Act allowed residents of both the Kansas and Nebraska territories to vote on whether or not to allow slavery.

2. After the Act was passed, proslavery and antislavery settlers flooded into Kansas to try to influence the decision. The violence that followed led to the state being called "Bleeding Kansas."

3. Smith County is the geographical center of the lower 48 states.

4. Kansas has more than 500 caves.

5. The first Pizza Hut opened in Wichita in 1958.

6. In 2003, scientists proved that Kansas is actually flatter than a pancake.

7. Scientists at the University of Kansas in 1905 identified helium, previously thought to rarely be found on Earth, in natural gas deposits from the Great Plains.

8. The first woman mayor in the United States was Susanna Madora Salter, who was elected in Argonia in 1887.

9. A grain elevator in Hutchinson is half a mile long and holds 46 million bushels of grain.

10. Kansas is the largest wheat-producing state. It produces almost one-fifth of all the wheat grown in the U.S.

30
STATE FACTS ABOUT
KENTUCKY

1	Abbreviation: KY
2	Date of Statehood: June 1, 1792
3	Nickname: Bluegrass State
4	Population: 4,505,836
5	Total Area: 40,408 square miles (104,656 sq km)
6	Area Rank: 37
7	Capital: Frankfort
8	Largest City: Louisville
9	Motto: "United We Stand, Divided We Fall"
10	Bird: Northern cardinal
11	Game Animal: Gray squirrel
12	Butterfly: Viceroy butterfly
13	Insect: Honeybee
14	Flower: Goldenrod
15	Tree: Tulip tree

5 Famous People
From Kentucky

1. Muhammad Ali, boxer
2. George Clooney, actor
3. Jennifer Lawrence, actress
4. Abraham Lincoln, U.S. president
5. Diane Sawyer, journalist

1. The eastern part of present-day Kentucky was once part of Virginia.

2. Abraham Lincoln and Jefferson Davis, presidents of the United States and Confederate States during the American Civil War, were born less than one year and 100 miles apart in the state.

3. Thomas Edison worked for two years as a telegraph operator in Louisville's Western Union office.

4. The song "Happy Birthday to You" was written in Louisville in the late 1800s by a teacher and her sister.

5. In 1959, a B-52 bomber carrying two nuclear weapons collided in midair with a refueling aircraft near Hardinsburg. One of the weapons was damaged but neither detonated.

6. In 1997, the Kentucky Department of Fish and Wildlife Resources began reintroducing elk into easter Kentucky, where they had been hunted out of existence more than 100 years earlier.

7. Kentucky's Mammoth Cave is the longest known cave system in the world.

8. The Kentucky Derby is the oldest continuously held major sporting event in the U.S. The horse race ha: been run every year since 1875.

9. The Derby, for three-year-old thoroughbred horses, has been call "the greatest two minutes in sports

10. The Harland Sanders Cafe and Museum in Corbin honors the location where the founder of KFC developed his now-world-famous chicken recipe.

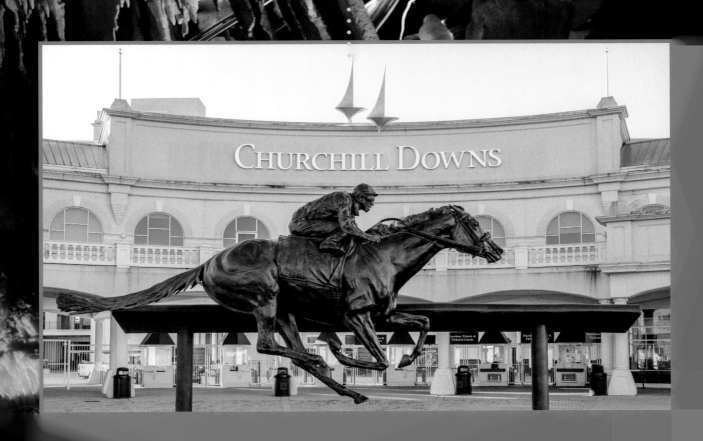

30 STATE FACTS ABOUT LOUISIANA

15 Fast Facts

1. Abbreviation: LA
2. Date of Statehood: April 30, 1812
3. Nickname: Pelican State
4. Population: 4,657,757
5. Total Area: 52,378 square miles (135,658 sq km)
6. Area Rank: 31
7. Capital: Baton Rouge
8. Largest City: New Orleans
9. Motto: "Union, Justice, and Confidence"
10. Bird: Eastern Brown Pelican
11. Mammal: Black bear
12. Reptile: Alligator
13. Insect: Honeybee
14. Flower: Magnolia blossom
15. Tree: Bald cypress

5 Famous People From Louisiana

1. Truman Capote, novelist
2. Ellen DeGeneres, talk-show host
3. Fats Domino, musician
4. Huey Newton, civil rights activist
5. Britney Spears, singer

1. Louisiana Territory was named after King Louis XIV of France.

2. The highest point in Louisiana is only 535 feet (163 m) above sea level.

3. The lowest point is New Orleans, which is eight feet (2.4 m) below sea level.

4. Louisiana has one of the largest alligator populations in the U.S.

5. Mardi Gras is a huge parade and party held in New Orleans on Fat Tuesday, the day before the Christian season of Lent begins.

6. New Orleans is called "Big Easy" because of its relaxed lifestyle. It is also known as "the Crescent City" or NOLA.

7. Because New Orleans is surrounded by swamps and marshes, it relies on a system of levees to protect it from flooding.

8. Those levees failed disastrously during Hurricane Katrina in 2005, leading to city-wide flooding and destruction.

9. The Lake Pontchartrain Causeway is the world's longest bridge over a body of water, stretching for almost 24 miles (39 km).

10. The Catahoula Leopard Dog is Louisiana's state dog and originated in Louisiana.

30
STATE FACTS ABOUT
MAINE

15 Fast Facts

1	Abbreviation: ME
2	Date of Statehood: March 15, 1820
3	Nickname: Pine Tree State
4	Population: 1,362,359
5	Total Area: 35,380 square miles (91,634 sq km)
6	Area Rank: 39
7	Capital: Augusta
8	Largest City: Portland
9	Motto: "I Direct"
10	Bird: Black-capped chickadee
11	Mammal: Moose
12	Crustacean: Lobster
13	Insect: Honeybee
14	Flower: White pinecone and tassel
15	Tree: White pine

1. Maine was once part of the Massachusetts Bay Colony and joined the U.S. as part of Massachusetts.

2. Maine is the only U.S. state with a one-syllable name.

3. Maine is the only state that shares its border with just one other state.

4. 90 percent of the U.S. lobster supply is caught off of Maine's coast.

5. Maine is also the largest producer of blueberries in the U.S.

6. The University of Maine has a Lobster Institute, dedicated to learning more about these animals.

7. About 76,000 moose live in Maine.

8. The Maine Coon Cat, the state's official cat, is the largest domestic cat breed.

9. No one is sure how Maine got its name. It was the name of a historic French province but might also come from sailors who called it the "mainland."

10. Eastport is the most eastern city in the United States and the first place in the U.S. to see sunrise.

5 Famous People
From Maine

1. L.L. Bean, entrepreneur
2. Anna Kendrick, actress
3. Stephen King, author
4. Henry Wadsworth Longfellow, poet
5. Margaret Chase Smith, U.S. senator

30 STATE FACTS ABOUT MARYLAND

15 Fast Facts

1   Abbreviation: MD

2   Date of Statehood: April 28, 1788

3   Nickname: Old Line State

4   Population: 6,177,224

5   Total Area: 12,406 square miles (32,131 sq km)

6   Area Rank: 42

7   Capital: Annapolis

8   Largest City: Baltimore

9   Motto: "Strong Deeds, Gentle Words"

10 Bird: Baltimore oriole

11 Reptile: Diamondback terrapin

12 Crustacean: Blue crab

13 Insect: Baltimore checkerspot butterfly

14 Flower: Black-eyed Susan

15 Tree: White oak

5 Famous People From Maryland

1. Frederick Douglass, abolitionist

2. Thurgood Marshall, Supreme Court justice

3. Jada Pinkett Smith, actress

4. Babe Ruth, baseball player

5. Harriet Tubman, leader of Underground Railroad

1. Maryland does not have a state mammal, but it does have a state horse (Thoroughbred), dog (Chesapeake Bay Retriever), and cat (Calico).

2. Annapolis was the capital of the U.S. between November 1783 and August 1784.

3. The state gave up part of its land to create Washington, D.C.

4. The Mason-Dixon line between Maryland and Pennsylvania was considered the line dividing north and south prior to the American Civil War.

5. Maryland was an important part of the Underground Railroad.

6. Although it is a Southern state, Maryland did not join the Confederacy during the Civil War.

7. The Maryland State House is the oldest state capitol building in continuous use.

8. George Washington gave Maryland its "Old Line" nickname after troops called the Maryland Line proved brave and dependable during the American Revolution.

9. The first telegraph message was sent in 1844 from Washington, D.C., to Baltimore.

10. The U.S. Naval Academy was founded in Annapolis in 1845.

30

STATE FACTS ABOUT
MASSACHUSETTS

15 Fast Facts

1	Abbreviation: MA
2	Date of Statehood: February 6, 1788
3	Nickname: Bay State
4	Population: 7,029,917
5	Total Area: 10,554 square miles (27,335 sq km)
6	Area Rank: 44
7	Capital: Boston
8	Largest City: Boston
9	Motto: "By the Sword We Seek Peace, But Peace Only Under Liberty"
10	Bird: Black-capped chickadee
11	Marine Mammal: Right whale
12	Reptile: Reptile
13	Insect: Ladybug
14	Flower: Mayflower
15	Tree: American elm

1. The chocolate chip cookie was invented by Ruth Wakefield at the Toll House Inn in Whitman.

2. Fig Newton cookies are named after the town of Newton.

3. Four U.S. presidents were born in Massachusetts: John Adams, John Quincy Adams, John F. Kennedy, and George H.W. Bush.

4. Boston Common is the nation's oldest public park. It dates to 1634.

5. The first telephone call in history was made between inventor Alexander Graham Bell and his assistant, Thomas Watson, on March 10, 1876, in Boston.

6. Basketball was invented in Springfield in 1891.

7. The first U.S. subway system was established in Boston in 1897.

8. Webster's Lake Chargoggagoggmanchauggagoggchaubunagungamaugg has the longest lake name in the world.

9. The Boston terrier is the Massachusetts state dog.

10. Massachusetts observes a legal holiday called Patriots' Day on the third Monday of April. It commemorates the first battles of the American Revolution at Lexington and Concord on April 19, 1775.

5 Famous People From Massachusetts

1. Ben Affleck, actor and director

2. Louisa May Alcott, author

3. Alexander Graham Bell, inventor

4. Mindy Kaling, actress and writer

5. Dr. Seuss (Theodor Seuss Geisel), author

30 STATE FACTS ABOUT MICHIGAN

15 Fast Facts

1. Abbreviation: MI
2. Date of Statehood: January 26, 1837
3. Nickname: Wolverine State
4. Population: 10,077,331
5. Total Area: 96,714 square miles (250,488 sq km)
6. Area Rank: 11
7. Capital: Lansing
8. Largest City: Detroit
9. Motto: "If You Seek a Pleasant Peninsula, Look About You"
10. Bird: American robin
11. Mammal: White-tailed deer
12. Reptile: Painted turtle
13. Fish: Trout
14. Flower: Apple blossom
15. Tree: White pine

5 Famous People From Michigan

1. Kristen Bell, actress
2. Gerald Ford, U.S. president
3. Henry Ford, automotive pioneer
4. Magic Johnson, basketball player and entrepreneur
5. Diana Ross, singer

1. Mastodon fossils have been found in many places in Michigan, and it is the official state fossil.

2. Four flags have flown over Michigan: French, English, Spanish, and the United States.

3. People from Michigan are called Michiganders.

4. The state is made up of two peninsulas.

5. People in Michigan's Upper Peninsula ("U.P.") are sometimes called "Yoopers."

6. Detroit was nicknamed "Motor City" as the center of the automobile industry.

7. Michigan is the only place in the U.S. with a floating post office. The *J.W. Westcott II*, a tugboat, has its own zip code and delivers mail to ships passing through the Detroit River.

8. Michigan has more than 11,000 inland lakes.

9. Michigan borders four of the five Great Lakes.

10. The name "Michigan" comes from a Chippewa word "Michi-gama," which means "large lake."

30

STATE FACTS ABOUT
MINNESOTA

HERE 1475 FT
ABOVE
THE OCEAN
THE MIGHTY
MISSISSIPPI
BEGINS
TO FLOW
ON ITS
WINDING WAY
2552 MILES
TO THE
GULF OF
MEXICO

15 Fast Facts

1	Abbreviation:	MN
2	Date of Statehood:	May 11, 1858
3	Nickname:	North Star State
4	Population:	5,706,494
5	Total Area:	86,936 square miles (225,163 sq km)
6	Area Rank:	12
7	Capital:	St. Paul
8	Largest City:	Minneapolis
9	Motto:	"The Star of the North"
10	Bird:	Common loon
11	Mammal:	none
12	Fish:	Walleye
13	Butterfly:	Monarch butterfly
14	Flower:	Pink and white lady's slipper
15	Tree:	Red pine

5 Famous People From Minnesota

1. Bob Dylan, musician
2. Judy Garland, actress
3. Chris Pratt, actor
4. Prince, musician
5. Charles Schulz, cartoonist

1. Minnesota was the first state to volunteer troops to serve the Union during the Civil War.

2. Although it is sometimes known as the "Land of 10,000 Lakes," Minnesota actually has 11,842 lakes.

3. Bloomington's Mall of America is the largest shopping mall in the country.

4. The Mississippi River begins in tiny Lake Itasca in northern Minnesota.

5. Masking tape, Scotch tape, Wheaties cereal, Bisquick baking mix, Aveda beauty products, and Green Giant vegetables were all invented in Minnesota.

6. The Mayo Clinic, one of the best medical facilities in the world, is located in Rochester.

7. Tonka trucks were developed in Minnesota.

8. Minnesota's waters flow outward in three directions: north to Hudson Bay in Canada, east to the Atlantic Ocean, and south to the Gulf of Mexico.

9. Author Laura Ingalls Wilder spent part of her childhood in Walnut Grove.

10. "Minnesota" comes from a Native American word meaning "cloudy water" or "sky-tinted water."

30 STATE FACTS ABOUT MISSISSIPPI

15 Fast Facts

1	Abbreviation: MS
2	Date of Statehood: December 10, 1817
3	Nickname: Magnolia State
4	Population: 2,961,279
5	Total Area: 48,432 square miles (125,438 sq km)
6	Area Rank: 32
7	Capital: Jackson
8	Largest City: Jackson
9	Motto: "By Valor and Arms"
10	Bird: Mockingbird
11	Mammals: White-tailed deer and red fox
12	Reptile: American alligator
13	Insect: Honeybee
14	Flower: Magnolia
15	Tree: Magnolia

1. The state is named after the Mississippi River.

2. The city of Jackson, founded in 1821, was named in honor of future president Andrew Jackson and his actions during the War of 1812.

3. The 13th Amendment, which abolished slavery in 1865, was not ratified by Mississippi until 2013.

4. In 1963, Dr. James Hardy performed the first human lung transplant at the University of Mississippi.

5. Mississippi produces more farm-raised catfish than any other state.

5 Famous People From Mississippi

1. Jim Henson, puppeteer
2. James Earl Jones, actor
3. Jerry Rice, football player
4. Ida B. Wells, journalist
5. Oprah Winfrey, TV host and entrepreneur

6. The 26-mile (42 km) section of the Mississippi Gulf Coast that stretches from Biloxi to Henderson Point is the longest human-engineered beach in the world.

7. Blues music was born in the Mississippi Delta, and the state was home to many blues pioneers.

8. Although Coca-Cola was invented in Georgia, it was first bottled in Vicksburg in 1894.

9. The teddy bear's name was coined after President Theodore Roosevelt refused to shoot a bear under what he considered unsportsmanlike terms during a hunt in Mississippi.

10. There are more churches per capita in Mississippi than in any other state.

30
STATE FACTS ABOUT
MISSOURI

1	Abbreviation: MO
2	Date of Statehood: August 10, 1821
3	Nickname: Show Me State
4	Population: 6,154,913
5	Total Area: 69,707 square miles (180,540 sq km)
6	Area Rank: 21
7	Capital: Jefferson City
8	Largest City: Kansas City
9	Motto: "Let the Welfare of the People Be the Supreme Law"
10	Bird: Eastern bluebird
11	Mammal: Missouri mule
12	Amphibian: American bullfrog
13	Insect: Honeybee
14	Flower: Hawthorn
15	Tree: Flowering dogwood

5 Famous People From Missouri

1. Maya Angelou, poet
2. Chuck Berry, musician
3. Ellie Kemper, actress
4. Harry S. Truman, U.S. president
5. Mark Twain (Samuel Clemens), author

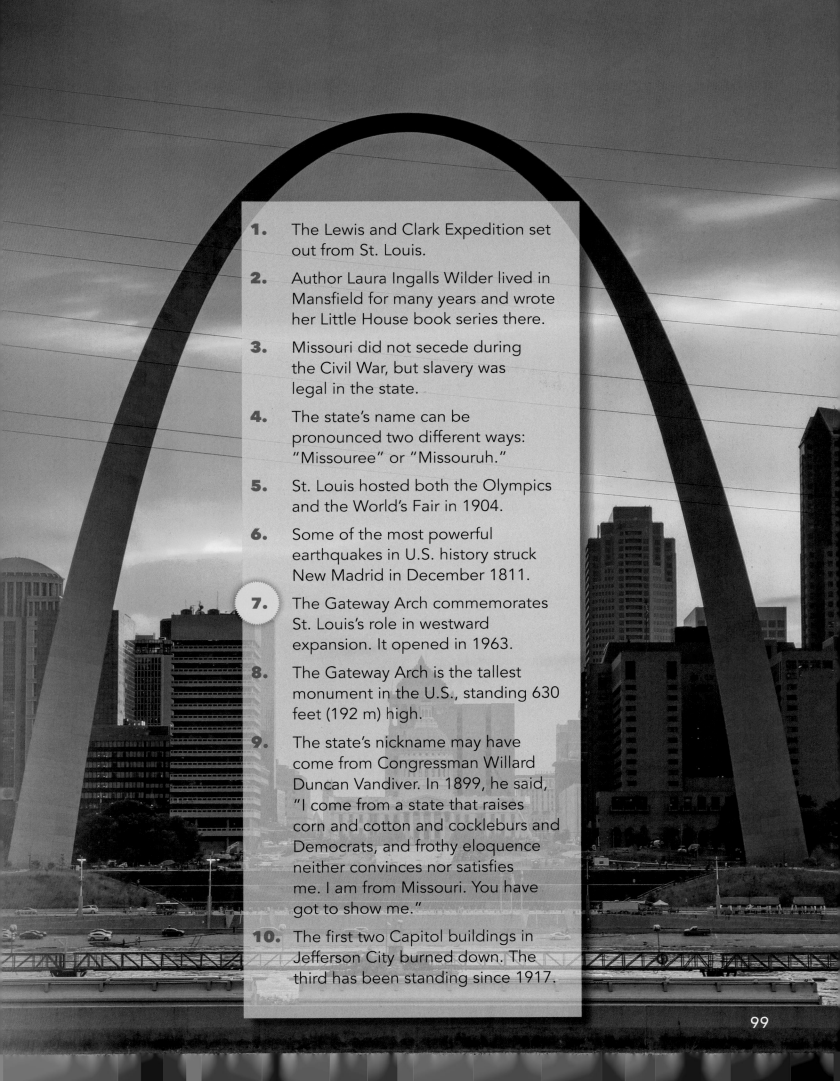

1. The Lewis and Clark Expedition set out from St. Louis.

2. Author Laura Ingalls Wilder lived in Mansfield for many years and wrote her Little House book series there.

3. Missouri did not secede during the Civil War, but slavery was legal in the state.

4. The state's name can be pronounced two different ways: "Missouree" or "Missouruh."

5. St. Louis hosted both the Olympics and the World's Fair in 1904.

6. Some of the most powerful earthquakes in U.S. history struck New Madrid in December 1811.

7. The Gateway Arch commemorates St. Louis's role in westward expansion. It opened in 1963.

8. The Gateway Arch is the tallest monument in the U.S., standing 630 feet (192 m) high.

9. The state's nickname may have come from Congressman Willard Duncan Vandiver. In 1899, he said, "I come from a state that raises corn and cotton and cockleburs and Democrats, and frothy eloquence neither convinces nor satisfies me. I am from Missouri. You have got to show me."

10. The first two Capitol buildings in Jefferson City burned down. The third has been standing since 1917.

30 STATE FACTS ABOUT MONTANA

15 Fast Facts

1. Abbreviation: MT
2. Date of Statehood: November 8, 1889
3. Nickname: Treasure State
4. Population: 1,084,225
5. Total Area: 147,040 square miles (380,832 sq km)
6. Area Rank: 4
7. Capital: Helena
8. Largest City: Billings
9. Motto: "Gold and Silver"
10. Bird: Western meadowlark
11. Mammal: Grizzly bear
12. Fish: Blackspotted cutthroat trout
13. Butterfly: Mourning cloak
14. Flower: Bitterroot
15. Tree Ponderosa pine

5 Famous People From Montana

1. Gary Cooper, actor
2. Phil Jackson, basketball player and coach
3. David Lynch, filmmaker
4. Jeannette Rankin, U.S. congresswoman
5. Michelle Williams, actress

1. The famous Battle of Little Bighorn was fought between Native American tribes and the U.S. Army in 1876.

2. Many people flocked to Montana after gold was discovered there in the 1850s.

3. Montana is also called "Big Sky Country."

4. The name "Montana" comes from the Spanish word for mountains.

5. From Triple Divide Peak, water can flow in three directions: north to Hudson Bay, east to the Atlantic Ocean, and west to the Pacific Ocean.

6. Montana is home to more than 100 different species of mammals.

7. Bannack, founded in 1862 during the Gold Rush, was the first capital of Montana Territory. Today it is a ghost town.

8. The largest observed snowflake fell during a storm in 1887 in Montana. It was measured at 15 inches (38 cm) wide.

9. The most visited place in Montana is Glacier National Park.

10. There are more elk, deer, and antelope in Montana than there are people.

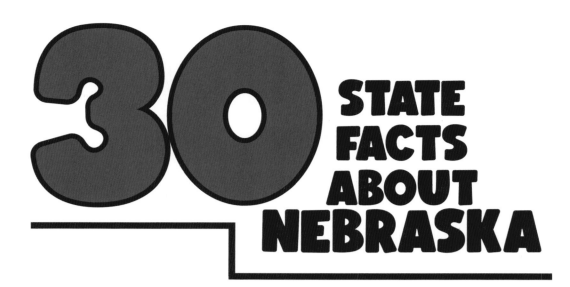

30 STATE FACTS ABOUT NEBRASKA

15 Fast Facts

1. Abbreviation: NE
2. Date of Statehood: March 1, 1867
3. Nickname: Cornhusker State
4. Population: 1,961,504
5. Total Area: 77,348 square miles (200,330 sq km)
6. Area Rank: 16
7. Capital: Lincoln
8. Largest City: Omaha
9. Motto: "Equality Before the Law"
10. Bird: Western meadowlark
11. Mammal: White-tailed deer
12. Fish: Channel catfish
13. Insect: Honeybee
14. Flower: Goldenrod
15. Tree: Cottonwood

5 Famous People
From Nebraska

1. Fred Astaire, actor and dancer
2. Warren Buffett, investor and philanthropist
3. Gerald Ford, U.S. president
4. Gabrielle Union, actress
5. Malcolm X, civil-rights activist

1. Many people settled in Nebraska as they traveled through it on the Oregon Trail.

2. Others arrived after the U.S. government passed the Homestead Act.

3. The state's name comes from a Native American word for "flat water." This name refers to the state's Platte River.

4. The University of Nebraska Cornhuskers football games are often attended by more than 90,000 people.

5. The first Arbor Day was held in Nebraska in 1872.

6. Because Nebraska had few trees, cottonwoods often served as landmarks on the Nebraska prairie.

7. A sculpture near Alliance called Carhenge features 39 cars arranged like the stone monoliths at Stonehenge.

8. Kool-Aid was invented in Nebraska and is the state's official soft drink.

9. Nebraska has the only unicameral, or single-house, legislature in the United States.

10. Famous aviator Charles Lindbergh took his first flying lessons in Nebraska.

30 STATE FACTS ABOUT NEVADA

15 Fast Facts

1. Abbreviation: NV
2. Date of Statehood: October 31, 1864
3. Nickname: Silver State
4. Population: 3,104,614
5. Total Area: 110,572 square miles (286,380 sq km)
6. Area Rank: 7
7. Capital: Carson City
8. Largest City: Las Vegas
9. Motto: "All For Our Country"
10. Bird: Mountain bluebird
11. Mammal: Desert bighorn sheep
12. Reptile: Desert tortoise
13. Insect: Vivid dancer damselfly
14. Flower: Sagebrush
15. Trees: Single-leaf piñon and bristlecone pine

1. The discovery of the Comstock Lode, in 1859, led to large-scale silver mining in Nevada.

2. Las Vegas has more hotel rooms than any other city in the world.

3. The top-secret Air Force facility Area 51 has long been the subject of rumors about UFOs and extraterrestrials.

4. In recent years, Nevada has produced more gold than any other U.S. state.

5. Nevada was originally inhabited by the Paiute, Shoshone, and Washoe tribes.

6. The first permanent non-native settlement was built by the Mormons in 1851.

7. Nevada is the driest state in the U.S. It receives less than 10 inches (25 cm) of precipitation per year.

8. About 86 percent of the land in Nevada is owned by the federal government.

9. Hoover Dam was originally called Boulder Dam. It was renamed after former President Herbert Hoover.

10. U.S. Route 50 in Nevada has been called "the loneliest road in America" because it travels through vast stretches with no towns or people.

5 Famous People From Nevada

1. Andre Agassi, tennis player

2. Kurt Busch, race-car driver

3. Kyle Busch, race-car driver

4. Patricia Ryan Nixon, first lady

5. Sarah Hopkins Winnemucca, author and activist

30

STATE FACTS ABOUT NEW HAMPSHIRE

15 Fast Facts

1. Abbreviation: NH
2. Date of Statehood: June 21, 1788
3. Nickname: Granite State
4. Population: 1,377,529
5. Total Area: 9,349 square miles (24,214 sq km)
6. Area Rank: 46
7. Capital: Concord
8. Largest City: Manchester
9. Motto: "Live Free or Die"
10. Bird: Purple finch
11. Mammal: White-tailed deer
12. Amphibian: Red-spotted newt
13. Insect: Ladybug
14. Flower: Purple lilac
15. Tree: White birch

5 Famous People From New Hampshire

1. Christa McAuliffe, teacher and astronaut
2. Mandy Moore, actress and singer
3. Franklin Pierce, U.S. president
4. Adam Sandler, actor
5. Alan Shepard, astronaut

1. New Hampshire was the first colony to set up its own government and constitution prior to the American Revolution.

2. For years, a rock formation called the Old Man of the Mountain was a beloved New Hampshire symbol. On May 3, 2003, the Old Man of the Mountain collapsed and fell.

3. In 1905, New Hampshire became the only U.S. state to host the formal conclusion of a foreign war when the treaty ending the Russo-Japanese War was signed in Portsmouth.

4. The state is named after Hampshire County in England.

5. On December 30, 1828, about 400 mill girls walked out of the Dover Cotton Factory in the first women's labor strike in the United States.

6. Despite being among the original 13 U.S. colonies, New Hampshire did not have an official state flag until 1909.

7. The weather station on Mount Washington has recorded some of the coldest temperatures and strongest winds in the continental United States.

8. Scottish settlers around Londonderry planted the first potato crop in America in 1719.

9. New Hampshire resident Sarah Josepha Hale wrote "Mary Had a Little Lamb" and also worked to make Thanksgiving a national holiday.

10. New Hampshire has the shortest coastline of any ocean-bordering state, at just 13 miles (21 km).

30 STATE FACTS ABOUT NEW JERSEY

15 Fast Facts

1. Abbreviation: NJ
2. Date of Statehood: December 18, 1787
3. Nickname: Garden State
4. Population: 9,288,994
5. Total Area: 8,723 square miles (22,592 sq km)
6. Area Rank: 47
7. Capital: Trenton
8. Largest City: Newark
9. Motto: "Liberty and Prosperity"
10. Bird: Eastern goldfinch
11. Mammal: Horse
12. Reptile: Bog turtle
13. Insect: Honeybee
14. Flower: Common violet
15. Tree: Red oak

5 Famous People From New Jersey

1. Edwin "Buzz" Aldrin, astronaut
2. Judy Blume, author
3. Peter Dinklage, actor
4. Grover Cleveland, U.S. president
5. Bruce Springsteen, musician

1. New Jersey has an official state microbe. *Streptomyces griseus* was discovered in the soil in 1916 and later was developed into an important antibiotic.

2. New Jersey has the highest population density of any state (more than 1,200 people per square mile).

3. Parts of the region were called New Netherlands and New Sweden before it was known as New Jersey.

4. The first baseball game was played in Hoboken in 1846.

5. New Jersey claims to be the "Diner Capital of the World."

6. More Revolutionary War battles were fought in New Jersey than in any other state.

7. In 1937, the German airship *Hindenburg* crashed and burned while landing at Lakehurst.

8. The streets in the Monopoly board game are named after real streets in Atlantic City.

9. There is an inactive volcano in Sussex County.

10. The light bulb, phonograph (record player), and motion picture projector were invented in Thomas Edison's Menlo Park laboratory.

30 STATE FACTS ABOUT NEW MEXICO

15 Fast Facts

1. Abbreviation: NM
2. Date of Statehood: January 6, 1912
3. Nickname: Land of Enchantment
4. Population: 2,117,522
5. Total Area: 121,590 square miles (314,917 sq km)
6. Area Rank: 5
7. Capital: Santa Fe
8. Largest City: Albuquerque
9. Motto: "It Grows As It Goes"
10. Bird: Roadrunner
11. Mammal: Black bear
12. Reptile: New Mexico whiptail
13. Insect: Tarantula hawk wasp
14. Flower: Yucca
15. Tree: Piñon pine

1. The original living Smokey Bear was found as a cub after a forest fire in Capitan. He went on to become the symbol for fire prevention by the U.S. Forest Service.

2. Santa Fe is the highest state capital, at 7,199 feet (2,194 m) above sea level.

3. People have lived in Taos Pueblo for more than 1,000 years.

4. The first atomic bomb was detonated in New Mexico.

5. The Albuquerque International Balloon Fiesta is the largest hot-air balloon festival in the world.

6. The Rio Grande is New Mexico's longest river and runs the entire length of the state.

7. New Mexico is unofficially a bilingual state, with one out of three families speaking Spanish.

8. New Mexico's official state question is "Red or green?" The colors refer to different chile varieties.

9. In 1950, the town of Hot Springs changed its name to Truth or Consequences, the title of a popular radio quiz program.

10. White Sands National Park is visited by some 600,000 people every year.

5 Famous People
From New Mexico

1. Jeff Bezos, entrepreneur
2. William Hanna, animator
3. Neil Patrick Harris, actor
4. Dolores Huerta, labor leader
5. Demi Lovato, singer

30

STATE FACTS ABOUT NEW YORK

15 Fast Facts

1. Abbreviation: NY
2. Date of Statehood: July 26, 1788
3. Nickname: Empire State
4. Population: 20,201,249
5. Total Area: 54,555 square miles (141,297 sq km)
6. Area Rank: 27
7. Capital: Albany
8. Largest City: New York City
9. Motto: "Ever Forward"
10. Bird: Eastern bluebird
11. Mammal: Beaver
12. Reptile: Snapping turtle
13. Insect: Ladybug
14. Flower: Rose
15. Tree: Sugar maple

5 Famous People From New York

1. Lucille Ball, actress
2. Lady Gaga, actress and singer
3. Jennifer Lopez, actress and singer
4. Grace Murray Hopper, computer scientist
5. Denzel Washington, actor

1. Five U.S. presidents were born in New York: Martin Van Buren, Millard Fillmore, Theodore Roosevelt, Franklin D. Roosevelt, and Donald Trump.

2. Many historians believe that New York's nickname comes from George Washington calling the state "the seat of the empire."

3. In 1807, the first successful steamboat, the *Clermont*, traveled up the Hudson River from New York City to Albany at a then-impressive 5 mph (8 km/h).

4. Nearly half of the length of the Hudson River is a tidal estuary, where salty seawater mixes with freshwater.

5. New York City was the first capital of the United States when the U.S. Constitution was ratified.

6. Hartsdale has the oldest and largest pet cemetery in the U.S.

7. New York's apple farmers claim to grow more varieties of the fruit than any other state.

8. Buffalo has hosted the National Buffalo Wing Festival since 2002.

9. Uncle Sam, the character who represents the United States, may have been based on a real person: Sam Wilson, a meatpacker from Troy.

10. Niagara Falls, on the border between Canada and New York, consists of American Falls, Bridal Veil Falls, and the Canadian Falls, also called Horseshoe Falls.

30 STATE FACTS ABOUT NORTH CAROLINA

15 Fast Facts

1. Abbreviation: NC
2. Date of Statehood: November 21, 1789
3. Nickname: Tar Heel State
4. Population: 10,439,388
5. Total Area: 53,819 square miles (139,391 sq km)
6. Area Rank: 28
7. Capital: Raleigh
8. Largest City: Charlotte
9. Motto: "To Be Rather Than To Seem"
10. Bird: Cardinal
11. Mammal: Grey squirrel
12. Reptile: Eastern box turtle
13. Insect: Honeybee
14. Flower: Dogwood
15. Tree: Pine

5 Famous People From North Carolina

1. Dale Earnhardt Jr., race-car driver
2. Andy Griffith, actor
3. Michael Jordan, basketball player
4. James K. Polk, U.S. president
5. Nina Simone, singer and musician

114

1. North Carolina's nickname comes from workers who sold tar and other products made from the state's pine trees to be used in wooden ship maintenance.

2. "Tar Heels" is also the nickname of the University of North Carolina's sports teams.

3. The Wright brothers tested their airplane on a North Carolina beach because it was remote, had steady winds, and the sand would provide a soft landing.

4. America's largest mansion, the Biltmore Estate, is in Asheville.

5. Pepsi was invented in New Bern.

6. The Outer Banks is nicknamed "the Graveyard of the Atlantic" because its sandbars and strong currents have sunk more than 1,000 vessels since 1526.

7. The first Krispy Kreme doughnut shop was in Winston-Salem.

8. The first English colony in North America was on Roanoke Island. Its settlers later disappeared under mysterious circumstances.

9. Babe Ruth hit his first professional home run in Fayetteville.

10. North Carolina is the nation's largest producer of sweet potatoes.

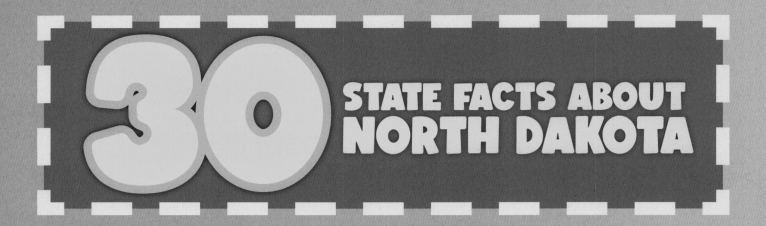

30 STATE FACTS ABOUT NORTH DAKOTA

15 Fast Facts

1. Abbreviation: ND
2. Date of Statehood: November 2, 1889
3. Nickname: Peace Garden State
4. Population: 779,094
5. Total Area: 70,698 square miles (183,107 sq km)
6. Area Rank: 19
7. Capital: Bismarck
8. Largest City: Fargo
9. Motto: "Liberty and Union, Now and Forever, One and Inseparable"
10. Bird: Western meadowlark
11. Mammal: Nokota horse
12. Fish: Northern pike
13. Insect: Ladybug
14. Flower: Wild prairie rose
15. Tree: American elm

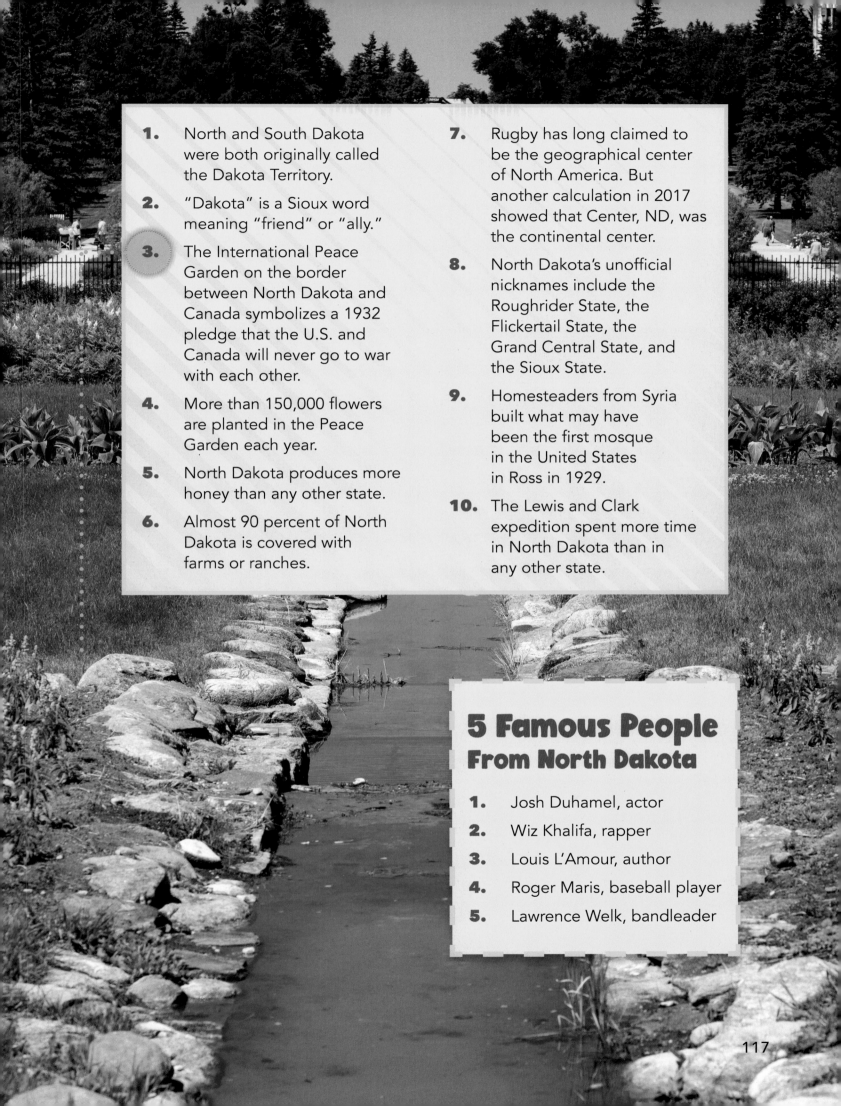

1. North and South Dakota were both originally called the Dakota Territory.

2. "Dakota" is a Sioux word meaning "friend" or "ally."

3. The International Peace Garden on the border between North Dakota and Canada symbolizes a 1932 pledge that the U.S. and Canada will never go to war with each other.

4. More than 150,000 flowers are planted in the Peace Garden each year.

5. North Dakota produces more honey than any other state.

6. Almost 90 percent of North Dakota is covered with farms or ranches.

7. Rugby has long claimed to be the geographical center of North America. But another calculation in 2017 showed that Center, ND, was the continental center.

8. North Dakota's unofficial nicknames include the Roughrider State, the Flickertail State, the Grand Central State, and the Sioux State.

9. Homesteaders from Syria built what may have been the first mosque in the United States in Ross in 1929.

10. The Lewis and Clark expedition spent more time in North Dakota than in any other state.

5 Famous People From North Dakota

1. Josh Duhamel, actor

2. Wiz Khalifa, rapper

3. Louis L'Amour, author

4. Roger Maris, baseball player

5. Lawrence Welk, bandleader

36 STATE FACTS ABOUT OHIO

15 Fast Facts

1. Abbreviation: OH

2. Date of Statehood: March 1, 1803

3. Nickname: Buckeye State

4. Population: 11,799,448

5. Total Area: 44,826 square miles (116,099 sq km)

6. Area Rank: 34

7. Capital: Columbus

8. Largest City: Columbus

9. Motto: "With God, All Things Are Possible"

10. Bird: Northern cardinal

11. Mammal: White-tailed deer

12. Reptile: Black racer snake

13. Insect: Ladybug

14. Flower: Red carnation

15. Tree: Ohio buckeye

1. Ohio is sometimes called "Mother of Presidents."

2. Seven U.S. presidents were born in Ohio: Ulysses S. Grant, Rutherford B. Hayes, James Garfield, Benjamin Harrison, William McKinley, William Howard Taft, and Warren Harding.

3. The state gets its nickname from the buckeye tree. The tree's nuts look like a deer's (buck's) eye.

4. Parts of the Cuyahoga River have caught fire at least 13 times, usually when sparks from trains fell into the polluted water. The government began working to clean up the river beginning in the late 1960s.

5. Although Ohio was declared a state in 1803, it didn't formally become a state until 1953 when President Dwight D. Eisenhower signed the official approval. (Eisenhower was nice enough to back-date the declaration to the original date.)

6. The state gets its name from the Iroquois word "ohi-yo," which means "great river."

7. Ohio has the only nonrectangular state flag in the U.S.

8. Ohio is the only state to have an official rock song: "Hang On Sloopy."

9. Oberlin College was the first college in the U.S. to admit both men and women from the time of its founding, in 1833, and Black students, in 1835.

10. The first professional football league formed in Canton in 1920.

5 Famous People From Ohio

1. Neil Armstrong, astronaut

2. Halle Berry, actress

3. LeBron James, basketball player

4. John Legend, musician

5. Toni Morrison, author

30
STATE FACTS ABOUT
OKLAHOMA

15 Fast Facts

1. Abbreviation: OK
2. Date of Statehood: November 16, 1907
3. Nickname: Sooner State
4. Population: 3,959,353
5. Total Area: 69,899 square miles (181,038 sq km)
6. Area Rank: 20
7. Capital: Oklahoma City
8. Largest City: Oklahoma City
9. Motto: "Labor Conquers All Things"
10. Bird: Scissor-tailed flycatcher
11. Mammal: Bison
12. Reptile: Collared lizard
13. Insect: Honeybee
14. Flower: Oklahoma rose
15. Tree: Redbud

1. Oklahoma's nickname comes from those who rushed into the territory to stake land claims before it was legal to do so. These early birds were called "Sooners," and some of the claims were challenged.

2. Oklahoma's official state meal is black-eyed peas, chicken-fried steak, okra, squash, corn on the cob, cornbread, barbecue pork, biscuits, sausage and gravy, grits, strawberries and pecan pie.

3. The nation's first tornado warning alert was issued in Oklahoma on March 25, 1948.

4. Cimarron County is the only county in the U.S. that borders four states: Colorado, New Mexico, Texas, and Kansas.

5. Oklahoma has the largest Native American population of any state.

6. Tahlequah is the tribal capital of the Cherokee Nation.

7. Oklahoma has more human-made lakes than any other state.

8. Per square mile, Oklahoma has the most tornadoes of any state.

9. Earthquakes began occurring with greater frequency in Oklahoma beginning in 2009. The state's rate of magnitude 3 and larger earthquakes was greater than California's from 2014 through 2017.

10. Oklahoma's state capitol building is the only one in the world with an oil well under it.

5 Famous People From Oklahoma

1. Garth Brooks, musician

2. Woody Guthrie, musician and songwriter

3. Wilma Mankiller, Cherokee leader

4. Maria Tallchief, dancer

5. Carrie Underwood, singer and songwriter

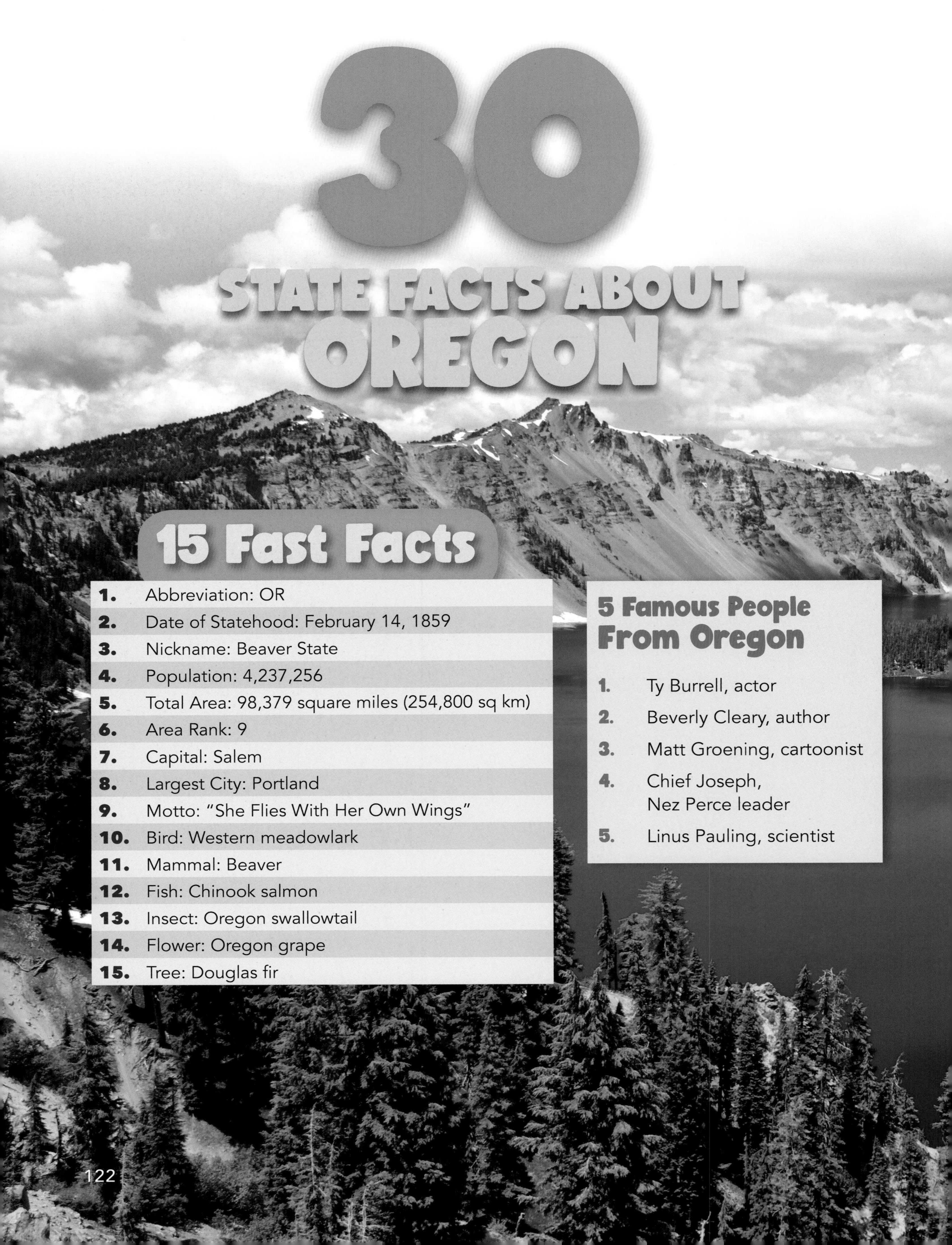

30
STATE FACTS ABOUT
OREGON

15 Fast Facts

1. Abbreviation: OR
2. Date of Statehood: February 14, 1859
3. Nickname: Beaver State
4. Population: 4,237,256
5. Total Area: 98,379 square miles (254,800 sq km)
6. Area Rank: 9
7. Capital: Salem
8. Largest City: Portland
9. Motto: "She Flies With Her Own Wings"
10. Bird: Western meadowlark
11. Mammal: Beaver
12. Fish: Chinook salmon
13. Insect: Oregon swallowtail
14. Flower: Oregon grape
15. Tree: Douglas fir

5 Famous People From Oregon

1. Ty Burrell, actor
2. Beverly Cleary, author
3. Matt Groening, cartoonist
4. Chief Joseph, Nez Perce leader
5. Linus Pauling, scientist

1. No one is sure how Oregon got its name. Some people think the state is named after the French word "ouragan," which means "hurricane." Others believe the name comes from the Chinook word "oolighan," which was a type of fish.

2. Oregon is nicknamed the Beaver State because beavers once drew fur traders and trappers to the region.

3. Crater Lake is the deepest lake in the U.S., with an average depth of 1,148 feet (350 m). It was formed when a volcano collapsed about 7,700 years ago.

4. Oregon is home to the biggest mushroom on Earth. The honey fungus covers about 2.4 miles (3.9 km) in Malheur National Forest.

5. During the Great Depression, North Bend used wooden coins as currency.

6. Oregon has the only state flag with a different design on each side.

7. During World War II, the Japanese military launched balloon bombs toward the U.S. On May 5, 1945, six people were killed near Bly when they found one of these balloons.

8. Mill Ends Park in Portland is the smallest park in the world. It measures just two feet (0.6 m) across and has one tree.

9. The sportswear company Nike started in Oregon and has its headquarters in Beaverton.

10. The John Day Fossil Beds National Monument is one of the richest fossil sites in the world.

30 STATE FACTS ABOUT PENNSYLVANIA

15 Fast Facts

1. Abbreviation: PA
2. Date of Statehood: December 12, 1787
3. Nickname: Keystone State
4. Population: 13,002,700
5. Total Area: 46,054 square miles (119,279 sq km)
6. Area Rank: 33
7. Capital: Harrisburg
8. Largest City: Philadelphia
9. Motto: "Virtue, Liberty, and Independence"
10. Bird: Ruffed grouse
11. Mammal: White-tailed deer
12. State Fish: Brook trout
13. Insect: Firefly
14. Flower: Mountain laurel
15. Tree: Eastern hemlock

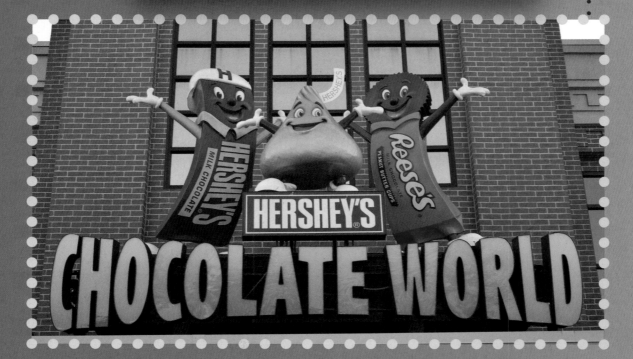

1. "Pennsylvania" means "Penn's woods." It was named in honor of colony founder William Penn's father, not Penn himself.

2. The Great Dane is the official state dog. William Penn had one of these big dogs, and its portrait hangs in the state capitol.

3. Pennsylvania is called the Keystone State because of its central position among the colonies. "Keystone" is an architecture term for a central, wedge-shaped stone in an arch.

4. Hershey claims to be the chocolate capital of the United States.

5. Pennsylvania is the only original colony not bordered by the Atlantic Ocean.

6. Punxsutawney Phil has been forecasting the weather on Groundhog Day since 1886. His handlers swear it's been the same groundhog all along.

7. Because so many players were serving in the military during World War II, the Philadelphia Eagles and the Pittsburgh Steelers merged to form the Steagles for one season in 1943.

8. The first polio vaccine was developed at the University of Pittsburgh.

9. Sylvester Stallone, star of the Rocky series of boxing movies, donated the Rocky Balboa statue at the Philadelphia Museum of Art to the city of Philadelphia in 1982.

10. The "pretzel belt" in the southeast is where a number of popular snack foods are produced, including Snyder's of Hanover pretzels and Herr's and UTZ potato chips.

5 Famous People From Pennsylvania

1. Rachel Carson, author and environmentalist
2. Margaret Mead, anthropologist
3. Fred Rogers, TV host
4. Will Smith, actor
5. Andy Warhol, artist

30 STATE FACTS ABOUT RHODE ISLAND

15 Fast Facts

1. Abbreviation: RI
2. Date of Statehood: May 29, 1790
3. Nickname: Ocean State
4. Population: 1,097,379
5. Total Area: 1,545 square miles (4,002 sq km)
6. Area Rank: 50
7. Capital: Providence
8. Largest City: Providence
9. Motto: "Hope"
10. Bird: Rhode Island Red chicken
11. Marine Mammal: Harbor seal
12. Fish: Striped bass
13. Insect: American burying beetle
14. Flower: Common blue violent
15. Tree: Red maple

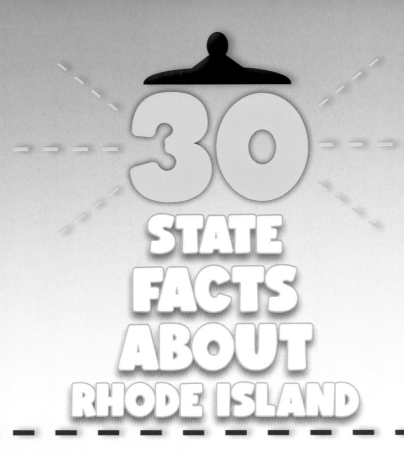

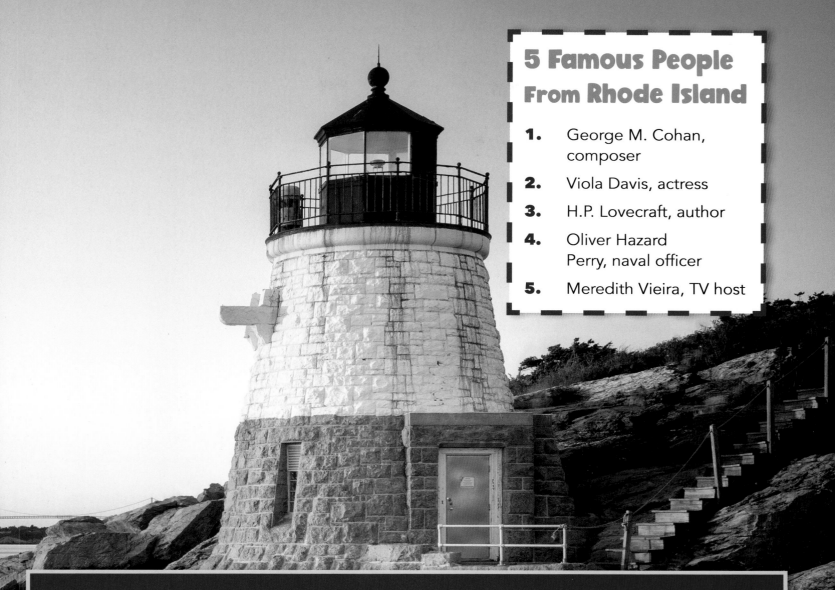

5 Famous People From Rhode Island

1. George M. Cohan, composer

2. Viola Davis, actress

3. H.P. Lovecraft, author

4. Oliver Hazard Perry, naval officer

5. Meredith Vieira, TV host

1. Rhode Island is the smallest of the 50 states.

2. The state is sometimes called "Little Rhody."

3. Rhode Island was last of the 13 original colonies to sign the Constitution.

4. Delegates wanted a Bill of Rights to be added before they would sign the Constitution.

5. Calamari is the official state appetizer, thanks to Rhode Island having the largest squid-fishing fleet on the East Coast.

6. The Touro Synagogue in Newport is the oldest synagogue in North America. It was built in 1763.

7. The state's official name was the State of Rhode Island and Providence Plantations until voters elected to drop "and Providence Plantations" in a ballot measure held in 2020.

8. The state may have gotten its name from the Dutch explorer Adrian Block, who named it "Roodt Eylandt," or "red island," after the red clay along the area's shoreline.

9. The American textile industry was born in 1790, when the first water-powered cotton mill began operating in Pawtucket.

10. The official state drink, coffee milk, is made by mixing coffee syrup into milk.

30
STATE FACTS ABOUT
SOUTH CAROLINA

15 Fast Facts

1. Abbreviation: SC
2. Date of Statehood: May 23, 1788
3. Nickname: Palmetto State
4. Population: 5,118,425
5. Total Area: 32,020 square miles (82,931 sq km)
6. Area Rank: 40
7. Capital: Columbia
8. Largest City: Columbia
9. Motto: "While I Breathe, I Hope"
10. Bird: Carolina wren
11. Mammal: White-tailed deer
12. Reptile: Loggerhead sea turtle
13. Insect: Carolina mantis
14. Flower: Yellow jessamine
15. Tree: Palmetto

5 Famous People From South Carolina

1. Mary McLeod Bethune, educator
2. Chadwick Boseman, actor
3. Chubby Checker, musician
4. Stephen Colbert, TV host
5. Althea Gibson, tennis player

1. King Charles II of England named South Carolina after his father, King Charles I.

2. Originally, North and South Carolina were one colony.

3. During the Revolutionary War, palmetto trees were used to build forts because their soft wood could absorb cannonball impacts.

4. South Carolina was the first state to secede from the Union just before the Civil War.

5. A 7.8 magnitude earthquake that struck near Charleston on August 31, 1886, is still the strongest ever to affect the southeastern U.S.

6. During the early 1930s, South Carolina was called "the Iodine State," because its fruits and vegetables were believed to have a high natural content of iodine.

7. South Carolina's Low Country is home to a Black population with a distinct culture and language known as Gullah.

8. Many of the Gullah's ancestors were brought to South Carolina from West and Central Africa as enslaved workers to exploit their knowledge of rice cultivation.

9. The Angel Oak is a famous old tree growing on Johns Island near Charleston. The sprawling tree is about 500 years old and produces shade that covers 17,200 square feet (1,600 sq m).

10. A colony of about 4,000 Rhesus monkeys lives on Morgan Island.

30 STATE FACTS ABOUT SOUTH DAKOTA

15 Fast Facts

1. Abbreviation: SD
2. Date of Statehood: November 2, 1889
3. Nickname: Mount Rushmore State
4. Population: 886,667
5. Total Area: 77,116 square miles (199,730 sq km)
6. Area Rank: 17
7. Capital: Pierre
8. Largest City: Sioux Falls
9. Motto: "Under God, the People Rule"
10. Bird: Ring-necked pheasant
11. Mammal: Coyote
12. State Fish: Walleye
13. Insect: Honeybee
14. Flower: Pasque flower
15. Tree: Black Hills spruce

5 Famous People From South Dakota

1. Becky Hammon, basketball player and coach
2. Crazy Horse, Lakota leader
3. Hubert Humphrey, U.S. vice president
4. January Jones, actress
5. Sitting Bull, Lakota leader

1. South Dakota has many unofficial nicknames, including the Coyote State, the Artesian State, the Blizzard State, The Land of Plenty, and The Land of Infinite Variety.

2. Rodeo is the official state sport.

3. The first Europeans in South Dakota were the Vérendrye brothers, who claimed the land for France in 1743.

4. In 1803, France sold the Dakotas to the U.S. as part of the Louisiana Purchase.

5. The word "Dakota" comes from the Sioux language and means "friend" or "ally."

6. Agriculture and mining are South Dakota's two most important industries.

7. Mount Rushmore is South Dakota's most famous landmark. It was carved into the Black Hills to increase tourism in the area. The work took over a decade to complete, 1927 to 1941.

8. Several volumes of Laura Ingalls Wilder's "Little House" series are set in South Dakota.

9. The Corn Palace in Mitchell is covered in murals made from multicolored local corn, grain, and grasses. The mural designs change every year.

10. One of the world's most famous dinosaurs, Sue the T. Rex, was discovered near the Badlands in 1990.

30

STATE FACTS ABOUT TENNESSEE

15 Fast Facts

1. Abbreviation: TN
2. Date of Statehood: June 1, 1796
3. Nickname: Volunteer State
4. Population: 6,910,840
5. Total Area: 42,144 square miles (109,152 sq km)
6. Area Rank: 36
7. Capital: Nashville
8. Largest City: Memphis
9. Motto: "Agriculture and Commerce"
10. Bird: Mockingbird
11. Mammal: Raccoon
12. Reptile: Eastern box turtle
13. Insects: Firefly, honeybee, ladybug
14. Flower: Iris
15. Tree: Tulip poplar

5 Famous People From Tennessee

1. Davy Crockett, frontiersman, politician
2. Aretha Franklin, singer
3. Morgan Freeman, actor
4. Benjamin Hooks, civil-rights leader
5. Dolly Parton, singer

1. Spanish explorer Hernando de Soto was the first European known to see the land now called Tennessee, in 1540.

2. Tennessee's name may come from Native American villages called Tanasi and Tanasqui.

3. The state got its nickname from the many troops who volunteered to fight during the War of 1812.

4. Tennessee was the last state to secede from the Union during the Civil War and the first state to be readmitted after the war.

5. Reelfoot Lake was formed after a series of earthquakes in 1811–1812.

6. The Grand Ole Opry radio show has been broadcasting from Nashville every Friday and Saturday night since 1925, making it the longest-running radio show in history.

7. Oak Ridge was nicknamed Atomic City as a site used for the Manhattan Project, which created the atomic bomb.

8. Great Smoky Mountains National Park and Dollywood, an amusement park partially owned by country singer Dolly Parton, attract millions of visitors every year.

9. A replica of the Parthenon, the famous ancient Greek building in Athens, Greece, stands in Nashville's Centennial Park.

10. Tennessee has more official state songs than any other state: nine state songs and one bicentennial rap.

30 STATE FACTS ABOUT TEXAS

Don't Mess® With Texas

UP TO $2000 FINE FOR LITTERING

15 Fast Facts

1.	Abbreviation: TX
2.	Date of Statehood: December 29, 1845
3.	Nickname: Lone Star State
4.	Population: 29,145,505
5.	Total Area: 268,596 square miles (295,660 sq km)
6.	Area Rank: 2
7.	Capital: Austin
8.	Largest City: Houston
9.	Motto: "Friendship"
10.	Bird: Northern mockingbird
11.	Mammals: Longhorn, armadillo
12.	Reptile: Horned lizard
13.	Insect: Monarch butterfly
14.	Flower: Bluebonnet
15.	Tree: Pecan

1. Texas has flown the flags of six different nations: Spain, France, Mexico, the Republic of Texas, the United States of America, and the Confederate States of America.

2. The Six Flags chain of amusement parks is named after Texas.

3. The state's name comes from the Caddo word "Tay-yas," which means "friends."

4. Texas is called the Lone Star State because the Republic of Texas flag had a single star on it.

5. The state capital is named after "father of Texas" Stephen F. Austin, who brought 300 families to Texas in 1825.

6. Dr. Pepper, Fritos, handheld calculators, and 3-D printing were all invented in Texas.

7. Some 20 million Mexican free-tailed bats live seasonally in Bracken Cave near San Antonio. Tourists gather to watch them fly out of the cave each evening.

8. The famous Battle of the Alamo took place in Texas in 1836.

9. The expression "Don't mess with Texas" was born as an anti-littering slogan.

10. Texas is the second-largest state in the U.S. in both population and size.

5 Famous People From Texas

1. Drew Brees, football player

2. Kelly Clarkson, singer and TV host

3. Lyndon Johnson, U.S. president

4. Beyoncé Knowles, singer

5. Sandra Day O'Connor, Supreme Court justice

30
STATE FACTS ABOUT
UTAH

1. Abbreviation: UT
2. Date of Statehood: January 4, 1896
3. Nickname: Beehive State
4. Population: 3,271,616
5. Total Area: 84,897 square miles (219,882 sq km)
6. Area Rank: 13
7. Capital: Salt Lake City
8. Largest City: Salt Lake City
9. Motto: "Industry"
10. Bird: California gull
11. Mammal: Rocky Mountain elk
12. Reptile: Gila monster
13. Insect: Honeybee
14. Flower: Sego lily
15. Tree: Blue spruce

5 Famous People From Utah

1. Nolan Bushnell, inventor and entrepreneur
2. Philo Farnsworth, inventor
3. J. Willard Marriott, entrepreneur
4. Donny Osmond, singer
5. Chrissy Teigen, TV host and author

1. Utah is nicknamed the Beehive State because bees represented hard work and industry.

2. The Church of Jesus Christ of Latter-Day Saints, also known as the Mormon Church, is headquartered in Salt Lake City.

3. In 1847, Brigham Young led a group of Mormons to Utah in search of religious freedom.

4. Salt Lake City is the only state capital that is three words long.

5. The transcontinental railroad was completed with a ceremonial spike at Promontory in 1869.

6. Arches National Park features more than 2,000 striking natural sandstone arches.

7. Every county in Utah contains part of a national forest.

8. The California gull is the state bird because, according to legend, seagulls helped save the lives of early Utah farmers by consuming swarms of crickets that threatened to wipe out their crops.

9. The Utahraptor, one of the largest raptors that ever lived, was discovered in Utah and named after the state.

10. Parts of the Great Salt Lake are nine times saltier than the ocean.

30 STATE FACTS ABOUT VERMONT

15 Fast Facts

1. Abbreviation: VT
2. Date of Statehood: March 4, 1791
3. Nickname: Green Mountain State
4. Population: 643,077
5. Total Area: 9,616 square miles (24,905 sq km)
6. Area Rank: 45
7. Capital: Montpelier
8. Largest City: Burlington
9. Motto: "Freedom and Unity"
10. Bird: Hermit thrush
11. Mammal: Morgan horse
12. Reptile: Painted turtle
13. Insect: Honeybee
14. Flower: Red clover
15. Tree: Sugar maple

5 Famous People From Vermont

1. Chester Arthur, U.S. president
2. Calvin Coolidge, U.S. president
3. John Deere, inventor
4. Damon Wayans, Jr., actor
5. Jody Williams, activist and Nobel Peace Prize laureate

1. Vermont was once part of New York. In 1777, it declared its independence from New York.

2. Between 1777 and 1791, Vermont had its own currency, postal service, constitution, and president.

3. Vermont was the first state to join the U.S. after the 13 original colonies.

4. "Vermont" comes from two French words meaning "green mountain."

5. Vermont is the largest producer of maple syrup in the U.S.

6. Montpelier is the smallest state capital in the nation.

7. The Morgan horse was developed in Vermont by a farmer named Justin Morgan.

8. Billboards have been illegal in Vermont since 1968.

9. Ben and Jerry's ice cream first opened in a former gas station in Burlington in 1978.

10. The Vermont Teddy Bear factory in Shelburne offers tours to thousands of visitors every year.

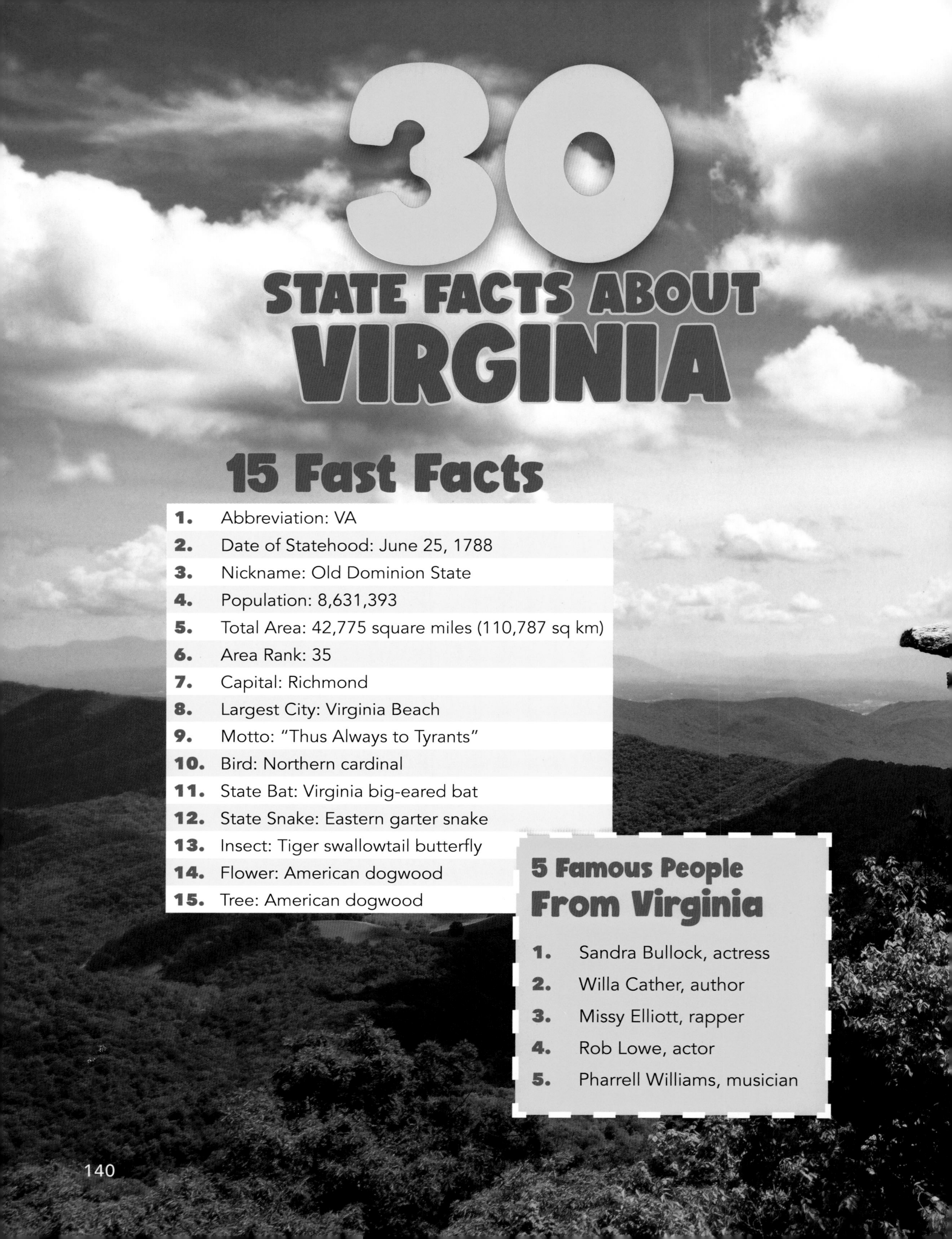

30

STATE FACTS ABOUT VIRGINIA

15 Fast Facts

1. Abbreviation: VA
2. Date of Statehood: June 25, 1788
3. Nickname: Old Dominion State
4. Population: 8,631,393
5. Total Area: 42,775 square miles (110,787 sq km)
6. Area Rank: 35
7. Capital: Richmond
8. Largest City: Virginia Beach
9. Motto: "Thus Always to Tyrants"
10. Bird: Northern cardinal
11. State Bat: Virginia big-eared bat
12. State Snake: Eastern garter snake
13. Insect: Tiger swallowtail butterfly
14. Flower: American dogwood
15. Tree: American dogwood

5 Famous People From Virginia

1. Sandra Bullock, actress
2. Willa Cather, author
3. Missy Elliott, rapper
4. Rob Lowe, actor
5. Pharrell Williams, musician

1. More presidents were born in Virginia than any other state.

2. Those eight presidents are George Washington, Thomas Jefferson, James Madison, James Monroe, William Henry Harrison, John Tyler, Zachary Taylor and Woodrow Wilson.

3. Virginia was named after Queen Elizabeth I, who was called the Virgin Queen.

4. Virginia was part of England's dominions, or territories, which is why it is called the Old Dominion State.

5. In 1903, Maggie Lena Walker, a Black woman, became the first woman to own a bank when she opened the St. Luke Penny Savings Bank in Richmond.

6. Mountain Dew was created in Virginia.

7. More miles of the Appalachian Trail cross Virginia than any other state.

8. One of the first American dog breeds, the American Foxhound, was developed in Virginia by George Washington.

9. Every year, wild ponies on Assateague Island are rounded up to swim across a channel to Chincoteague Island.

10. Virginia is the largest state without any major professional sports teams.

30

STATE FACTS ABOUT
WASHINGTON

15 Fast Facts

1. Abbreviation: WA
2. Date of Statehood: November 11, 1889
3. Nickname: Evergreen State
4. Population: 7,705,281
5. Total Area: 71,298 square miles (184,661 sq km)
6. Area Rank: 18
7. Capital: Olympia
8. Largest City: Seattle
9. Motto: "By and By"
10. Bird: Willow goldfinch
11. State Endemic Mammal: Olympic marmot
12. State Fish: Steelhead trout
13. Insect: Green darner dragonfly
14. Flower: Coast rhododendron
15. Tree: Western hemlock

5 Famous People From Washington

1. Kurt Cobain, musician
2. John Elway, football player and executive
3. Bill Gates, entrepreneur
4. Hope Solo, soccer player
5. Hilary Swank, actress

1. Washington produces more apples, raspberries, and sweet cherries than any other state.

2. Washington is the only state named after a U.S. president.

3. The state's nickname comes from its many evergreen forests.

4. Seattle landmark the Space Needle was built for the 1962 World's Fair.

5. The Hoh Rain Forest, located in Olympic National Park, is one of only a few rain forests in the U.S.

6. The games Pictionary, Cranium, and pickleball were all invented in Washington.

7. Jeff Bezos started Amazon in a converted garage in Bellevue in 1994.

8. Longview has several bridges built for squirrels to cross roads.

9. Starbucks was founded in Seattle in 1971.

10. Father's Day was created by Spokane resident Sonora Smart Dodd in 1910.

143

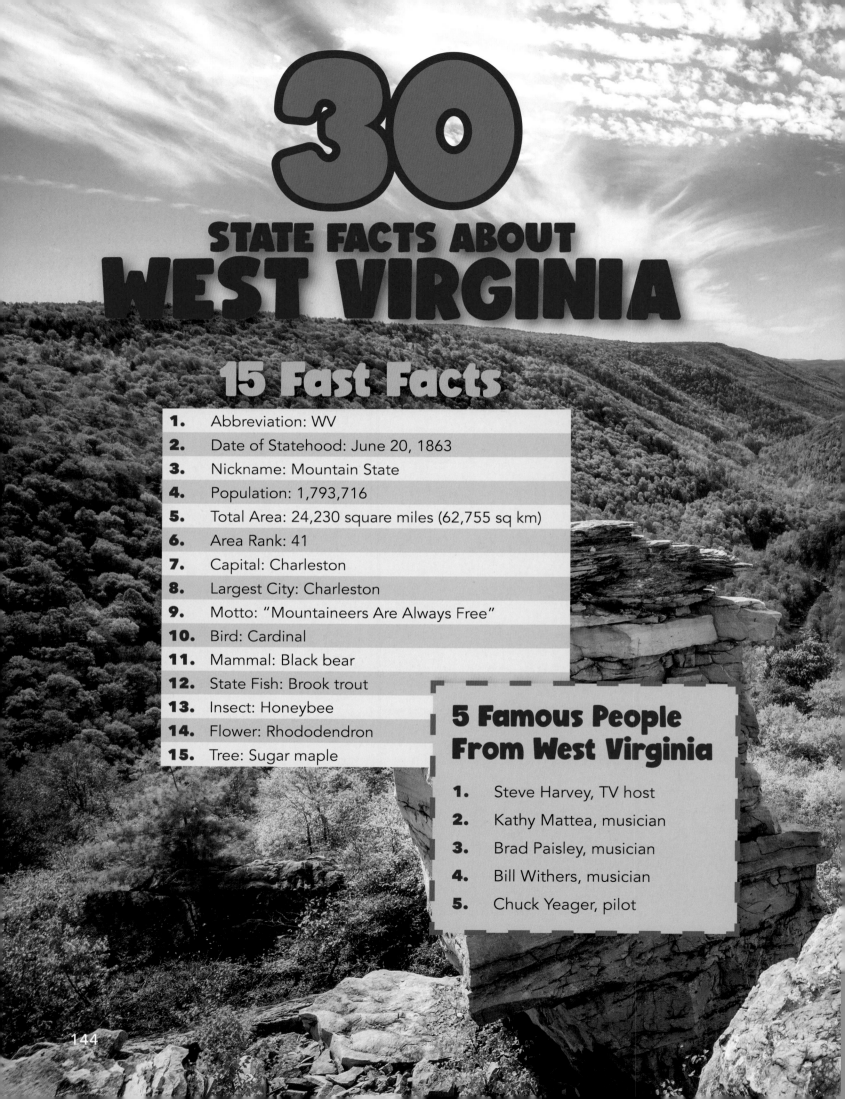

30 STATE FACTS ABOUT WEST VIRGINIA

15 Fast Facts

1. Abbreviation: WV
2. Date of Statehood: June 20, 1863
3. Nickname: Mountain State
4. Population: 1,793,716
5. Total Area: 24,230 square miles (62,755 sq km)
6. Area Rank: 41
7. Capital: Charleston
8. Largest City: Charleston
9. Motto: "Mountaineers Are Always Free"
10. Bird: Cardinal
11. Mammal: Black bear
12. State Fish: Brook trout
13. Insect: Honeybee
14. Flower: Rhododendron
15. Tree: Sugar maple

5 Famous People From West Virginia

1. Steve Harvey, TV host
2. Kathy Mattea, musician
3. Brad Paisley, musician
4. Bill Withers, musician
5. Chuck Yeager, pilot

1. West Virginia was part of Virginia until 1861.

2. Because it did not want to secede from the Union, West Virginia separated from Virginia. It became its own state in 1863.

3. President Lincoln declared West Virginia as a state, making it the only state admitted to the Union by presidential proclamation.

4. West Virginia has the highest elevation of any state east of the Mississippi.

5. In 1859, abolitionist John Brown staged a violent and unsuccessful raid on a federal arsenal at Harpers Ferry.

6. Almost 75 percent of the state is covered by forests.

7. Golden Delicious apples were first grown in West Virginia.

9. Coal mining used to be the state's biggest industry, but today tourism is tops.

9. On July 1, 1921, West Virginia became the first state to charge sales tax.

10. The largest diamond ever discovered in North America was found in Peterstown in 1928. The bluish-white Jones diamond measured about 34.5 carats.

30

STATE FACTS ABOUT
WISCONSIN

15 Fast Facts

1. Abbreviation: WI
2. Date of Statehood: May 29, 1848
3. Nickname: Badger State
4. Population: 5,893,718
5. Total Area: 65,496 square miles (169,634 sq km)
6. Area Rank: 23
7. Capital: Madison
8. Largest City: Milwaukee
9. Motto: "Forward"
10. Bird: American robin
11. Mammal: Badger
12. Fish: Muskellunge
13. Insect: Honeybee
14. Flower: Wood violet
15. Tree: Sugar maple

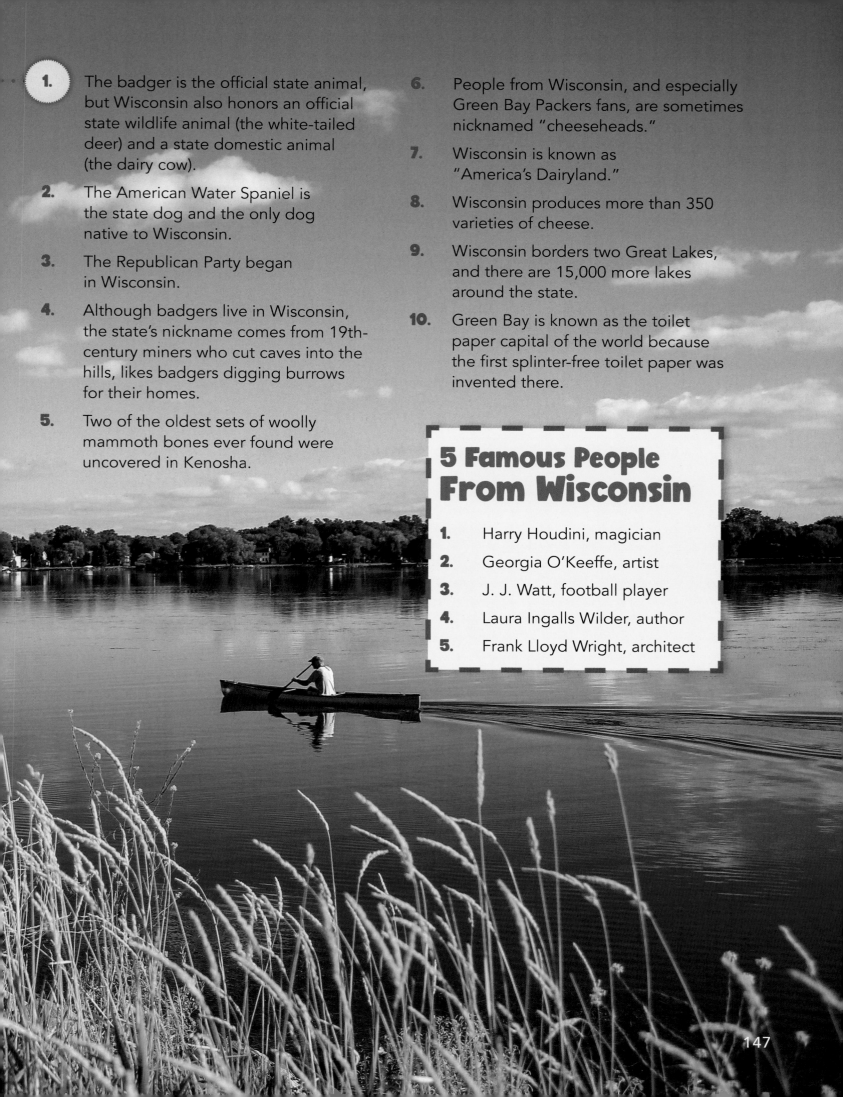

1. The badger is the official state animal, but Wisconsin also honors an official state wildlife animal (the white-tailed deer) and a state domestic animal (the dairy cow).

2. The American Water Spaniel is the state dog and the only dog native to Wisconsin.

3. The Republican Party began in Wisconsin.

4. Although badgers live in Wisconsin, the state's nickname comes from 19th-century miners who cut caves into the hills, likes badgers digging burrows for their homes.

5. Two of the oldest sets of woolly mammoth bones ever found were uncovered in Kenosha.

6. People from Wisconsin, and especially Green Bay Packers fans, are sometimes nicknamed "cheeseheads."

7. Wisconsin is known as "America's Dairyland."

8. Wisconsin produces more than 350 varieties of cheese.

9. Wisconsin borders two Great Lakes, and there are 15,000 more lakes around the state.

10. Green Bay is known as the toilet paper capital of the world because the first splinter-free toilet paper was invented there.

5 Famous People From Wisconsin

1. Harry Houdini, magician
2. Georgia O'Keeffe, artist
3. J. J. Watt, football player
4. Laura Ingalls Wilder, author
5. Frank Lloyd Wright, architect

30 STATE FACTS ABOUT WYOMING

15 Fast Facts

1. Abbreviation: WY
2. Date of Statehood: July 10, 1890
3. Nickname: Equality State
4. Population: 576,851
5. Total Area: 97,813 square miles (253,333 sq km)
6. Area Rank: 10
7. Capital: Cheyenne
8. Largest City: Cheyenne
9. Motto: "Equal Rights"
10. Bird: Meadowlark
11. Mammal: Bison
12. Reptile: Horned toad
13. Insect: Sheridan's green hairstreak butterfly
14. Flower: Indian paintbrush
15. Tree: Plains cottonwood

5 Famous People From Wyoming

1. Dick Cheney, U.S. vice president
2. Curt Gowdy, sportscaster
3. Leonard Hobbs, inventor
4. Patricia MacLachlan, author
5. Jackson Pollack, artist

1. The state's name probably comes from the Lenape Indian word "mecheweami-ing," which means "at (or on) the big plain."

2. Wyoming's nickname comes from it being the first state to give women the right to vote, hold public office, and serve on juries.

3. Shoshone National Forest was the nation's first national forest.

4. In 1925, Wyoming became the first state to have a woman governor.

5. Wyoming is the least populated state in the U.S.

6. People from Wyoming are called Wyomingites.

7. Most of Yellowstone National Park is in Wyoming.

8. There are only two escalators in the entire state. Both are located in Casper.

9. There were so many dinosaur bones in southeast Wyoming that a former sheep rancher built a "fossil cabin" out of them.

10. Although Wyoming has no coastline, it has more than 32 islands in its lakes and rivers.

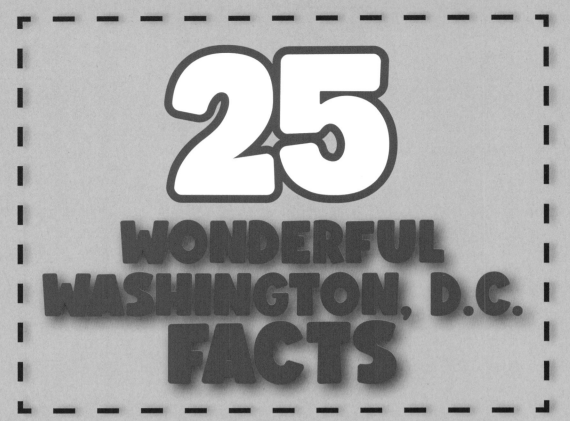

25 WONDERFUL WASHINGTON, D.C. FACTS

10 Fast Facts

1.	Abbreviation: DC	
2.	Population: 689,545	
3.	Total Area: 68 square miles (176 sq km)	
4.	Area Rank: 51	
5.	Motto: "Justice For All"	
6.	Bird: Wood thrush	
7.	Fruit: Cherry	
8.	Rock: Potomac bluestone	
9.	Flower: American beauty rose	
10.	Tree: Scarlet oak	

1. D.C. stands for "District of Columbia."

2. The name "Washington" honors George Washington, while "Columbia" honors Christopher Columbus.

3. D.C.'s location was chosen in part because it was then in the middle of the new nation.

4. D.C. residents can vote in federal elections, but their representatives in Congress are only permitted a vote in committees, not on legislation.

5. In 1898, construction workers discovered a dinosaur bone while working on sewers. One hundred years later, the find, Capitalsaurus, became the District's official dinosaur.

6. In 1912, Japan donated 3,000 cherry trees to D.C., and each spring the district celebrates a Cherry Blossom Festival.

7. D.C. has more than 175 embassies and international cultural centers.

8. Woodrow Wilson is the only president buried in Washington, D.C.

9. There is an empty crypt under the Capitol building, where George Washington was supposed to be buried. Instead, he was buried at his home, Mount Vernon.

10. D.C. has more residents than the states of Wyoming and Vermont.

5 Famous People From Washington, D.C.

1. Benjamin Oliver Davis, military leader

2. Kevin Durant, basketball player

3. Taraji P. Henson, actress

4. Samuel L. Jackson, actor

5. Christopher Meloni, actor

20 TERRIFIC FACTS ABOUT U.S. TERRITORIES

1. The U.S. has five major territories: American Samoa, Guam, Commonwealth of the Northern Mariana Islands, Commonwealth of Puerto Rico, and the U.S. Virgin Islands.

2. Citizens of the territories can vote in primary elections for president, but they cannot vote in the general elections for president.

3. A total of 3,569,284 people live in those five territories.

4. Of the five, Puerto Rico has the largest population, and American Samoa has the smallest population.

5. American Samoa, Guam, and the Northern Marianas are in the Pacific Ocean, while Puerto Rico and the U.S. Virgin Islands lie between the Atlantic Ocean and the Caribbean Sea.

6. An agreement between Great Britain, Germany, and the U.S. gave American Samoa to the U.S. in 1899.

7. The U.S. Navy controlled American Samoa between 1900 and 1951.

8. Five of American Samoa's seven islands are volcanic.

9. Guam's motto is, "Where America's Day Begins."

10. Guam was seized by Japan in 1941, but the U.S. regained control in 1944.

11. Sometime between 1945 and 1952, nonnative brown tree snakes were introduced to Guam, probably as stowaways on ships. They quickly became a destructive threat to native wildlife, especially birds.

12. The Northern Marianas are made up of 14 islands, but only six are inhabited.

13. The U.S. gained control over the Northern Marianas, Guam, and Puerto Rico in 1898, after the Spanish-American War.

14. Famous Puerto Ricans include actress and singer Jennifer Lopez, *Hamilton* creator and star Lin-Manuel Miranda, actress Rita Moreno, baseball player Roberto Clemente, and singer Ricky Martin.

15. In 2020, Puerto Rico voted to become a U.S. state, but the results of the vote were not binding.

16. The U.S. bought the Virgin Islands from Denmark in 1917 for $25 million.

17. In the late 17th century, the Virgin Islands were known as a haven for pirates.

18. Virgin Islands National Park takes up about two-thirds of the entire island of St. John.

19. The U.S. also controls nine other small islands: Midway Atoll, Palmyra Atoll, Baker Island, Howland Island, Jarvis Island, Johnston Atoll, Kingman Reef, Wake Island, and Navassa Island.

20. Most of these islands are uninhabited and serve as nature conservancies.

Entertainment

50 FACTS ABOUT AMERICAN MUSIC

1. U.S. popular music has been influenced by Native American, African American, Latin American, and European traditions.

2. The blues are recognized as the root of most contemporary American music.

3. Early blues recordings called "race records" were marketed to Black audiences.

4. In 1903, bandleader W.C. Handy claimed to hear the first blues music being played by a street guitarist at a train station in Mississippi.

5. Early blues music included a mixture of traditional instruments and household items, including homemade drums, washboards, spoons, guitars, mandolins, banjos, kazoos, double basses, harmonicas, and fiddles.

6. The blues has roots in the music enslaved Africans brought to America. This music included spirituals and work songs.

7. The blues got its name from "blue devils," an 18th-century description of sadness.

8. Mamie Smith made history in February 1920 when she became the first Black singer to record a blues song, "That Thing Called Love." The record sold a million copies within a year.

9. Myth has it that legendary blues musician Robert Johnson sold his soul to the devil in exchange for his guitar-playing skills.

10. Jazz was born in New Orleans, Louisiana.

11. The first jazz record was released by the Original Dixieland Jass Band in 1917.

12. Jazz became very popular in the 1920s and 1930s.

13. Later, different styles of jazz developed, including bebop, smooth jazz, and cool jazz.

14. Rhythm and blues (R&B) music combined blues with the strong rhythms of jazz music.

15. Country music is considered to be America's oldest musical genre.

16. Country's roots include English folk ballads, Irish fiddle tunes, Mississippi Delta blues, French/Cajun music, Southern gospel music, and more.

17. Jimmie Rodgers has been called "the Father of Country Music."

18. Rodgers mixed singing with rhythmic yodeling in his performances.

19. The Grand Ole Opry radio program, which started broadcasting in the 1920s, brought country music all over the United States.

20. Kitty Wells was the first woman to become a major country music star, releasing her first hit record in 1952.

21. Bluegrass is a type of country music influenced by jazz and blues.

22. Bluegrass usually highlights creative banjo and guitar playing and high-pitched vocal harmonies.

23. Bill Monroe became known as the "Father of Bluegrass" after he began playing that style of music in 1945.

24. During the 1950s, rockabilly music became popular.

25. Notable rockabilly performers included Elvis Presley, the Everly Brothers, Jerry Lee Lewis, and Brenda Lee.

26. Rock and roll combined blues, gospel, and R&B into a new kind of music.

27. Early rock and roll pioneers included Chuck Berry, Fats Domino, Elvis Presley, and Bill Haley and His Comets.

28. American rock music influenced—and was influenced by—"British invasion" groups like The Beatles and The Rolling Stones.

29. A smooth style called doo-wop was popular in the 1950s and 1960s. It featured tight harmonies and often included nonsense syllables and phrases.

30. Soul music combined rhythm and blues with gospel music.

31. Berry Gordy, Jr., founded Motown Records in 1959 and became a leading producer of soul music.

32. Motown was located in—and named after—Detroit, the Motor City.

33. Motown became known for its many popular artists, including the Supremes (with Diana Ross), the Four Tops, and the Jackson 5, to name just a few.

34. Hip hop music began at informal dance parties in the Bronx, New York City.

35. Hip hop pioneer DJ Kool Herc was the first person to loop instrumental breaks in records so they played over and over, while people danced to them.

36. Hip hop is also called rap music.

37. Rap music focuses on a person rapping, or talking, often in rhyme, over a beat.

38. On January 5, 1980, "Rapper's Delight" by the Sugarhill Gang was the first hip hop record to reach the *Billboard* Top 40.

39. Tejano music mixes Mexican, European, and U.S. musical styles. It is especially popular in Texas and the southwestern United States.

40. EDM, or Electronic Dance Music, developed in Chicago and Detroit beginning in the 1980s.

Bestselling American Recording Artists of All Time

1. Garth Brooks
2. Elvis Presley
3. The Eagles
4. Michael Jackson
5. Billy Joel
6. George Strait
7. Barbra Streisand
8. Aerosmith
9. Mariah Carey
10. Bruce Springsteen

35 FACTS ABOUT AMERICAN NEWS AND MEDIA

1. Americans today get their news from a variety of sources, including radio, TV, newspapers and magazines, websites, and social media.

2. Newspapers were a vital source of information during colonial times and during the American Revolution.

3. Many newspapers had a political voice and were used to spread information about British misdeeds and encourage people to fight against the British government.

4. After the American Revolution, newspapers were believed to be an important tool for democracy and keeping voters informed.

5. During the late 1800s, Joseph Pulitzer's *New York World* became the first tabloid paper.

6. The *New York World* featured sensational news reports and highlighted crimes and scandals.

7. This type of news became known as "yellow journalism."

8. CBS and NBC began broadcasting news on the radio during the 1920s.

9. Warren Harding was the first U.S. president to regularly give speeches over the radio.

10. President Franklin D. Roosevelt was famous for his radio speeches, which were called "fireside chats."

11. The 1960 election featured the first televised presidential debate, between John F. Kennedy and Richard Nixon.

12. TV news broadcaster Walter Cronkite was once called "the most trusted man in America" because so many people relied on him to tell them what was happening.

13. Before the 1980s, there were just three major television networks: CBS, NBC, and ABC.

14. On June 1, 1980, CNN became the world's first 24-hour television news network.

15. Its first story was a report on the attempted assassination of civil rights leader Vernon Jordan.

16. The 24-hour news cycle led to a constant demand for new information.

17. Rupert Murdoch, an Australian newspaper magnate, launched Fox News Channel in October 1996.

18. By the mid 1990s, many newspapers and TV news sources were also publishing their stories online.

19. During the early 2000s, newspapers began to lose advertising income. This led to cuts in news reporting and smaller papers. Some newspapers stopped publishing altogether.

20. A 2021 study shows 86 percent of Americans get news online "often" or "sometimes."

21. Facebook is the most popular social media site for consuming news. In a 2020 study, 36 percent of people said they got their news from Facebook.

22. YouTube, WhatsApp, Twitter, and Instagram are other popular sites for finding news.

23. Many people getting news stories from online sources have trouble identifying whether the stories are biased or inaccurate.

24. Fake news can spread faster than real news.

25. A 2016 study found that the top 20 fake news stories generated more online views than the top 20 stories from major news outlets.

26. Some polls show that more than half of Americans don't trust the media to tell them the truth.

27. Social media can place journalism in the hands of the people.

28. Citizen journalism occurs when ordinary people document events and post about them on the internet.

29. Some major news stories might have gone unreported or under-reported if it were not for people sharing videos and photos documenting them using social media.

30. In 1940, there were 1,878 daily newspapers, with a total circulation of 41.1 million.

31. By 2018, those numbers had dropped to 1,254 newspapers with a circulation of 25.7 million.

32. The largest newspaper in the United States is *USA Today*, with more than two million readers.

33. Other top U.S. newspapers include the *Wall Street Journal*, *New York Times*, *Los Angeles Times*, and *New York Post*.

34. *USA Today* is also the most popular newspaper on the web, with more than 147 million monthly visitors.

35. The top news/information website in 2020 was the Yahoo/HuffPost News Network, with more than 171 million monthly visitors.

35

FACTS ABOUT RADIO AND TV HISTORY

1. In 1820, Hans Christian Oersted discovered that sending electric current through a wire created electromagnetic waves.

2. By the 1880s, scientists proved that electromagnetic waves could be sent through the air.

3. In 1895, Guglielmo Marconi began sending broadcasts over short distances.

4. On December 24, 1906, physicist Reginald Fessenden sent the first long-distance transmission of human voice and music from a station at Brant Rock, Massachusetts.

5. Fessenden's signal was received as far away as Norfolk, Virginia.

6. In 1907, American inventor Lee De Forest introduced the Audion signal detector, which amplified radio signals.

7. KDKA became the first commercial radio station when it began broadcasting from Pennsylvania in 1920.

8. On September 25, 1926, the Radio Corporation of America (RCA) formed the National Broadcasting Company (NBC) to take over its network broadcasting business.

9. In early 1927, the Columbia Broadcasting System (CBS) was established.

10. In 1943, the government forced NBC to sell a part of its system to Edward J. Noble, who formed the American Broadcasting Corporation (ABC).

11. Local radio stations got most of their shows from the major networks.

12. The period between the 1920s and 1950s is called the Golden Age of Radio.

13. Millions of radio listeners enjoyed comedies, dramas, soap operas, concerts, game shows, and informational broadcasts during this time.

14. One of the most dramatic moments in radio history occurred on October 30, 1938, when CBS broadcast an Orson Welles production of "The War of the Worlds." Some listeners thought the sci-fi story of a Martian invasion was a news report.

15. In 1921, there were only five radio stations in the United States.

16. By 1940, that number had grown to 765 stations.

17. As of 2020, there were 11,215 radio stations broadcasting in the United States.

18. Country music was the most popular radio format, followed by news/talk radio and classic rock.

19. Many radio stations stream online, which allows them to reach audiences all over the world.

20. Television was first demonstrated in San Francisco by Philo Taylor Farnsworth in 1927.

21. While he was still in high school, Farnsworth figured out a way to scan images with a beam of electrons, change them into radio waves, and then transform them back into a picture on a screen.

22. Radio giant RCA invested $50 million in the development of television.

23. The first official TV broadcast in the United States was President Franklin Roosevelt's speech at the opening of the 1939 World's Fair in New York.

24. In May 1939, RCA broadcast the first televised baseball game, between two college teams.

25. Early television sets showed blurry black-and-white pictures on a tiny screen.

26. Actors had to work under hot lights and wear black and green makeup in order to show up on the screen.

27. National commercial TV broadcasts began in 1947.

28. Many popular radio comedies and dramas moved over to television. Some of their actors and actresses did too.

29. The number of television sets in the U.S. rose from 6,000 in 1946 to about 12 million by 1951.

30. By 1955, half of all U.S. homes had a television set.

31. In 1967, Congress created a public broadcasting system (PBS) to broadcast educational programs.

32. Eighteen of the top twenty most-watched TV broadcasts of all time have been Super Bowls.

33. The highest-rated TV show broadcast of all time was the final episode of *M.A.S.H.* in 1983.

34. The longest-running scripted prime-time TV series is *The Simpsons*. The animated series was introduced in December 1989.

35. The longest-running live-action scripted prime-time TV series are *Gunsmoke* and *Law & Order*, which each broadcast 635 episodes over 20 seasons.

35 FASCINATING FACTS ABOUT AMERICAN MOVIES

1. The first moving picture cameras were invented in the 1890s.

2. Thomas Edison invented a camera called the kinetoscope in 1893.

3. Early movies were silent and only included a single scene.

4. The first moving picture ever made was 1878's *The Horse in Motion*.

5. *The Horse in Motion* was made to settle a bet about whether all four of a horse's feet were off the ground at the same time when it is galloping.

6. A dancer named Carmen "Carmencita" Dauset Moreno may have been the first woman to ever appear in an American film. Her movie, the 21-second-long *Carmencita*, was released in 1894.

7. The first feature-length film was a documentary called *The Corbett-Fitzsimmons Fight*. It was released in the U.S. in 1897.

8. The first movie theater opened in Pittsburgh in 1905.

9. Before that, movies were shown at carnivals.

10. Thomas Edison's Edison Trust controlled the movie industry in the early 1900s.

11. In 1907, Edison filmed a movie in Fort Lee, New Jersey. For a short time, Fort Lee became the movie capital of the world.

12. In time, some studios moved to California to take advantage of the good weather, and to get away from legal restrictions.

13. The first film made in Hollywood was *Old California*, directed by D.W. Griffth and released in 1910.

14. *Old California* was shot in just two days.

15. Nestor Studios built the first Hollywood studio in 1911.

16. The first full-length movie that included spoken dialogue was *The Jazz Singer*, released in 1927.

17. This new style of film was called "talking pictures" or "talkies."

18. Many actors lost their careers when "talkies" became popular because they did not have appealing or strong voices.

19. Mel Brooks's *Silent Movie*, released in 1976, has only one word of dialogue: "No."

20. Movie stars in Hollywood's "Golden Age" up to the early 1960s were usually under contract to one studio and appeared in multiple films for that studio every year.

21. John Wayne played the most leading roles, starring in 153 movies.

22. John Carradine has the most screen credits with appearances in more than 230 movies.

23. The first Academy Awards for film, or Oscars, were awarded in 1929. *Wings*, a silent film starring Clara Bow, won Best Picture.

24. George Lucas's original *Star Wars* became the model for a new type of blockbuster in 1977.

25. The first feature film created solely with computer-generated imagery (CGI) was 1995's *Toy Story*.

The American Film Institute's 10 Best American Movies of All Time

1. Citizen Kane (1941)
2. The Godfather (1972)
3. Casablanca (1942)
4. Raging Bull (1980)
5. Singin' in the Rain (1952)
6. Gone With the Wind (1939)
7. Lawrence of Arabia (1962)
8. Schindler's List (1993)
9. Vertigo (1958)
10. The Wizard of Oz (1939)

UNIVERSAL
STUDIOS
HOLLYWOOD

35 FOOT-TAPPING FACTS ABOUT THEATER AND DANCE

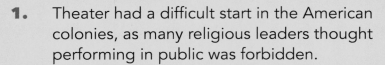

1. Theater had a difficult start in the American colonies, as many religious leaders thought performing in public was forbidden.

2. Anti-British feeling was so high in the colonies that a riot broke out during one performance when it was discovered a British soldier was in the cast.

3. Shakespeare's plays were the most popular performances in theater during the 1800s.

4. As interest in theater grew, New York City became the center of live performances.

5. Vaudeville shows were popular in the early 1900s. Vaudeville shows featured a variety of performers and acts.

6. In order to qualify as a Broadway theater, the theater must have 500 seats and be located in New York between 40th Street and 54th Street, and from west of 6th Avenue to east of Eighth Avenue, including Times Square.

7. Theaters that have between 99 and 499 seats are called Off-Broadway.

8. Only four Broadway theaters are actually on the street named Broadway.

9. New York's theater district is also nicknamed the Great White Way.

10. The nickname comes from the area being among the first parts of the city to be illuminated by electric lights in the 1890s.

11. Broadway theaters do not have a row "I," because the letter is often confused with the number "1."

12. The American Theatre Wing was founded during World War II to provide entertainment for soldiers.

13. In 1947, the American Theatre Wing presented the first Antoinette Perry Awards for Excellence in Theatre, commonly known as the Tony Awards.

14. Julie Taymor was the first woman to win a Tony for Best Director of a Musical. She won for *The Lion King*.

15. During the 2018–2019 season, Broadway shows earned $1.8 billion.

16. In 2018, there were 3,533 live-performance theaters in the U.S.

17. *Phantom of the Opera* is the longest-running Broadway show. It had 13,370 performances between its opening in 1988 and the Broadway shutdown in March 2020.

18. The box office earnings for *Phantom of the Opera* are higher than any film or stage play in history, including *Titanic*, *E.T.*, *Star Wars*, and *Avatar*.

19. *Chicago* is the longest-running revival on Broadway. It ran for 9,692 performances between 1996 and March 2020.

20. The plot of *Chicago* is based on a sensational murder case from 1924.

21. *The Lion King* is the highest-grossing show in Broadway history, and the first to gross more than $1 billion.

22. 66 percent of Broadway audiences are female.

23. Dancing was an important part of Native American culture.

24. The first known ballet in America was presented in 1735.

25. Before the 1900s, most dancing was done at home or at community events.

26. Vaudeville shows featured tap, and toe dancing, comic dance sketches, ballroom dancers, ethnic numbers in various ethnic styles.

27. Tap dancing developed in the U.S. from a fusion of the step-dancing traditions of many cultures, including West African.

28. Metal tap shoes became popular during the 1920s.

29. *Shuffle Along*, a hugely popular all-Black Broadway show that premiered in 1921, featured jazz tap dancing.

30. The Nicholas Brothers were famous tap dancers who made that style of dance popular in movies.

31. Couples were drawn to dance marathons during the 1930s as a way to make money.

32. Breakdancing was created during the 1970s in the Bronx, New York City, as a nonviolent way for young people to challenge each other.

33. The hustle became a popular dance during the disco era of the 1970s.

34. Many popular disco dance styles have Latin roots.

35. The TV show *Dancing With the Stars* premiered in 2005 and brought renewed interest to traditional dance styles, such as the waltz, tango, and quickstep.

20 FUN FACTS ABOUT VIDEO GAMES AND GAMERS

1. More than 214 million Americans play video games for at least an hour per week.

2. 70 percent of people under the age of 18 play video games.

3. The first video game was *Tennis for Two*.

4. *Tennis for Two* was created at Brookhaven Labs in New York in 1958.

5. In 1962, a college student invented *Spacewar!*, the first game that could be played on multiple computers.

6. In 1972, Nolan Bushnell and Ted Dabney formed Atari, Inc., and released an updated version of *Tennis for Two*, called *Pong*.

7. Nintendo introduced its mobile gaming console, Game Boy, in 1989.

8. PlayStation 2, released in 2000, sold more than 155 million units and is believed to be the bestselling console of all time.

9. By the early 2010s, many video games could be played on standard mobile devices, which made it easier for even more people to enjoy gaming.

10. In 2020, the video game industry was worth more than $60 billion.

TOP SELLING VIDEO GAMES IN 2019

1. Call of Duty: Modern Warfare
2. Grand Theft Auto V
3. Madden NFL 20
4. NBA 2K20
5. Mortal Kombat 11
6. Star Wars Jedi: Fallen Order
7. NBA 2K 19
8. Borderlands 3
9. Tom Clancy's Rainbow Six: Siege
10. Super Smash Bros. Ultimate

40
AMAZING BLACK ENTERTAINERS

1. **Alvin Ailey** (1931–1989)—A visionary dancer and choreographer who was one of the first to create an integrated modern dance company.

2. **Marian Anderson** (1897–1993)—Anderson's 1939 performance on the steps of the Lincoln Memorial in front of an integrated audience of more than 75,000 people was one of the greatest moments in the fight for equality.

3. **Louis Armstrong** (1901–1971)—This trumpet player was a key figure in the sound of modern jazz.

4. **Harry Belafonte** (1927–)—The first Black entertainer to win an Emmy and the first to win a Tony, Belafonte was also a singer and civil rights activist.

5. **Chadwick Boseman** (1976–2020)—A dynamic actor and star of the Marvel Universe, Boseman's life was cut short by cancer at the height of his career.

6. **Diahann Carroll** (1935–2019)—The first Black woman to win a Tony and the first to star in her own TV show in a non-stereotypical role.

7. **Sam Cooke** (1931–1964)—This popular soul singer used his success to fight for equality and control of his art.

8. **Misty Copeland** (1982–)—Copeland made history when she became the first Black principal dancer of the American Ballet Theatre.

9. **Dorothy Dandridge** (1922–1965)—A pioneer in the entertainment industry, Dandridge was the first Black woman to be nominated for a Best Actress Oscar and Best Actress Golden Globe.

10. **Bo Diddley** (1928–2008)—Diddley's unique blues guitar influenced countless musicians.

11. **Ella Fitzgerald** (1917–1996)—Known as the "First Lady of Song," Fitzgerald's singing style brought new life to jazz.

12. **Aretha Franklin** (1942–2018)—"The Queen of Soul" brought her powerful voice to gospel and soul music. Franklin was the first woman inducted into the Rock and Roll Hall of Fame.

13. **Whoopi Goldberg** (1955–)—An author, actress, comedian, and talk show host, Goldberg has won almost every entertainment award, including an EGOT (Emmy, Grammy, Oscar, and Tony).

14. **Arsenio Hall** (1956–)—This actor and comedian was the first Black host of a late-night talk show.

15. **Jimi Hendrix** (1942–1970)—Hendrix brought an intensity and style to guitar playing that influenced musicians in many different genres.

16. **Billie Holiday** (1915–1959)—One of the greatest singers of all time, Holiday also spoke out against lynching through her powerful song "Strange Fruit."

17. **Lena Horne** (1917–2010)—A singer, actress, and civil-rights activist who refused racist roles, Horne was one of the most important stars of her time.

18. **Beyoncé Knowles** (1981–)—"Queen Bey" is one of the most powerful women in the music industry in the 21st century.

19. **Spike Lee** (1957–)—This writer, actor, director, and filmmaker has created honest portrayals of the Black experience for more than 40 years.

20. **John Legend** (1978–)—Musician, singer, and producer Legend was the first Black man to win an EGOT—an Emmy, Grammy, Oscar, and Tony.

21. **Hattie McDaniel** (1893–1952)—The first Black person to win an Oscar, for Best Supporting Actress.

22. **Oscar Micheaux** (1884–1951)—A pioneering feature film director and producer, Micheaux made both silent and sound films with all-Black casts.

23. **Arthur Mitchell** (1934–2018)—Mitchell created the first African American classical ballet company, Dance Theatre of Harlem.

24. **Eddie Murphy** (1961–)—One of the most popular comedians and actors from the 1980s on.

25. **Lupita Nyong'o** (1983–)—Nyong'o won a Best Supporting Actress Oscar in 2014 and went on to star in the *Star Wars* universe, *Black Panther*, and other films.

26. **Jordan Peele** (1979–)—A talented director, actor, and writer, Peele was the first Black writer to win an Oscar for Best Original Screenplay and has created memorable and ground-breaking films.

27. **Tyler Perry** (1969–)—After creating and starring in the "Madea" stage plays and movies, Perry went on to build his own movie studio and become one of the richest and most powerful men in the entertainment industry.

28. **Sidney Poitier** (1927–)—The first Black man to win an Oscar for Best Actor, and one of the most important actors of his generation.

29. **Prince** (1958–2016)—Prince was a huge creative force beginning in the 1980s, combining soul, funk, and rock music in a whole new way.

30. **Ma Rainey** (1886–1939)—Called "the Mother of the Blues," Rainey was one of the first Black women to have her music recorded.

31. **Nina Simone** (1933–2003)—A talented classical pianist from childhood, Simone brought together many styles of music in her work.

32. **John Singleton** (1968–2019)—A groundbreaking and award-winning filmmaker who made his first hit movie right after graduating from film school.

33. **Will Smith** (1968–)—Smith started as a rapper and went on to become one of the highest-paid and most popular movie stars.

34. **Sister Rosetta Tharpe** (1915–1973)—"The Godmother of Rock and Roll" started playing electric guitar in the 1930s and transformed gospel into a new kind of music.

39.

35. **Tina Turner** (1939–)—Turner's incredible stage presence and powerful voice gave strength to listeners everywhere.

36. **Cicely Tyson** (1924–2021)—A brilliant actress who refused to play stereotypical roles and served as an inspiration to entire generations of performers.

37. **Dinah Washington** (1924–1963)—A popular recording artist in the 1950s, Washington paved the way for future Black singers.

38. **Ethel Waters** (1896–1977)—A singer and actress who was the first Black woman in an integrated Broadway cast and starred in her own TV variety show in 1939.

39. **Oprah Winfrey** (1954–)—Winfrey was the first Black woman to own her own production company and is also a successful actress, talk-show host, and entrepreneur.

40. **Stevie Wonder** (1950–)—Singer, songwriter, and musician Wonder began making ground-breaking hit records when he was 13 years old.

26.

30

IMPORTANT LATINX ENTERTAINERS

1. **Christina Aguilera** (1980–)—One of the most successful pop stars of the 2000s, Aguilera won five Grammys and sold millions of albums.

2. **Marc Anthony** (1968–)—This multiple Grammy winning musician also holds the Guinness World Record for being the bestselling salsa artist of all time.

3. **Desi Arnaz** (1917–1986)—As Lucille Ball's husband and producing partner, Arnaz rose to fame playing Lucy's husband on her classic TV comedy *I Love Lucy*.

4. **Bad Bunny** (1994–)—This Puerto Rican rapper, singer, and songwriter makes music combining many styles.

5. **Camila Cabello** (1997–)—This popular singer got her start as a member of the girl group Fifth Harmony and went on to become a solo star.

6. **Gloria Estefan** (1957–)—Born in Cuba and raised in Miami, Estefan became an international star as the singer for Miami Sound Machine.

7. **José Ferrer** (1912–1992)—Born in Puerto Rico, Ferrer was the first Hispanic man to win an Oscar.

8. **America Ferrera** (1984–)—This actress, born in Los Angeles to Honduran parents, starred in the TV show *Ugly Betty* and starred in and produced the TV show *Superstore*.

9. **Selena Gomez** (1992–)—This popular singer and actress launched her career on the children's television show *Barney & Friends* while she was still in grade school.

10. **Oscar Isaac** (1979–)—This Guatemalan American actor's films include the *Star Wars* sequel trilogy, as well as roles in dramas and thrillers.

11. **John Leguizamo** (1964–)—A New York City native, Leguizamo works to portray the Latin-American experience through his plays and movies.

12. **Eva Longoria** (1975–)—This actress has starred in and produced many TV dramas.

13. **George Lopez** (1961–)—This Mexican American comedian has starred in movies and his own TV shows.

14. **Jennifer Lopez** (1969–)—One of the most well-known performers in pop culture, Lopez's talents shine in both the music and movie worlds.

15. **Mario Lopez** (1973–)—Lopez rose to fame in the classic TV show *Saved By the Bell* and went on to become a popular TV host.

16. **Lin-Manuel Miranda** (1980–)—The creator and star of the hit Broadway musicals *Hamilton* and *In the Heights*, Miranda has also appeared in many films and TV shows.

17. **Rita Moreno** (1931–)—The first Hispanic performer to win an Oscar, Emmy, Grammy, and a Tony, Moreno first shot to fame in the 1961 movie *West Side Story*.

18. **Edward James Olmos** (1947-)—Mexican American actor Olmos won an Emmy and a Golden Globe. A lot of his work focuses on telling stories from Hispanic communities.

19. **Kenny Ortega** (1950–)—Ortega choreographed and directed *High School Musical, Hocus Pocus*, and Disney's *Descendants* series.

20. **Pitbull** (1981–)—The stage name of Armando Christian Pérez, also known as "Mr. Worldwide," Pitbull is one of the most popular pop stars in the world.

21. **Freddie Prinze** (1954–1977)—Prinze starred in *Chico and the Man*, the first TV series set in a Mexican American neighborhood, and was also a popular stand-up comic.

22. **Selena Quintanilla** (1971–1995)—The queen of Tejano music, Selena was poised to achieve even more success when she was tragically murdered.

23. **Richard "Cheech" Marin** (1946–)—A Mexican American with a long career in comedy and films, Marin also owns one of the largest Hispanic art collections in the world.

16.

24. **Christopher Lee Rios** (1971–2000)—Known as "Big Pun," Rios is considered one of the greatest Latino rappers of all time.

25. **Linda Ronstadt** (1946–)—This Mexican American singer's long career includes hits on the country, Latin, and pop charts, and she has won ten Grammy awards.

26. **Zoe Saldana** (1978–)—This actress has made a name for herself appearing in major films, including the Avatar and Star Trek series.

27. **Carlos Santana** (1947–)—One of the greatest guitarists of all time, Santana has been performing for more than 50 years.

28. **Jimmy Smits** (1955–)—This actor's many firsts include the first Latino actor in the Star Wars franchise and the first to play an American president in a TV show (*The West Wing*).

29. **Danny Trejo** (1944–)—Trejo is known as a popular actor (sometimes working with his cousin, acclaimed director Robert Rodriguez) and restaurateur.

30. **Ritchie Valens** (1941–1959)—This Mexican American singer became a teen pop idol with several hits before he was killed in a tragic plane crash.

17.

35 AWESOME ASIAN AMERICAN ENTERTAINERS

1. **Philip Ahn** (1905–1978)—One of the most popular Asian actors of his time, Ahn was the first Korean American actor to receive a star on Hollywood's Walk of Fame.

2. **Michele Selene Ang** (1983–)—Born in Indonesia to Chinese parents, Ang moved to the U.S. as a teenager and became famous appearing in the series *13 Reasons Why*.

3. **Aziz Ansari** (1983–)—This South Carolina-born writer, actor, and comedian became known for his role on *Parks and Recreation* and featured his India-born parents in his series *Master of None*.

4. **Joan Chen** (1961–)—Born in China, Chen became a well-known actress, producer, and director.

5. **John Cho** (1972–)—Born in South Korea, this actor became famous in the Harold and Kumar films and several Star Trek films.

6. **Sessue Hayakawa** (1886–1973)—A pioneering star of the silent film era, Hayakawa formed his own company, Hayworth Pictures, to produce and star in his own films. He later appeared in the classic movie *The Bridge on the River Kwai*.

7. **Mindy Kaling** (1979–)—This actress, writer, producer, and director first gained recognition writing for and starring in the NBC sitcom *The Office*.

8. **Padma Lakshmi** (1970–)—India-born Lakshmi started her career as a model and went on to write cookbooks and host the popular TV show *Top Chef*.

9. **Lucy Liu** (1968–)—Liu shot to fame on TV series *Ally McBeal* and went on to star in *Elementary* and in Charlie's Angels films.

10. **Keye Luke** (1904–1991)—A founding member of the Screen Actors Guild, Luke starred in many movies, including the Charlie Chan and Green Lantern series.

11. **Norah Lum** (1988–)—Usually credited as Awkwafina, this actress has become famous for her funny and sensitive roles.

16. **Randall Park** (1974–)—Park shot to fame as a star of TV series *Fresh Off the Boat* and then joined the Marvel Cinematic Universe.

17. **Kal Penn** (1977–)—Well-known as a TV and movie actor, Penn was also part of the White House staff during President Barack Obama's administration.

18. **Beulah Quo** (1923–2002)—After appearing in many movie and TV roles, Quo co-founded the famed East West Players, the first Asian American repertory theater in the country, in 1965.

19. **Lea Salonga** (1971–)—The Philippines-born Salonga, the first Asian woman to win a Tony Award, also provided the singing voice for two different Disney princesses (Jasmine in *Aladdin* and the title role in *Mulan*).

12. **Mako Iwamatsu** (1933–2006)—Usually credited as Mako, this actor appeared in many film and Broadway roles and also voiced Iroh in *Avatar: The Last Airbender*.

13. **Pat Morita** (1932–2005)—A popular actor in many movies and TV shows, Morita is maybe best known for playing Mr. Miyagi in the Karate Kid movies.

14. **Sandra Oh** (1971–)—Korean Canadian-born actress Oh has been nominated for a dozen Emmys, won two Golden Globes, and became an American citizen in 2018.

15. **Soon-Tek Oh** (1932–2018)—Oh acted on Broadway and in the James Bond film *The Man With the Golden Gun*, then voiced the father in *Mulan*. He also co-founded the East West Players with Beulah Quo.

20. **Nico Santos** (1979–)—Born in the Philippines, Santos became popular for his acting in movies and on TV, including in the series *Superstore*.

21. **James Shigeta** (1929–2014)—Shigeta started his career as a singer and went on to appear in many movies, including the classic *Die Hard*.

22. **Phillipa Soo** (1990–)—Soo originated the role of Eliza in *Hamilton*, which went on to win 11 Tony Awards and numerous other honors.

23. **George Takei** (1937–)—After spending part of his childhood in a Japanese internment camp, Takei appeared in the original Star Trek series and went on to become a popular actor and activist.

24. **Kelly Marie Tran** (1989–)—Tran shot to international fame for her work in the *Star Wars* sequel trilogy films and in *Raya and the Last Dragon*.

25. **Miyoshi Umeki** (1929–2007)—The Japanese American actress won an Academy Award in 1957, the first Oscar for an Asian actress.

26. **Ming-Na Wen** (1963–)—This Chinese American actress is best known for voicing Fa Mulan in the animated films *Mulan* and *Mulan II* and for starring in *Agents of S.H.I.E.L.D.*

27. **Anna May Wong** (1905–1951)— Considered to be the first Chinese American movie star, Wong's career included silent films, sound movies, radio, television, and the stage.

28. **Constance Wu** (1982–)—Wu's breakthrough role came on the popular television series *Fresh Off the Boat*. She went on to star in major movies such as *Crazy Rich Asians*.

29. **Steven Yeun** (1983–)—Yeun made history as the first Asian American nominated for a Best Actor Award, for family drama *Minari*, at the 2021 Oscars.

30. **Chloé Zhao** (1982–)—A writer and director, Zhao was born in China and studied filmmaking at New York University. In 2021, she was the first Asian woman to win a Best Director Oscar, and she joined the Marvel Cinematic Universe with *Eternals*.

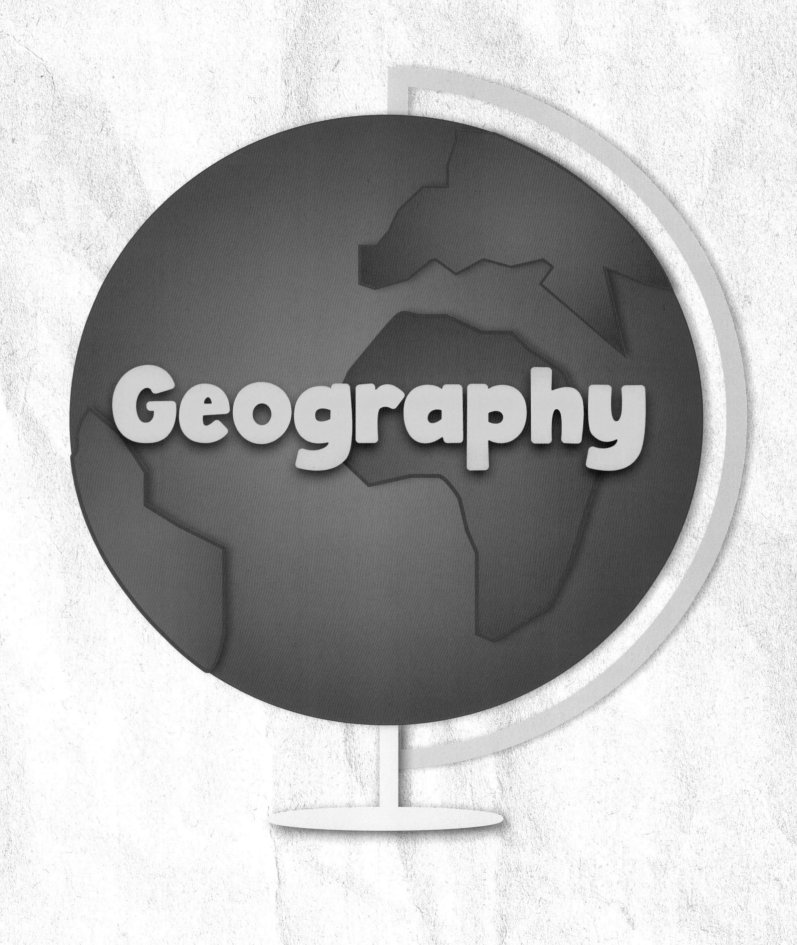

Geography

35
DRY DESERT FACTS

1. A desert is a region that receives less than 10 inches (25 cm) of precipitation a year.

2. The U.S. has four major deserts: the Great Basin, Mojave, Sonoran, and Chihuahuan.

3. All North American deserts are located in an area called the Basin and Range Province.

4. The Basin and Range Province covers much of the inland western U.S. and extends south into Mexico.

5. The Basin and Range Province features mountain ranges with flat desert basins in between.

6. The mountains create a rain shadow that leads to deserts.

7. The Great Basin Desert is the largest North American desert.

8. It covers about 200,000 square miles (520,000 sq km).

9. The Great Basin Desert covers most of Nevada, along with parts of Utah, California, and Idaho.

10. The Great Basin is the northernmost and highest desert in the U.S.

11. This desert includes mountains higher than 9,800 feet (3,000 m) and valleys above 3,900 feet (1,200 m).

12. Because of its elevation and location, the Great Basin is classified as a cold desert.

13. Most of the precipitation in the Great Basin Desert falls as snow in the mountains.

14. The Mojave Desert is the driest and smallest desert in North America.

15. The Mojave covers about 48,000 square miles (124,000 sq km).

16. The Mojave is located in southern Nevada and southeastern California.

17. The Sonoran Desert is located along the shores of the Gulf of California.

18. This desert is located in California, southern Arizona, and part of Mexico.

19. The Sonoran covers about 100,000 square miles (260,000 sq km).

20. The Sonoran is home to a large saltwater lake called the Salton Sea.

21. The Sonoran is the only North American desert to contain sand dunes.

22. North America's fourth desert, the Chihuahuan, is the most eastern and southern of the continent's deserts.

23. The Chihuhuan covers parts of New Mexico, Arizona, and Texas, but most of it lies in Mexico.

24. The types of plants that can grow in deserts are limited by the lack of moisture, extreme temperatures, and soil types.

25. The Great Basin has the fewest plant species.

26. The most common plants in the Great Basin are sagebrush, saltbushes, and grass.

27. Cacti and Joshua trees are common in the Mojave.

28. The Joshua tree only grows in the Mojave.

29. Joshua trees are also known as yucca palm, tree yucca, and palm tree yucca.

30. The saguaro cactus only grows in the Sonoran Desert.

31. Saguaros are covered with protective spines. They grow white flowers in the late spring and red fruit in summer.

32. Animals that live in the desert get their water from food.

33. Most desert animals are active at night to avoid the hot daytime temperatures.

34. Scientists have recorded 350 species of birds, 20 species of amphibians, more than 100 reptile species, more than 1,000 species of bees, and even 30 different kinds of fish in the Sonoran Desert.

35. The Sonoran also contains more than 2,000 species of plants.

40 MONUMENTAL MOUNTAIN AND VOLCANO FACTS

1. Colorado has 56 mountains taller than 14,000 feet (4,267 m)

2. Alaska has 19 mountains taller than 14,000 feet (4,267 m)

3. The 16 highest mountains in the U.S. are all located in Alaska.

4. Alaska's Denali is the highest mountain in North America, standing 20,310 feet (6,190 m) tall.

5. California's Mount Whitney is the tallest mountain in the lower 48 states.

6. Mount Whitney is 14,505 feet (4,421 m) tall.

7. There are three major mountain ranges in the United States.

8. Those mountain ranges are the Sierra Nevada, the Rocky Mountains, and the Appalachian Mountains.

9. The Sierra Nevada runs north-to-south in California and Nevada.

10. The Sierra Nevada range is about 400 miles (644 km) long and 70 miles (113 km) wide.

11. Mount Whitney is the highest point in the Sierra Nevada Mountains.

12. The Sierra Nevada Mountains are fault-block mountains. They formed along a fault in the Earth's crust.

13. The Rocky Mountains are the longest mountain range in North America and the second-longest range in the world.

14. The Rockies stretch for 3,000 miles (4,828 km) from New Mexico into Canada.

15. The highest peak in the Rocky Mountains is Mount Elbert in Colorado.

16. Mount Elbert is 14,440 feet (4,401 m) tall.

17. There are several smaller mountain ranges within the Rockies.

18. The Rockies are fold mountains. They formed where two tectonic plates meet.

19. The Appalachian Mountains stretch for 1,500 miles (2,414 km) from northern Alabama to Maine.

20. The highest point of the Appalachians is Mount Mitchell in North Carolina, which is 6,683 feet (2,037 m) high.

21. During the early days of the United States, the Appalachians were a barrier to westward expansion from the original 13 colonies.

22. Smaller ranges within the Appalachians include the Great Smoky Mountains, the Blue Ridge Mountains, the Green Mountains, the White Mountains, and the Berkshires.

23. The Appalachians are much lower than the Rockies or Sierra Nevada Mountains because they are older and have been worn down by erosion.

24. Other mountain ranges in the U.S. include the Adirondacks (New York State), Alaska's Brooks Range and Alaska Range, the Ozarks (southern Missouri and northern Arkansas), and the Cascades along the northwestern coast.

25. The Cascades are part of the Ring of Fire, a region along much of the Pacific Ocean marked by frequent earthquakes and active volcanoes.

26. Washington State's volcano, Mount Saint Helens, located in the Cascades, erupted in 1980.

27. The Mount St. Helens eruption in 1980 killed 57 people and sent clouds of ash over a dozen western states.

28. Mount St. Helens has had many periods of activity since the 1700s.

29. A volcano is considered active if it has erupted recently or has the potential to erupt again.

30. The U.S. has 169 active volcanoes.

31. Only Indonesia and Japan have more active volcanoes than the U.S.

32. Washington's Mount Rainier hasn't erupted in 1,100 years, but it is still considered active.

33. Hawaii has five active volcanoes: Kilauea, Mauna Loa, Mauna Kea, Hualalai, and Haleakala.

34. Kilauea erupted as recently as December 2020.

35. Mauna Loa is the largest active volcano in the world.

36. Only three volcanoes in the lower 48 states have erupted since the U.S. was founded.

37. After being dormant for over 1,000 years, Oregon's Mount Hood had a period of eruptions between 1781 and 1791.

38. Residents also reported minor eruptions of Mount Hood in the mid-1800s.

39. Lassen Peak in California was active between 1914 and 1917, and it erupted in 1915.

40. Crater Lake, in Oregon, formed from the eruption of Mount Mazama in about 5700 BC.

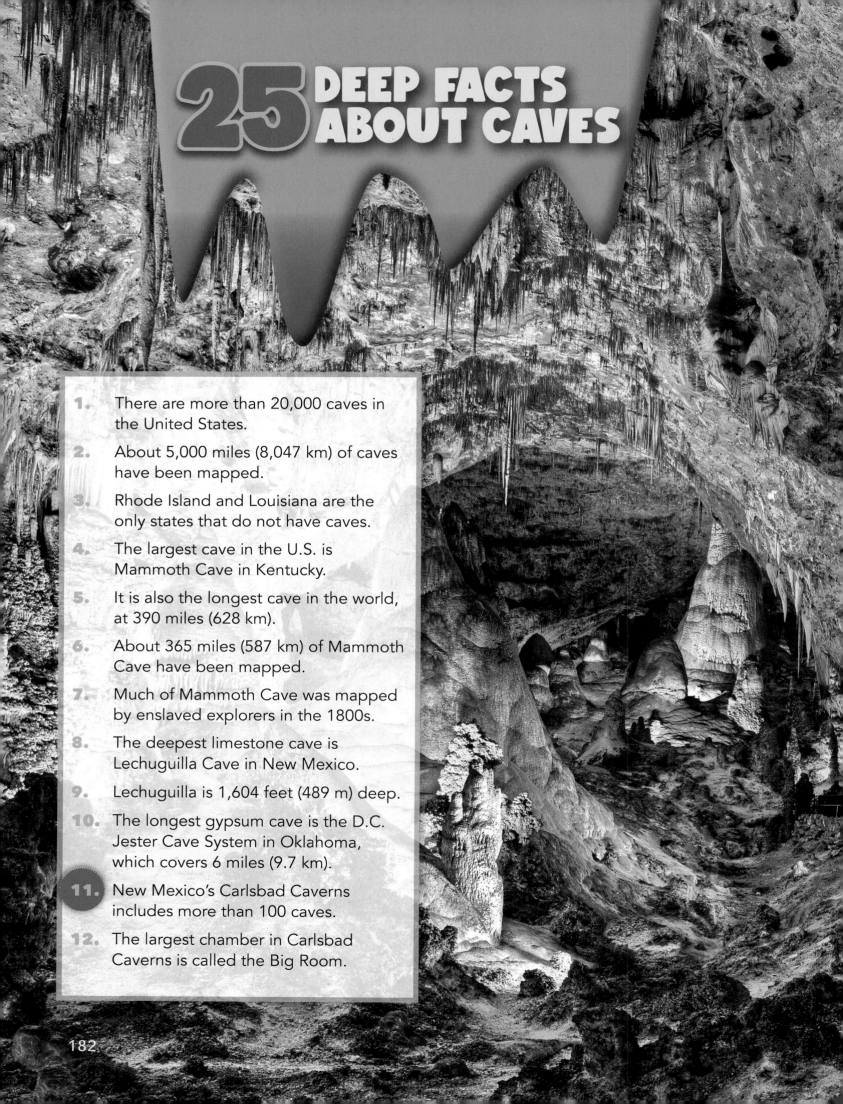

25 DEEP FACTS ABOUT CAVES

1. There are more than 20,000 caves in the United States.

2. About 5,000 miles (8,047 km) of caves have been mapped.

3. Rhode Island and Louisiana are the only states that do not have caves.

4. The largest cave in the U.S. is Mammoth Cave in Kentucky.

5. It is also the longest cave in the world, at 390 miles (628 km).

6. About 365 miles (587 km) of Mammoth Cave have been mapped.

7. Much of Mammoth Cave was mapped by enslaved explorers in the 1800s.

8. The deepest limestone cave is Lechuguilla Cave in New Mexico.

9. Lechuguilla is 1,604 feet (489 m) deep.

10. The longest gypsum cave is the D.C. Jester Cave System in Oklahoma, which covers 6 miles (9.7 km).

11. New Mexico's Carlsbad Caverns includes more than 100 caves.

12. The largest chamber in Carlsbad Caverns is called the Big Room.

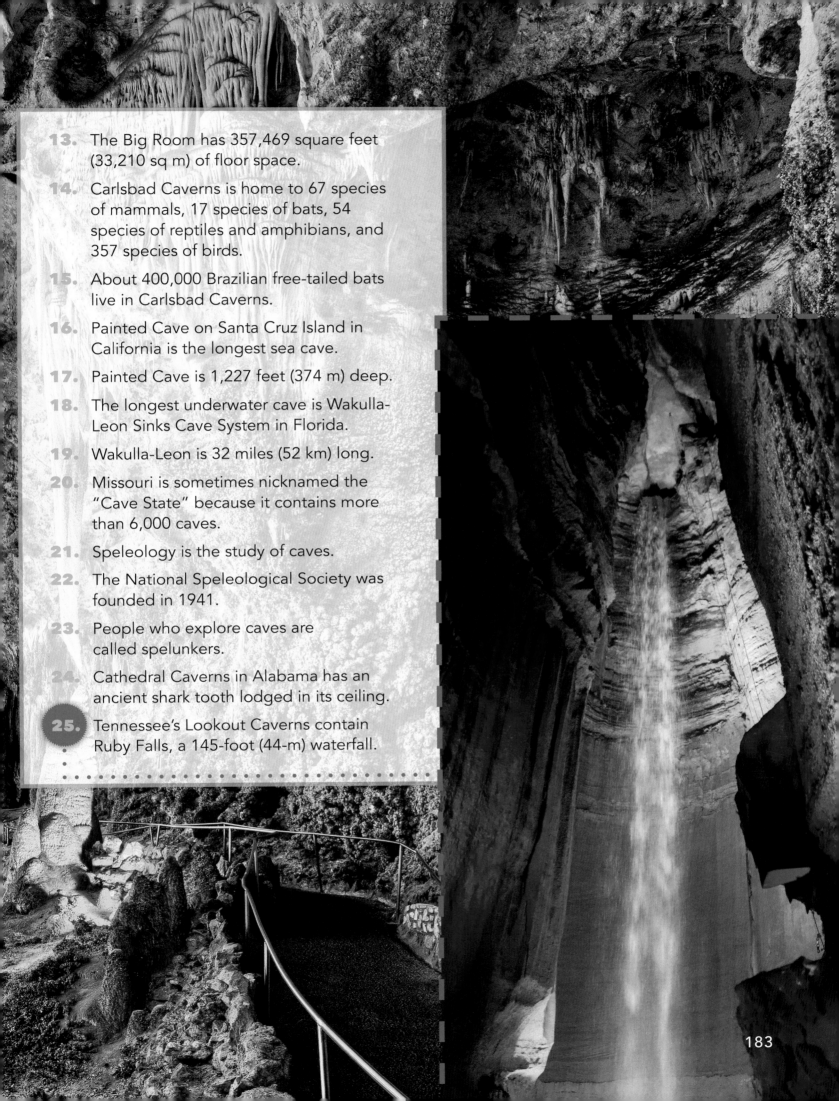

13. The Big Room has 357,469 square feet (33,210 sq m) of floor space.

14. Carlsbad Caverns is home to 67 species of mammals, 17 species of bats, 54 species of reptiles and amphibians, and 357 species of birds.

15. About 400,000 Brazilian free-tailed bats live in Carlsbad Caverns.

16. Painted Cave on Santa Cruz Island in California is the longest sea cave.

17. Painted Cave is 1,227 feet (374 m) deep.

18. The longest underwater cave is Wakulla-Leon Sinks Cave System in Florida.

19. Wakulla-Leon is 32 miles (52 km) long.

20. Missouri is sometimes nicknamed the "Cave State" because it contains more than 6,000 caves.

21. Speleology is the study of caves.

22. The National Speleological Society was founded in 1941.

23. People who explore caves are called spelunkers.

24. Cathedral Caverns in Alabama has an ancient shark tooth lodged in its ceiling.

25. Tennessee's Lookout Caverns contain Ruby Falls, a 145-foot (44-m) waterfall.

40 WET FACTS ABOUT LAKES AND RIVERS

10 Longest Rivers in the U.S.

#	Name	Location	Length
1.	Missouri River	MT, ND, SD, NE, IA, KS, MS	2,540 miles (4,088 km)
2.	Mississippi River	MN, WI, IA, IL, MS, KY, TN, AR, MS, LA	2,340 miles (3,766 km)
3.	Yukon River	Alaska and Canada	1,980 miles (3,187 km)
4.	Rio Grande	NM, TX, and Mexico	1,900 miles (3,058 km)
5.	St. Lawrence River	New York and Canada	1,900 miles (3,058 km)
6.	Arkansas River	CO, KS, OK, AR	1,460 miles (2,350 km)
7.	Colorado River	CO, UT, AZ, NV, CA, and Mexico	1,450 miles (2,334 km)
8.	Atchafalaya River	Louisiana	1,420 miles (2,285 km)
9.	Ohio River	IL, IN, KY, OH, PA, WV	1,310 miles (2,108 km)
10.	Red River	TX, OK, AR, LA	1,290 miles (2,076 km)

10 Largest Lakes in the U.S.

#	Name	Location	Size in Area
1.	Lake Superior	MN, WI, MI and Canada	31,700 sq miles (82,103 sq km)
2.	Lake Huron	Michigan and Canada	23,000 sq miles (59,570 sq km)
3.	Lake Michigan	WI, IL, IN, MI	22,300 sq miles (57,757 sq km)
4.	Lake Erie	MI, OH, PA, NY and Canada	9,910 sq miles (25,667 sq km)
5.	Lake Ontario	New York and Canada	7,340 sq miles (19,011 sq km)
6.	Great Salt Lake	Utah	2,117 sq miles (5,483 sq km)
7.	Lake of the Woods	Minnesota and Canada	1,485 sq miles (3,846 sq km)
8.	Iliamna Lake	Alaska	1,014 sq miles (2,626 sq km)
9.	Lake Oahe	North and South Dakota	685 sq miles (1,774 sq km)
10.	Lake Okeechobee	Florida	662 sq miles (1,715 sq km)

1. The five largest lakes in the U.S. are the Great Lakes.

2. Lake Superior is the largest freshwater lake in the world.

3. Lake Superior's average depth is 500 feet (152 m), but some places are 1,333 feet (406 m) deep.

4. More than 20 percent of all the world's fresh water is in the Great Lakes, making them the largest freshwater system in the world.

5. Lake Tahoe, in California and Nevada, is directly behind the Great Lakes in largest freshwater lakes by volume of water.

6. Utah's Great Salt Lake is saltier than the ocean.

7. Because it is so salty, no fish live in the Great Salt Lake, only brine shrimp and algae.

8. Crater Lake in Oregon is the deepest lake in the United States at 1,943 feet (592 m) deep.

9. The depth of Crater Lake was first measured in 1886 using a lead pipe attached to piano wire.

10. Crater Lake formed from land that collapsed at the center of a volcano.

11. Florida's Lake Okeechobee may be big, but it is only about 9 feet (3 m) deep.

12. Fire on Ohio's Cuyahoga River helped pave the way for environmental reforms and cleaner water.

13. The Mississippi River, at about 2,340 miles (3,766 km) long, is an important transportation route.

14. The Missouri River is a tributary of the Mississippi River.

15. The Yukon River was one of the most important transportation routes during the 1893–1906 Klondike Gold Rush.

16. The St. Lawrence River forms part of the border between New York and Ontario, Canada, while the Rio Grande forms the border between part of Texas and Mexico.

17. About 83 different land and aquatic mammals live in the St. Lawrence River and the Gulf of St. Lawrence.

18. Over millions of years, the Colorado River carved out the Grand Canyon.

19. The Colorado River is an important source of water and power for the southwest United States.

20. The Hoover Dam, which was built on the Colorado River in 1936, formed Lake Mead and provides power to the city of Las Vegas.

35
FUN FACTS ABOUT FORESTS

1. About one-third of the United States is forested.

2. Forests cover about 750 million acres (303,514,232 hectares) of the U.S.

3. Forests can be owned by companies or individuals, or by federal, state, or tribal governments.

4. More than 56 percent of U.S. forests are privately owned.

5. Privately owned forests supply 91 percent of the wood harvested in the U.S.

6. National Forests provide 66 million people with their water supply.

7. In 1891, President Theodore Roosevelt created the U.S. Forest Service, which manages National Forests.

8. Yellowstone was the first National Forest in the U.S.

9. Later, Yellowstone's National Forest lands were broken down into separate forests.

10. The Forest Service manages 154 National Forests, covering 188,336,179 acres (76,216,948 hectares).

11. California has the most national forests.

12. Only Connecticut, Delaware, Hawaii, Iowa, Kansas, Maryland, Massachusetts, New Jersey, North Dakota, and Rhode Island do not have a National Forest within their borders.

13. Logging and other resource harvesting is permitted in National Forests, but the fastest growing use of National Forests is recreation.

14. Tongass National Forest is the largest National Forest in the U.S.

15. Tongass covers more than 500 miles (805 km) in southeastern Alaska and is roughly the same size as West Virginia.

16. The smallest National Forest is Tuskegee in Alabama. It covers 11,000 acres (4,452 hectares).

17. El Yunque in Puerto Rico is the only tropical rainforest in the National Forest system.

187

18. Adak "National Forest," in Alaska, is made up of exactly 33 trees.

19. Adak's 33-tree forest is not officially part of the National Forest system.

20. Adak was created when a military base commander planted pine trees to cheer up troops stationed there over Christmas during World War II.

21. Timber products are the most valuable agricultural crop in the U.S.

22. The Hoh Rain Forest in Washington State receives up to 140 inches (356 cm) of precipitation per year.

23. The Hoh Rain Forest is one of the last remaining examples of a temperate rainforest in the U.S.

24. At one time, the Pacific Northwest rainforest stretched from southeastern Alaska to the central coast of California.

25. The Forest Inventory and Analysis (FIA) Program of the U.S. Forest Service conducts a forest census to monitor forests.

10 Biggest National Forests in the U.S.

#	Name	Location	Area
1.	Tongass	Alaska	17,000,000 acres (6,900,000 ha)
2.	Chugach	Alaska	6,900,000 acres (2,800,000 ha)
3.	Humboldt-Toiyabe	Nevada and California	6,700,000 acres (2,700,000 ha)
4.	Salmon-Challis	Idaho	4,200,000 acres (1,700,000 ha)
5.	Bridger-Teton	Wyoming	3,400,000 acres (1,400,000 ha)
6.	Superior	Minnesota	3,200,000 acres (1,300,000 ha)
7.	Mark Twain	Missouri	3,000,000 acres (1,200,000 ha)
8.	Tonto	Arizona	2,900,000 acres (1,736,000 ha)
9.	Boise	Idaho	2,900,000 acres (1,736,000 ha)
10.	Gila	New Mexico	2,700,000 acres (1,000,000 ha)

Living
Things

50 BEAUTIFUL BIRD FACTS

1. About 1,100 species of birds live in the lower 48 states.

2. Another 521 bird species live in Alaska.

3. There are more than 7 billion wild birds in the U.S. and Canada.

4. That's a lot less than the 10 billion birds in those countries in 1970.

5. Scientists count the number of birds through bird watching and by tracking groups of birds on radar.

6. Loss of habitat is the number one reason bird populations are declining.

7. Other threats include cats and other predators who kill birds, and deadly collisions with windows.

8. The largest bird in the U.S. is the California condor. Its wingspan is 10 feet (3 m) wide, and its body is 4.5 feet (1.4 m) long.

9. The California condor is also one of the rarest birds in the U.S. Captive breeding has brought their numbers up.

10. The calliope hummingbird is the smallest bird in the U.S. It measures just over 3 inches (8 cm) long. It weighs only one-tenth of an ounce.

11. Owls are the most dangerous birds in North America. These top predators have powerful talons and are expert hunters.

12. Seeing a robin is one of the traditional first signs of spring in the northern part of the U.S.

13. However, not all robins migrate south for the winter.

14. The northern cardinal is the most popular state bird and is also the mascot for several sports teams.

15. While blue jays are common in the eastern part of the U.S., Stellar's jays are found in the West.

16. Crows are considered highly intelligent.

17. European starlings are very common in the U.S., thanks to Eugene Schieffelin, who introduced the bird to the U.S. in 1890.

18. Schieffelin thought that America should have every bird mentioned in Shakespeare's plays.

19. After Schieffelin released some European starlings in New York City's Central Park, they spread across the nation.

20. Northern mockingbirds can mimic other bird songs, as well as the sounds of frogs, toads, car alarms, music, and machinery.

21. The tufted titmouse is not named after mice. The term "mouse" comes from an Old English word for a small bird.

22. House sparrows live in groups led by the male with the biggest black patch on its chest.

23. Male house wrens build several nests, then let their partners choose which nest they like best.

24. House finches used to be found only in the Southwest.

25. In 1940, New York pet shops got in trouble for selling finches illegally, so some released their birds in the wild.

26. Finches are now common all over the United States.

27. Woodpeckers have a large and reinforced brain case and a thick skull. These features protect the brain from being injured when the bird pecks against wood.

28. Woodpeckers also have extra muscles behind the beak to act like shock absorbers.

29. Woodpeckers have extra-long tongues to reach insects through holes.

30. Woodpecker tongues coil inside of their skull when pulled back.

20 Most Common Birds in the U.S.

1. Mourning Dove
2. Northern Cardinal
3. American Robin
4. American Crow
5. Blue Jay
6. Song Sparrow
7. Red-Winged Blackbird
8. European Starling
9. American Goldfinch
10. Canada Goose
11. House Finch
12. Downy Woodpecker
13. Mallard Dog
14. Red-Bellied Woodpecker
15. House Sparrow
16. Turkey Vulture
17. Black-Capped Chickadee
18. Tufted Titmouse
19. Dark-Eyed Junco
20. White-Breasted Nuthatch

65
MAGNIFICENT MAMMAL FACTS

1. Mammals are warm-blooded, air-breathing vertebrates. Their bodies are covered with hair.

2. Mammals typically give birth to live young and produce milk.

3. There are at least 428 different species of mammals in the U.S.

4. Almost half of those species—207—are rodents.

5. Rodents include rats, mice, voles, lemmings, squirrels, chipmunks, gophers, marmots, porcupines, and beavers.

6. At least 39 mammal species are carnivores.

7. Hoofed mammals make up at least 12 species.

8. Hoofed mammals include caribou, elk, deer, moose, pronghorn, peccary, sheep, mountain goat, musk ox, and bison.

9. There are 45 species of bats.

10. Rabbits, hares, and pikas make up 19 species.

11. Shrews and moles make up 46.

12. There are 43 species of whales, porpoises, and dolphins.

13. There are 14 species of sea lions, seals, and walruses.

14. There are 10 different species of skunks.

15. The U.S. has one species of opossum, one species of armadillo, and one species of manatee.

16. The bison is the largest land animal in the U.S. Adult males can weigh more than 2,000 pounds (907 kg).

17. Yellowstone National Park is the only place where bison have lived since prehistoric times.

18. Bison can run up to 35 miles (56 km) per hour.

19. They can also jump, spin around, and swim.

20. The moose is the largest member of the deer family. Adult males weigh more than 1,600 pounds (726 kg) and stand up to 6 feet (1.8 m) tall at the shoulder.

21. Moose are not normally aggressive toward people, but that can change if they feel threatened or tired.

22. More people are injured each year by encounters with moose than with bears.

23. Alaska is home to the two large carnivores: the Kodiak bear and the polar bear.

24. Kodiak bears only live in the Kodiak Archipelago of southeastern Alaska.

25. These big brown bears weigh up to 1,500 pounds (680 kg).

26. Polar bears can weigh up to 1,760 pounds (800 kg).

27. Cougars are the largest wild cat in North America.

28. About 30,000 cougars live in the western United States.

29. Cougars are also called mountain lions, pumas, and panthers.

30. Pygmy shrews are the smallest mammals in the U.S.

31. A pygmy shrew only weighs about 0.07 ounce (2 grams) and is less than two inches (5 cm) long.

32. Pygmy shrews may also be the hungriest mammal. These tiny creatures have to eat three times their body weight every day.

33. Pygmy shrews typically capture prey every 15–30 minutes.

34. Pygmy shrews have the fastest heartbeat (1,200 beats per minute) of any mammal.

35. They also have one of the shortest lifespans, only living for 11–13 months.

36. Not all mammals live on land. Marine mammals spend most of their lives in the ocean.

37. Marine mammals are protected by a law called the Marine Mammal Protection Act.

38. There are four types of marine mammals.

39. Cetaceans include dolphins, porpoises, and whales.

40. Pinnipeds include seals, sea lions, and walruses.

41. Pinnipeds use their flippers to move on land and in the water.

42. Sirenians include manatees and dugongs.

43. Sirenians are the only entirely herbivorous (plant-eating) group of marine mammals.

44. Sirenians are named for the group of dangerous sea creatures of Greek mythology, the Sirens.

45. Some people think rumored or reported mermaid sightings were actually just people seeing manatees.

46. Marine fissipeds are considered marine animals, even though they spend much of their time on land.

47. Polar bears and sea otters are fissipeds.

48. Elephant seals spend most of their lives in the ocean, but they sometimes come onshore along the Pacific coast.

49. Elephant seals can weigh up to 4,000 pounds (1,814 kg).

50. Opossums are the only marsupial species that lives in North America.

51. Marsupials are mammals that give birth to undeveloped young, then nurse them in a pouch for several months.

52. Opossums can eat up to 5,000 ticks a year.

53. Opossums are immune to almost all snake venom.

54. Unlike other mammals, opossums almost never get rabies.

55. Opossums can have up to 20 babies at a time.

56. Young opossums often ride on their mother's back.

57. A gray wolf can eat between 20 and 30 pounds (9 to 14 kg) in one meal.

58. Wolves typically hunt within territories.

59. A bat can eat up to 1,200 mosquitoes in an hour.

60. Bats use echolocation to find food in total darkness.

61. Some bats can fly faster than 60 miles (97 km) per hour.

62. The skunk family's scientific name, Mephitidae, means "stink."

63. Mammals often have special markings on their bodies to call attention to the weapons they use in a fight.

64. A skunk's stripes point toward their bottom, where their stinky spray comes from.

65. Stripes on a badger's face call attention to its sharp teeth.

30
FUN FISH FACTS

1. There are more than 1,150 species of fish in the United States.

2. About 800 of these species live in fresh water.

3. The white sturgeon is the largest freshwater fish in North America.

4. White sturgeons can grow between 15–20 feet (4.5–6 m) long.

5. The second-largest fish in North America is the alligator gar.

6. An alligator gar can be up to 8 feet (2.4 m) long and weigh up to 300 pounds (136 kg).

7. Alligator gars have been around since prehistoric times.

8. An alligator gar has special gills that let them process oxygen in water that many fish cannot live in.

9. Lake sturgeon once grew to more than 250 pounds (113 kg) in the Great Lakes.

10. A species of fish with the Latin name *Heterandria formosa* is the smallest fish in the United States.

11. *H. formosa* is just over 1 inch (2.5 cm) long.

12. These little fish live in the southeastern U.S. and are related to guppies.

13. Muskellunge or "muskie" are common in the lakes and rivers of the northern U.S.

14. Muskies can grow up to 7 feet (1.8 m) long and weigh almost 70 pounds (32 kg).

15. Muskies are top predators and feed on fish, frogs, snakes, ducklings, crayfish, and small mammals.

16. Scientists can figure out how old a fish is by counting growth rings on its scales or inner ear bones.

17. Atlantic salmon once swam from Long Island Sound up into New England, but today this fish in mostly found in Maine.

18. Atlantic salmon spend the first few years of their lives in rivers, then swim out to sea where there is more food for them to eat.

19. Salmon return to the same river where they were born to lay their eggs.

20. A female salmon lays between 2,500 and 7,000 eggs.

21. One type of Atlantic salmon, called the landlocked Atlantic salmon, lives in lakes and never migrates to the sea.

22. Landlocked Atlantic salmon are smaller than other salmon. They measure between 12 and 20 inches (30–51 cm) long.

23. Five species of Pacific salmon live off the U.S. and Canada: chinook or king, coho, pink, sockeye, and chum salmon.

24. Alaska's salmon fisheries are responsible for 90 percent of the salmon caught in North America.

25. Salmon have been an important part of Native American culture in the Pacific Northwest for centuries.

Top 5 Most Popular Freshwater Fish for Anglers

1. Largemouth and smallmouth bass
2. Crappie
3. Bluegill
4. Walleye
5. Trout

40 SCALY REPTILE AND AMPHIBIAN FACTS

1. The Greek word "amphibios" means having two lives.

2. Amphibians got this name because they have a larval stage and an adult stage that are often quite different from one another.

3. The word "reptile" comes from a Latin word meaning "crawl."

4. There are about 311 species of reptiles in the United States.

5. There are about 295 species of amphibians in the U.S.

6. Snakes are the most common reptile species, with 142 in the U.S.

7. Lizards come in second with 111 species.

8. There are 56 species of turtles.

9. Salamanders are the most common amphibians, with 191 species.

10. Frogs and toads add up to 104 different species.

11. Together, reptiles and amphibians are known as "herpetofauna."

12. The southwestern part of the U.S. is home to a large number of different reptiles and amphibians.

13. About 100 reptiles and 20 amphibian species live in the Sonoran Desert.

14. The Chihuahuan Desert is home to more than 170 different reptile and amphibian species.

15. Most reptiles and amphibians lay eggs.

16. Amphibians and reptiles are cold-blooded, or unable to regulate their body temperature.

17. To get warm, reptiles and amphibians bask in the sun, and they move underground or into the shade to get cool.

18. Being cold-blooded allows reptiles and amphibians to use less energy than warm-blooded animals.

19. Amphibians are an important part of a habitat's food web because they consume insects, worms, and other invertebrates, while also serving as food for many reptiles, fish, birds, and mammals.

20. An amphibian's skin is very thin, which makes them susceptible to toxins in the environment.

21. The presence of amphibians is a sign of a healthy habitat.

22. There are about 21 species of venomous snakes in the U.S.

23. The cottonmouth snake got its name because the inside of its mouth is white and looks like cotton.

24. Copperheads are the most likely to bite of all venomous snakes because they tend to strike instead of moving away when startled.

25. Scarlet kingsnakes have similar color bands as the venomous coral snake, but kingsnakes are not venomous.

26. Alligators are the largest reptiles in the U.S. They can grow up to 12 feet (3.6 m) long and weigh up to 1,000 pounds (450 kg).

27. The largest amphibian in the U.S. is the hellbender, an aquatic salamander that lives in the south.

28. Hellbenders can reach 29 inches (74 cm) in length.

29. Bullfrogs are the largest members of the frog family in the U.S.

30. Some salamanders do not have lungs and breathe through their skin instead.

Top 10* Venomous Snakes in the U.S.

*In no particular order

1. Cottonmouth
2. Timber rattlesnake
3. Black diamond rattlesnake
4. Tiger rattlesnake
5. Copperhead
6. Eastern coral snake
7. Western diamondback rattlesnake
8. Eastern diamondback rattlesnake
9. Prairie rattlesnake
10. Mojave rattlesnake

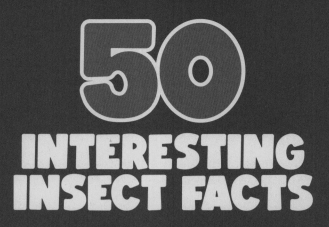

50 INTERESTING INSECT FACTS

1. The number of described insect species in the U.S. is about 91,000.

2. Scientists think there could be another 73,000 undescribed species.

3. Scientists estimate there are about 10 quintillion individual insects alive in the U.S. at any given time.

4. The giant water bug is the largest insect in the U.S. It can measure up to 4 inches (10 cm) long.

5. Another big insect is the giant salmonfly. It measures just over 3 inches (8 cm) long.

6. Despite their name, tarantula hawks are actually wasps. They measure about 2 inches (5 cm) long.

7. The tiny fairy wasp is believed to be the smallest insect in the U.S. at less than 0.04 inch (1 mm) long.

8. Many insects are dangerous to humans because they spread disease or damage crops.

9. Many insects are helpful to humans because they eat other insects that harm crops or spread disease.

10. Insects such as bees and butterflies pollinate plants.

11. Honeybees are the only insects that work to create a food eaten by humans.

12. A single honeybee colony can produce 220 pounds (100 kg) of honey a year.

13. Honeybees communicate through movement.

14. A bee's wings can beat 190 times a second.

15. Houseflies can find sugar with their feet.

16. Butterflies taste with their feet.

17. Houseflies have compound eyes that allow them to see in many directions at once.

18. Many insects have extra eyes, called ocelli, in the middle of their face.

19. As it takes in blood, a tick can grow from the size of a grain of rice to the size of a marble.

20. Beetles make up about one quarter of all known species of animals and plants.

21. Bugs and insects are not the same thing.

22. A bug is an insect, but not all insects are bugs.

23. True bugs have a mouth shaped like a straw or needle that allows them to suck juices, mostly from plants.

24. Bugs also have three life stages, while insects have four.

25. Cicadas spend almost all of their lives underground.

26. Cicadas emerge from underground in cycles after a number of years.

27. Billions of cicadas emerge at one time.

28. They only live above ground long enough to mate and lay eggs— about six weeks.

29. Male cicadas attract females by making a humming sound.

30. Cicadas make this sound by moving their organs.

31. A single ladybug can eat more than 5,000 insects in its lifetime.

32. Fireflies, or lightning bugs, are only found east of the Mississippi River.

33. Water striders use surface tension to walk on water.

34. A termite queen can lay up to 40,000 eggs in one day.

35. A cockroach can live up to three weeks without its head.

36. Mosquitoes flap their wings about 500 times a second. That's what makes the whining noise you often hear when a mosquito is close by.

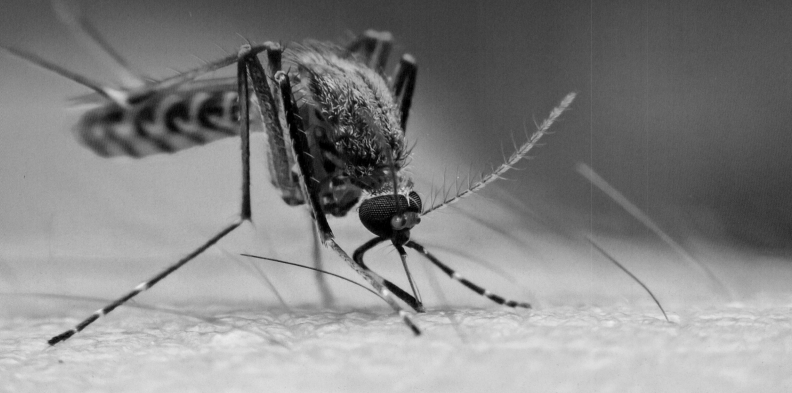

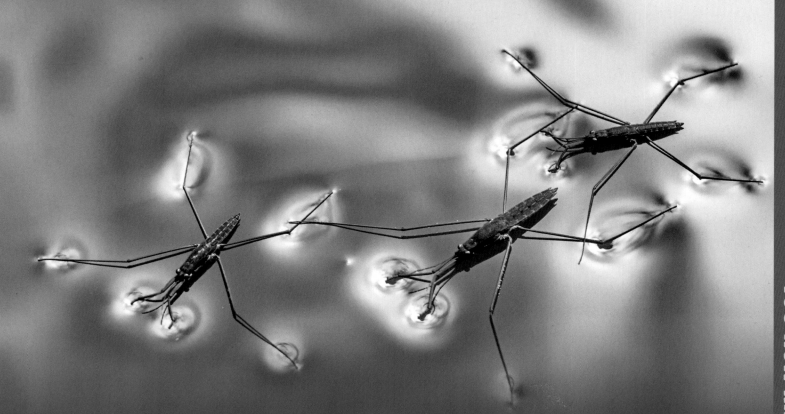

Helpful vs. Harmful Top 10

#	Helpful Insects	Harmful Insects
1.	Praying Mantis	Mosquito
2.	Honeybee	Africanized bee
3.	Ladybug	Yellow Jacket
4	Butterfly	Wasp
5.	Lacewing	Deer Tick
6.	Dragonfly	Fire Ant
7.	Earthworm	Horsefly
8.	Bumblebee	Kissing bug
9.	Ground beetle	Aphid
10.	Hoverfly	Centipede

By the Numbers:
The Four Orders of Insects

1. Coleoptera (Beetles): 23,700 species

2. Diptera (Flies): 19,600 species

3. Hymenoptera (Ants, Bees, Wasps): 17,500 species

4. Lepidoptera (Butterflies and Moths): 11,500 species

40 POPULAR PLANT FACTS

1. The U.S. has more than 18,700 species of plants.

2. There are about 16,500 species of flowering plants, or angiosperms.

3. There are 122 species of conifers.

4. There are 658 species of ferns.

5. Mosses and liverworts make up about 1,460 species.

6. Conifers are part of a group called gymnosperms.

7. Conifers reproduce without fruit or flowers.

8. Instead, conifers produce cones. Male cones produce pollen, while female cones grow seeds.

9. Pines are the largest group of conifers, numbering about 250 species.

10. Spruces, firs, junipers, larches, and ginkgoes are also conifers.

Top 10 Most Popular Flowers in the U.S.

1. Rose
2. Gladiolus
3. Hydrangea
4. Geranium
5. Tulip
6. Pansy
7. Gerbera Daisy
8. Daffodil
9. Dahlia
10. Carnation

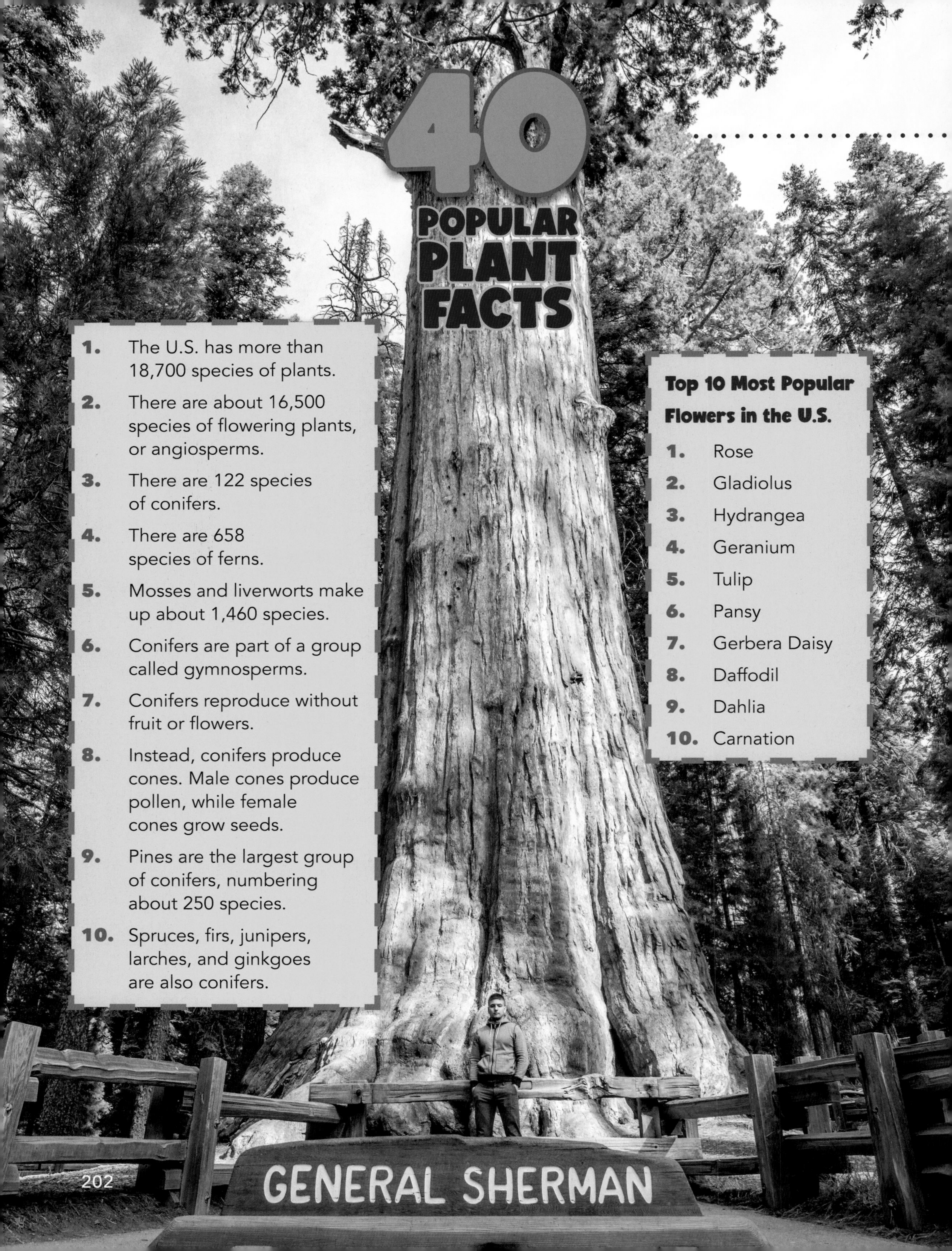

GENERAL SHERMAN

11. General Sherman is the largest tree in the world. It lives in a National Park in California.

12. General Sherman is 275 feet (83 m) tall, and over 36 feet (11 m) in diameter at the base.

13. The tallest tree in the world is Hyperion, a coast redwood in California. It measures about 380 feet (116 m) tall.

14. Hyperion's exact location is a secret from most people.

15. A bristlecone pine in California is the oldest-known tree on Earth. It is estimated to be over 5,000 years old.

16. Bamboo is the fastest-growing woody plant. It can grow up to 35 inches (89 cm) a day.

17. Poinsettias were brought to the U.S. from Mexico in 1825.

18. A sunflower looks like one large flower, but each head is composed of hundreds of tiny flowers called florets.

19. Each floret ripens and becomes a seed.

20. Other plants in the sunflower family include daisies, goldenrod, asters, and bachelor's buttons.

21. Apples, apricots, peaches, pears, quinces, and strawberries are all members of the rose family.

22. Strawberries are sometimes said to be the only fruit that bear seeds on the outside, but those "seeds" are actually tiny little individual fruits called achenes.

23. The average strawberry has 200 "seeds" on the outside.

24. Some plants, like the Venus Fly Trap, catch insects because they cannot get the nutrients they need from the soil where they grow.

25. The International Rose Test Garden in Portland, Oregon, is the oldest official, continuously operated public rose test garden in the United States.

26. The Rose Test Garden includes more than 10,000 roses.

27. The Rose Test Garden began in 1918 as a safe haven for hybrid roses grown in Europe during World War I.

28. The U.S. has many invasive plants. Invasive plants are those that threaten native plants.

29. The most common invasive plants are purple loosestrife, Japanese honeysuckle, Norway maples, and English ivy.

30. Kudzu is an invasive plant found in the South that can grow up to 1 foot (0.3 m) per day.

Business and Science

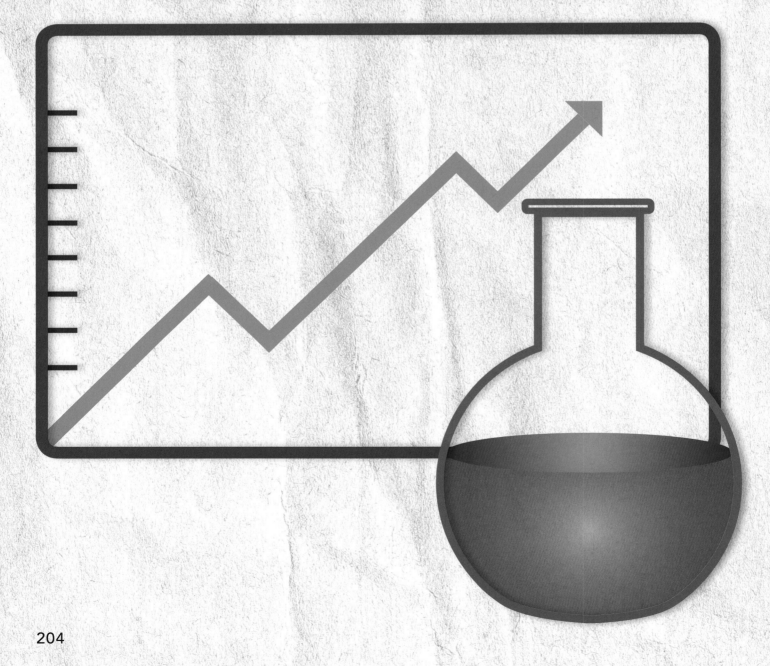

30 AMAZING FACTS ABOUT BLACK BUSINESS LEADERS

1. Madam C.J. Walker (born Sarah Breedlove) was the first American woman to become a millionaire in her own right.

2. In 1905, Walker developed a line of hair products specifically made for Black woman.

3. Walker opened her own factory in 1908.

4. Walker's beauticians became known as "Walker Agents" and traveled throughout Black communities to promote the company's products.

5. Oprah Winfrey started as a TV news anchor and went on to found Harpo, Inc., a multimedia company that has a magazine and a television network.

6. Winfrey was once fired from a job and called "unfit for television news."

7. Winfrey's net worth is over $2 billion, making her the richest Black American.

8. Daymond John had to close and restart his fashion business, Fubu, three times before it became successful.

9. Robert and Sheila Johnson founded Black Entertainment Television (BET) in the late 1970s. In 2001, he became the first Black American billionaire when he sold BET.

10. Johnson is principal owner of the NBA's Charlotte Bobcats, making him the first Black owner of a major pro sports team.

11. When Janice Bryant Howroyd founded the employment agency ActOne Group, she only had a telephone. By 2016, ActOne earned more than $1 billion in annual revenue.

12. Sean Combs (also known as a rapper with the stage names Puff Daddy, P. Diddy, Puffy, or Diddy) is an entrepreneur who owns a record label, a clothing line, a cable music network, and several restaurants.

13. By 2017, Combs was named the richest man in hip-hop, with a net worth of more than $820 million.

14. Rapper Jay-Z was described as the first hip-hop billionaire in 2019, with companies including Roc-A-Fella Records, Roc Nation, apparel line Rocawear, restaurant and beverage businesses, and Tidal, a music streaming service.

15. Jay-Z once rapped the lyric, "I'm not a businessman / I'm a business, man."

16. Jay-Z is married to singer and actress Beyoncé Knowles, who also runs several companies.

17. George Foreman was made famous as a boxer, but his business really took off when he pioneered the George Foreman Grill.

18. Foreman said he got the idea for his grill in a vision after being knocked out by boxer Muhammad Ali.

19. One of the richest Black men in the U.S. throughout the 1960s, Arthur Gaston established the Citizens Savings and Loan Association, the A.G. Gaston Construction Co., and CF Bancshares, a financial institution.

20. Gaston was also a leading employer of African Americans in Alabama.

21. Annie Malone became a millionaire in the early 1900s by developing and marketing hair products for Black women.

22. Malone and her employees sold her products door to door.

23. Malone's Poro Company created 75,000 jobs for women around the world.

24. Malone also founded Poro College, a cosmetology school, in 1917.

25. Former enslaved woman Clara Brown moved to Colorado during the 1850s Gold Rush. She started a successful laundry business and used that money to invest in real estate.

26. Brown eventually gave away a lot of her money. She also encouraged former enslaved men and women to move to Colorado.

27. Maggie Lena Walker was the first Black woman in the United States to charter a bank. She established St. Luke Penny Savings Bank in 1903 and also served as the bank's first president.

28. John Johnson used a $500 loan to start Johnson Publishing Co., which published *Ebony* and *Jet*, leading magazines for African Americans.

29. Reginald Lewis was considered the richest Black businessman throughout the 1980s. He founded the venture capital firm TLC Group LP in 1983.

30. Rosalind Brewer became the CEO of Walgreens Boots Alliance in 2021. She was ranked on *Fortune* magazine's list of the most powerful women in the world in 2020.

60

FACTS ABOUT LIFE-CHANGING INVENTIONS AND INVENTORS

10 TOP AMERICAN INVENTORS

1. **Benjamin Franklin**—Inventions include bifocal eyeglasses, the lightning rod, the odometer, and the Franklin stove.

2. **Thomas Edison**—Harnessed electricity to invent the incandescent light bulb, the phonograph, the movie camera, and the alkaline storage battery.

3. **George Eastman**—Brought photography to the general public through his invention of the Kodak camera.

4. **Nikola Tesla**—An electrical and mechanical genius who discovered alternating electrical current and new ways to generate electric power.

5. **George Washington Carver**—Carver's work with peanuts created 300 different products, including foods, dyes, inks, and more.

6. **John Deere**—Invented the first riding plow, allowing farmers to grow more crops more easily.

7. **Samuel Morse**—Invented the telegraph and Morse code, speeding up the ways people could communicate over long distances.

8. **Charles Goodyear**—Developed vulcanization, a process to treat rubber so it could be used to make tires.

9. **Henry Ford**—Invented the assembly line process that made building cars faster and cheaper.

10. **Steve Jobs**—Founded Apple and developed groundbreaking computers, phones, and streaming services.

20 THINGS YOU DIDN'T KNOW WERE INVENTED BY AMERICAN WOMEN

1. Circular saw (Tabitha Babbitt)
2. Wifi and GPS technology (Hedy Lamarr)
3. COBOL computer language (Grace Murray Hopper)
4. Kevlar "bulletproof" fiber (Stephanie Kwolek)
5. Paper bag machine (Margaret Knight)
6. Windshield wipers (Mary Anderson)
7. Disposable diaper (Marion O'Brien Donovan)
8. Life raft (Maria Beasley)
9. Electric refrigerator (Florence Parpart)
10. Street sweeper (Florence Parpart)
11. Dishwasher (Josephine Cochran)
12. Liquid paper (Bette Nesmith Graham)
13. Fire escape (Anna Connelly)
14. Car heater (Margaret A. Wilcox)
15. Medical syringe (Letitia Geer)
16. Micro-electrode (Ida Hyde)
17. Hydyne rocket fuel (Mary Sherman Morgan)
18. Home security system (Marie van Brittan Brown)
19. Word processor (Evelyn Berezin)
20. Caller ID (Shirley Ann Jackson)

3😀 INFLUENTIAL
AMERICAN INVENTIONS

1. Modern suspension bridge
2. Machine gun
3. Skyscraper
4. Airplane
5. Electric traffic light
6. Cotton gin
7. Frozen food
8. Nylon
9. Automatic transmission for cars
10. Microwave oven
11. Credit card
12. Integrated circuit
13. Laser
14. Compact disc
15. Sewing machine
16. Fiber-optic cable
17. Personal computer
18. ARPANET (which became the Internet)
19. Email
20. Transistor
21. 3-D printing
22. GPS
23. Motion pictures
24. Liquid fuel rocket
25. American sign language
26. Anesthesia
27. Safety elevator
28. Telephone
29. Air conditioning
30. Cell phone

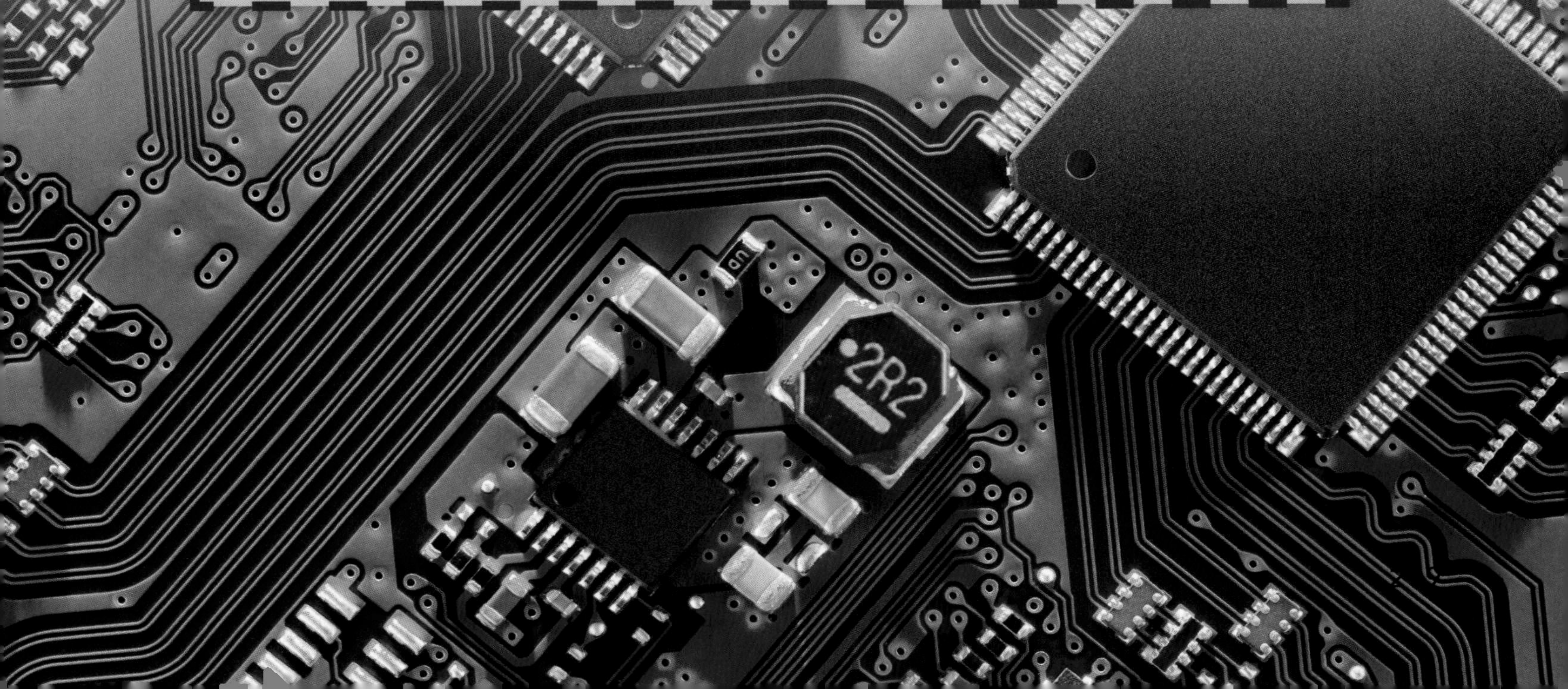

35 AGRICULTURE FACTS

1. There are more than two million farms in the United States.

2. 99 percent of those farms are family owned.

3. The average American farm size is 435 acres (176 hectares).

4. On average, each farm can yield enough food to feed 165 people.

5. About 30 percent of farmers are women.

6. More than 24 million Americans work in agriculture.

7. There are more than 800,000 ranchers and cattle producers in the U.S.

8. Corn is by far the most popular crop, with more than 13,691,561 bushels produced in 2019.

9. Total U.S. corn yield has increased more than 360 percent since 1950.

10. The U.S. is the top corn producer in the world.

11. The U.S. is also the top producer of beef and poultry.

12. About 914 million acres of land in the U.S. are dedicated to farming.

13. One in four people in Nebraska are employed in agriculture.

14. In 2018, $139.6 billion worth of American agricultural products were exported around the world.

15. The United States sells more food and fiber to world markets than it buys from other countries.

16. A quarter of farmers have been in the business for less than 10 years.

17. In 2020, livestock on U.S. farms included 94 million cattle, 79 million hogs and pigs, 9 million dairy cows, and 5 million sheep and lambs.

18. After factoring in costs, farmers only earn about eight cents for every dollar spent.

19. One acre of land can grow a variety of crops, including 50,000 pounds (22,680 kg) of strawberries or 2,784 pounds (1,263 kg) of wheat.

20. In a single day, one dairy cow can produce enough milk to make almost five pounds (2 kg) of butter, almost nine gallons (34 liters) of ice cream, or 10.5 pounds (4.8 kg) of cheese.

21. Agriculture contributes more than $100 billion to the U.S. economy.

22. Extreme weather causes 90 percent of the crop losses in the U.S.

23. Of the more than two million U.S. farms, only about 15,000 are certified as organic.

24. Organic food is only about 3 to 4 percent of total U.S. food sales.

25. About 41 percent of land in the continental U.S. is used to feed farm animals.

Top 5 Crops Produced in the U.S.

1. Corn
2. Soybeans
3. Wheat
4. Sugar beets
5. Sugar cane

Top 5 U.S. Farming States

1. Texas
2. Missouri
3. Iowa
4. Oklahoma
5. California

25 LARGEST COMPANIES IN THE U.S.

1. Walmart
2. Amazon
3. Exxon Mobil
4. Apple
5. CVS Health
6. Berkshire Hathaway
7. United Health Group
8. McKesson
9. AT&T
10. AmerisourceBergen
11. Alphabet
12. Ford Motor
13. Cigna
14. Costco Wholesale
15. Chevron
16. Cardinal Health
17. JP Morgan Chase
18. General Motors
19. Walgreens Boots Alliance
20. Verizon Communications
21. Microsoft
22. Marathon Petroleum
23. Kroger
24. Fannie Mae
25. Bank of America

50 HARD-WORKING FACTS ABOUT JOBS

1. Almost 161 million people are part of the civilian labor force in the U.S.

2. In April 2021, the unemployment rate was 6.2 percent.

3. In 1935, at the height of the Great Depression, the unemployment rate was over 20 percent.

4. In 1945, as World War II was ending, the unemployment rate was under 2 percent.

5. Experts estimate that the food service industry will have the largest gain in jobs between 2018 and 2028.

6. The biggest decline will be in the wired telecommunications industry.

7. On average, men make about $97 more per week than their female coworkers.

8. The gender pay gap is lower among younger workers.

9. On average, physicians, pharmacists, nurse practitioners, and physician's assistants are some of the highest-paying jobs in the United States.

10. About 490,000 Americans work as fast-food cooks.

11. As of 2018, there were about eight million undocumented immigrants working in the United States.

12. Undocumented immigrants make up about 5 percent of the U.S. labor force.

13. Manufacturing has decreased from 32 percent of the nation's jobs in 1953 to about 8 percent in 2019.

14. There were about 350,000 fewer jobs in the U.S. auto industry in 2019 than in 1994.

15. Some of the lowest-paying jobs in the United States include cashier, movie theater worker, farmhand, amusement park worker, and dishwasher.

16. The federal minimum wage was created in 1938.

17. Congress raised the federal minimum wage 22 times between 1938 and 2020.

18. 29 states have a minimum wage higher than the federal minimum wage.

19. About 88 percent of full-time workers in the United States have access to medical insurance through their work.

20. Only 21 percent of part-time workers have access to medical insurance through their work.

21. The workers reporting the fewest on-the-job injuries are librarians, secretaries, and salespeople.

22. As of 2019, 107.8 million people, or 71 percent of the workforce, were employed in private service-providing industries.

23. Service-providing industries include trade, transportation and utilities; education and health services; professional and business services; and leisure and hospitality.

24. About 22.5 million Americans work for local, state, or federal governments.

25. Almost 13 million Americans work in manufacturing.

26. About 16 million Americans are self-employed.

27. Only about a quarter of self-employed people had employees of their own.

28. The wage gap between college-educated workers and those with less education is the widest it has ever been.

29. The median salary for college graduates ages 25 to 37 working full time was about $24,700 more a year than those same young adults holding only a high school diploma.

30. Fewer teens are employed today than in the past.

31. In 2019, almost 20 percent of Americans ages 65 and older, or about 10.5 million people, were employed full- or part-time.

Top 10 Most Dangerous Jobs

1. Logging workers
2. Fishing workers
3. Pilots and flight engineers
4. Roofers
5. Sanitation workers and recycling collectors
6. Truck drivers
7. Agricultural workers
8. Iron and steel workers
9. Construction workers
10. Landscaping workers

32. Older workers represented 6.6 percent of all employed Americans.

33. Health-care industries are the fastest growing in the United States.

34. The ranks of nurse practitioners are expected to grow by more than 52 percent between 2019 and 2029.

35. The number of jobs for home health-care and personal-care aides is expected to grow by almost 34 percent between 2019 and 2029.

36. Workers in Santa Clara, CA, received the highest weekly wages by county in the U.S. in 2019.

37. Their average weekly wage in Santa Clara, CA, was $2,825.

38. Two other California counties—San Mateo and San Francisco—were ranked No. 2 and No. 3.

39. The lowest-paid workers in 2019 were in Cameron County, TX.

40. Cameron County workers earned an average of $701 per week.

50 SUPER SCIENCE DISCOVERIES IN EACH STATE

1. Electric hearing aids were invented in **Alabama** in 1895.

2. Scientists in **Alaska** track global climate patterns to discover information about climate change.

3. Clyde Tombaugh discovered Pluto at an observatory in **Arizona**.

4. The only U.S. diamond mine was developed in **Arkansas**.

5. Edwin Hubble discovered the universe was expanding while working in **California**.

6. Two teenagers discovered the fossils of a rare mastodon in **Colorado**.

7. Physicist Josiah Willard Gibbs was working at Yale University in **Connecticut** when he discovered chemical potential, the energy that fuels chemical reactions.

8. In **Delaware**, the DuPont chemical company developed new polymers, including nylon and Teflon.

9. The cancer drug Taxol was developed in **Florida**.

10. Ether was used to limit pain during surgery for the first time in **Georgia** in 1842.

11. The telescopes at **Hawaii**'s Keck Observatory have made many important discoveries about the universe.

12. Philo T. Farnsworth developed the predecessor to the television in **Idaho**.

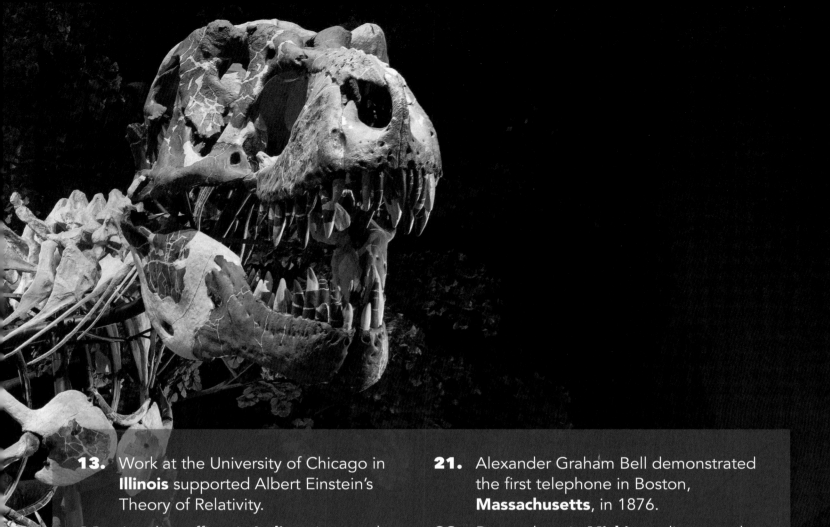

13. Work at the University of Chicago in **Illinois** supported Albert Einstein's Theory of Relativity.

14. A police officer in **Indiana** invented the Breathalyzer, which measures the alcohol level in a person's blood.

15. The discovery of quasicrystals in **Iowa** changed the way scientists look at matter.

16. Helium was discovered in **Kansas** in 1903.

17. A **Kentucky** inventor was the first to develop a wireless telephone in the early 1900s.

18. John Leonard Riddell invented the binocular microscope—a microscope fitted for two eyes—in **Louisiana**.

19. Telstar delivered the first transatlantic television signal from **Maine** to France in 1962.

20. A scientist in **Maryland** discovered telomeres, an important part of chromosomes.

21. Alexander Graham Bell demonstrated the first telephone in Boston, **Massachusetts**, in 1876.

22. Researchers in **Michigan** discovered super massive black holes.

23. Earl Bakken developed the first battery-powered, wearable pacemaker in **Minnesota** in 1968.

24. The first human lung transplant and heart transplant were performed by Dr. James D. Hardy in **Mississippi**.

25. Microchip technology was developed in **Missouri**.

26. The first Tyrannosaurus Rex was discovered in **Montana**.

27. A paleontologist discovered the remains of two prehistoric cats in **Nebraska**.

28. The first working solar cells were developed in **Nevada**.

29. The first mechanical alarm clock was invented in **New Hampshire** in 1787.

HOW RARE WAS T-REX?

THE TYRANT KING!

30. A professor in **New Jersey** changed the way we look at plate tectonics, the theory that the Earth is made of moving plates.

31. The first atomic bomb was detonated in the deserts of **New Mexico** in 1945.

32. The chromosomal theory of inheritance, which links traits to chromosomes, was confirmed at **New York**'s Columbia University.

33. The first airplane flight took place in **North Carolina**.

34. Paleontologists in **North Dakota** discovered a prehistoric creature they nicknamed "the Chicken from Hell" (it was dug up from the Hell Creek geological formation).

35. Synthetic rubber was invented in **Ohio**.

36. A pressurized suit for high-altitude flight was invented in **Oklahoma**.

37. Cave explorers found a new species of spider in **Oregon**.

38. Jonas Salk developed the polio vaccine in **Pennsylvania**.

39. **Rhode Island**'s Brown University developed the Zeroth Law of Thermodynamics, which explains how temperature is defined.

40. The first military submarine, the *Hunley*, was used in a Civil War battle in **South Carolina**.

41. The cyclotron particle accelerator, used to discover everything from new elements to cancer treatments, was invented in **South Dakota**.

42. Scientists at the Oak Ridge National Laboratory in **Tennessee** discovered the element promethium.

43. NASA led the mission to land astronauts on the moon from its space center in **Texas**.

44. The big-nosed dinosaur Nasutoceratops was discovered in **Utah**.

45. **Vermont**'s Wilson "Snowflake" Bentley was the first to take microscopic photos of snowflakes to show their structure.

46. A researcher in **Virginia** discovered that the lymphatic system is connected to the brain.

47. The Heimlich maneuver saved the life of a choking victim for the first time in **Washington** in 1974.

48. The first steamboat traveled down the Potomac River in **West Virginia** in 1787.

49. Important discoveries in stem cell research were made at the University of **Wisconsin**.

50. **Wyoming**'s Cosmo Bluff was the site of many important dinosaur discoveries.

27

45 SPACE PROGRAM FACTS

1. A spacesuit weighs about 280 pounds.

2. It takes 45 minutes to put on a spacesuit.

3. A complete NASA spacesuit costs $12 million.

4. Most of a spacesuit's cost is for the backpack and control module.

5. The first U.S. satellite was Explorer 1. It was launched in 1958.

6. It took 115 minutes for Explorer 1 to orbit the Earth.

7. NASA space shuttles were the world's first reusable spacecraft in 1981.

8. It took almost 528,000 gallons (2 million liters) of fuel to launch the space shuttle into space.

9. Each space shuttle astronaut was allowed 3.8 pounds (1.7 kg) of food per day.

10. All space food is individually packaged and precooked, except for fresh fruit and vegetables.

11. The final space shuttle mission was in 2011.

12. The International Space Station (ISS) launched in 1998. It was a joint venture between the United States and Russia.

13. The ISS cost more than $120 billion to build.

14. The ISS has been continually occupied by astronauts from different countries since 2000.

15. Many astronauts get "space sick." Symptoms include nausea, dizziness, headaches, and vomiting.

16. Many animals have been sent into space including dogs, monkeys, chimpanzees, mice, and frogs.

17. A spacecraft has to travel 15,000 miles (24,140 km) per hour to break free of Earth's gravity.

18. The first American to travel in space was Alan Shepard.

19. On July 20, 1969, Neil Armstrong and Buzz Aldrin became the first people to walk on the moon.

20. Armstrong, Aldrin, and Michael Collins traveled 250,000 miles (402,000) to the moon and back.

21. The footprints on the moon could be there for millions of years because there is no wind to blow them away.

22. Six *Apollo* missions landed on the moon between 1969 and 1972.

23. In spite of all the evidence, some people believe the 1969 moon landing was fake.

24. Astronauts reported the moon smells like wet ashes or gunpowder.

25. Cartoon dog Snoopy was a safety mascot for NASA.

26. *Apollo 10*'s command module was called "Charlie Brown" and the lunar module was called "Snoopy."

27. *Apollo 13* was supposed to land on the moon, but an explosion onboard meant it had to turn back to Earth.

28. *Apollo 16* spacecraft were named after stars. The command module was "Caspar," and the lunar module was "Orion."

29. Among the items taken to the moon on the *Apollo 16* mission were 25 U.S. flags and one state flag for each of the 50 states.

30. In 2012, NASA sent the Curiosity robot rover to Mars.

31. Curiosity weighed about a ton and was the size of a car.

32. Curiosity traveled around the surface of Mars, collected samples, and sent photos back to Earth.

33. Spacecraft travel so fast when they re-enter Earth's atmosphere that the friction creates intense heat.

34. Spacecraft have special tiles to reflect heat so the craft doesn't burn up on re-entry.

35. Sally Ride joined NASA in 1978 and became the first American woman in space in 1983.

36. The first Black woman in space was Dr. Mae Jemison. She served as a science mission specialist in 1992.

37. Eileen M. Collins was the first female commander of the space shuttle. She and her crew launched in July 1999.

38. On October 11, 1984, Katherine Sullivan was the first U.S. woman to walk in space.

39. Ellison Onizuka was the first Asian American in space in 1985.

40. There have been three major disasters in the American space program.

41. In 1967, three astronauts were killed in a launch pad fire onboard the *Apollo 1* space capsule.

42. In 1986, the space shuttle *Challenger* exploded after takeoff. All seven astronauts, including teacher Christa McAuliffe, were killed.

43. Seven astronauts died aboard space shuttle *Columbia* in 2003 when it disintegrated upon re-entering Earth's atmosphere.

44. A pilot applying to be a NASA astronaut must have completed 1,000 hours of flying time in a jet aircraft.

45. There is no set number of people in an astronaut candidate class; NASA selects candidates on an as-needed basis.

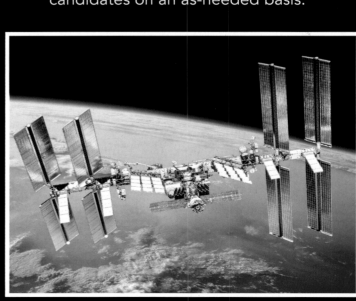

30 TECHNOLOGY TECHNICALITIES

1. ENIAC, the first computer, weighed more than 27 tons.

2. The first computer mouse was invented at Stanford Research Institute in the 1960s.

3. The first computer mouse was made of wood.

4. Its inventor named it "mouse" because the power cord looked like a rodent's tail.

5. The word "typewriter" is the longest word you can type using one row of a standard "QWERTY" keyboard.

6. "Stewardesses" is the longest word you can type with one hand using standard two-hand keyboard position.

7. Apple, Microsoft, Google, and HP all started in someone's garage.

8. The first spam email was sent in 1978.

9. More than 80 percent of daily emails in the U.S. are spam.

10. The worst U.S. security breach happened in 2008 when someone plugged in a USB flash drive they found in a parking lot.

11. The drive connected to the U.S. Central Command, a major military command post, and stole thousands of top-secret files.

12. The U.S. Postal Service uses computers to sort 95 percent of the mail.

13. For eight years, the password for the computer controls of nuclear missiles in the U.S was 00000000.

14. The first 1 GB hard disk drive weighed about 550 pounds (249 kg).

15. That first hard disk drive cost $40,000.

16. Windows operating system was originally called Interface Manager.

17. Microprocessors help computers make calculations extremely quickly.

18. Intel's first microprocessor was created to run a calculator.

19. RAM, or random access memory, stores all the information a computer needs to run.

20. Some computers have fans installed inside to keep them from overheating.

21. People usually blink 20 times a minute, but they only blink seven times a minute when looking at a computer screen.

22. 1980's IBM 5120 was the heaviest desktop computer ever made. It weighed about 105 pounds (48 kg).

23. The IBM 5120 also required a 130-pound (59-kg) external floppy drive.

24. The computer in a basic cell phone is a million times cheaper, a thousand times more powerful, and a hundred thousand times smaller than one computer at MIT in 1965.

25. More than 20,000 websites, mostly in the U.S., are hacked every day.

26. The first-ever hard disk drive was made in 1979, and could hold only 5MB of data.

27. Microsoft included solitaire in its operating systems to teach people how to use a mouse.

28. Asteroids and Lunar Lander were the first computer games made in the U.S. Both came out in 1980.

29. A computer virus is a program that self-replicates, or copies itself, endlessly.

30. The first computer virus was Creeper, created by an engineer named Bob Thomas in 1970.

35
FUN FACTS ABOUT APPS

1. The first mobile apps were games.

2. The first mobile app was a built-in version of the arcade game "Snake," included on the Nokia 6110 cell phone in 1977.

3. The first iPod came with built-in app games Solitaire and Brick.

4. The original App Store launched with just 500 apps.

5. Angry Birds is the most popular app of all time.

6. Angry Birds was released in 2015 and led to commercial tie-ins, movies, and theme-park rides.

7. About 56 percent of mobile phone users play games on their phones.

8. Over time, the most popular apps changed from games to social and lifestyle apps.

9. Mobile apps are used more than websites.

10. The two biggest platforms for mobile apps are iOS and Android.

11. Most apps are developed to work on multiple platforms.

12. The most popular source of revenue for apps is advertising.

13. Mobile apps generated $461.7 billion in the U.S. in 2019.

14. More than five million apps are available to download.

15. Google Play is the most popular app store.

16. In early 2020, Google Play contained 2.9 million apps.

17. Apple's App Store is the second-largest app store with approximately 1.85 million available apps for iOS.

18. Free apps with in-app purchase options are the most popular in Google Play Store.

19. The average U.S. adult spends 4 hours and 39 minutes a day using apps.

20. One of the most popular apps in the U.S., TikTok, had 89 million users in 2020.

Top 15 Most Popular Mobile Apps in the U.S. in 2021

1. YouTube
2. Facebook
3. Gmail
4. Google Search
5. Google Maps
6. Facebook Messenger
7. Amazon Mobile
8. Weather Channel
9. Google Play
10. Instagram
11. Find My
12. Apple News
13. Google Drive
14. Google Photos
15. Spotify

25 CREATIVE MOBILE PHONE FACTS

1. A cell phone is a portable telephone that is able to make and receive phone calls and text messages via a radio frequency.

2. Cell phones got their name from the towers, called "cells," that transmitted the signals.

3. A smartphone also has multi-purpose computing abilities.

4. The average cell phone today has more computing power than the computers used for the *Apollo 11* moon landing.

5. The first cell phone call was made in 1973 by Martin Cooper.

6. Cooper called a colleague at another company to brag about his new invention.

7. Cell phones reached the U.S. market in 1983.

8. Early cell phones cost $4,000.

9. IBM made the first smartphone in 1994.

10. The smartphone's code name while it was in development was Angler.

11. Apple introduced the first iPhone in 2007.

12. The first iPhone cost $499 for 4GB and $599 for 8GB.

13. Android operating systems control almost 85 percent of the market.

14. Apple and Samsung are the two biggest smartphone manufacturers.

15. 31 percent of smartphone users in the U.S. never turn off their phones.

16. 45 percent of Americans aged 10–12 have a smartphone.

17. 97 percent of Americans owned a mobile phone in 2021.

18. 81 percent of Americans owned a smartphone in 2021.

19. Smartphones are factors in 26 percent of car crashes in the U.S. every year.

20. Cell phones can use Bluetooth technology to connect wirelessly to other devices.

21. Bluetooth technology is named after Harald "Bluetooth" Gormsson, King of Denmark and Norway during the 10th century.

22. Bluetooth technology unites devices the same way King Harald united the tribes in Denmark.

23. Nomophobia is the fear of being without a mobile phone.

24. One study estimated people's mobile phones to have 18 times more bacteria than a toilet handle.

25. Americans sent almost three trillion text messages in 2019.

50 TOP GOOGLE SEARCHES IN U.S. IN 2020

Searches
1. Election results
2. Coronavirus
3. Kobe Bryant
4. Coronavirus update
5. Coronavirus symptoms

People
1. Joe Biden
2. Kim Jong Un
3. Kamala Harris
4. Jacob Blake
5. Ryan Newman

News
1. Election results
2. Coronavirus
3. Stimulus checks
4. Unemployment
5. Iran

Games
1. Among Us
2. Fall Guys: Ultimate Knockout
3. Valorant
4. Genshin Impact
5. Ghost of Tsushima

Athletes
1. Ryan Newman
2. Tom Brady
3. Bubba Wallace
4. Mike Tyson
5. Rudy Gobert

Sports Teams
1. Boston Celtics
2. Miami Heat
3. Kansas City Chiefs
4. Los Angeles Clippers
5. Dallas Stars

Movies

1. Parasite
2. 1917
3. Black Panther
4. Harley Quinn: Birds of Prey
5. Little Women

TV Shows

1. Tiger King
2. Cobra Kai
3. Ozark
4. The Umbrella Academy
5. The Queen's Gambit

Musicians/Bands

1. Shakira
2. August Alsina
3. Adele
4. Doja Cat
5. Grimes

Recipes

1. Sourdough bread
2. Whipped coffee
3. Disney churro
4. Dole Whip
5. Doubletree cookie

25 RICHEST PEOPLE IN THE U.S.

1. Jeff Bezos (Amazon)
2. Elon Musk (SpaceX, Tesla)
3. Bill Gates (Microsoft)
4. Mark Zuckerberg (Facebook)
5. Warren Buffett (Berkshire Hathaway)
6. Larry Ellison (software)
7. Larry Page (Google)
8. Sergei Brin (Google)
9. Steve Ballmer (Microsoft)
10. Alice Walton (Walmart)
11. Mackenzie Scott (Amazon)
12. Jim Walton (Walmart)
13. Rob Walton (Walmart)
14. Michael Bloomberg (Bloomberg LP)
15. Daniel Gilbert (Quicken)
16. Phil Knight (Nike)
17. Charles Koch (Koch Industries)
18. Julia Koch (Koch Industries)
19. Michael Dell (Dell Computers)
20. Miriam Adelson (casinos)
21. Len Blavatnik (oil, music)
22. Jacqueline Mars (candy, pet food)
23. John Mars (candy, pet food)
24. Leonard Lauder (cosmetics)
25. Thomas Peterffy (finance)

228

Places

50 TOP AMERICAN CITY FACTS

Top 25 Most Populous U.S. Cities

Rank	City	Population (2019)
1.	New York, NY	8,336,817
2.	Los Angeles, CA	3,979,576
3.	Chicago, IL	2,693,976
4.	Houston, TX	2,320,268
5.	Phoenix, AZ	1,680,992
6.	Philadelphia, PA	1,584,064
7.	San Antonio, TX	1,547,253
8.	San Diego, CA	1,423,851
9.	Dallas, TX	1,343,573
10.	San Jose, CA	1,021,795
11.	Austin, TX	978,908
12.	Jacksonville, FL	911,507
13.	Fort Worth, TX	909,585
14.	Columbus, OH	898,553
15.	Charlotte, NC	885,708
16.	San Francisco, CA	881,549
17.	Indianapolis, IN	876,384
18.	Seattle, WA	753,675
19.	Denver, CO	727,211
20.	Washington, DC	705,749
21.	Boston, MA	692,600
22.	El Paso, TX	681,728
23.	Nashville-Davidson, TN	670,820
24.	Detroit, MI	670,031
25.	Oklahoma City, OK	655,057

1. Part of Seattle sits on top of the remains of the original city from the 1800s.

2. Today, tourists in Seattle can follow a guide through three blocks of the underground city, including an old saloon, stores, and a hotel.

3. Some people in San Francisco travel to work on the city's historic cable cars, but the majority of riders are tourists.

4. Detroit sits on top of a salt mine that has provided road salt to other cities in the U.S. since 1910.

5. A big reason why Los Angeles is so big and spread-out is that the city controlled the entire area's water supply.

6. The city of Lexington, Kentucky, accepts canned food as payment for parking fines.

7. Boston has hidden poems on some sidewalks that are only visible when wet.

8. Miami is the only major American city that was officially founded by a woman.

9. Portland, Oregon, was named by a coin flip by the two founders who each wanted to name it after their hometown. Had the coin landed the other way, the city would have been named Boston, Oregon.

10. Pittsburgh has more bridges—446—than any other city in the world.

11. Nashville has a scale version of Greece's Parthenon.

12. As of 2019, there were 19,502 incorporated cities, towns, and villages in the United States.

13. Only 10 U.S. cities have populations above 1 million.

14. About 40% of the U.S. population lives in cities with 50,000 or more residents.

15. Thirty-four states have towns named Springfield.

16. Other popular city names are Midway, Fairview, and Riverside.

17. Although the Statue of Liberty is associated with New York City, it is officially located in Jersey City, NJ.

18. 182 places in the U.S. have "Christmas" in their name.

19. The 1893 World's Fair in Chicago featured almost 100,000 electric lights, allowing people there to imagine what all cities would look like in the future.

20. The Chicago World's Fair also introduced the Ferris wheel. It was meant to top the Eiffel Tower, built at the World's Fair in Paris, France, just a few years earlier.

21. A law passed in 1910 makes it impossible to build skyscrapers in Washington, D.C.

22. San Francisco has the oldest of many neighborhoods nicknamed Chinatown in the U.S.

23. Among the 20 cities or towns with the fastest growing populations between 2010 and 2019, 11 were in the South, 8 were in the West, and one was in the Midwest.

24. The five fastest-growing cities between 2010 and 2019 were Irvine, CA; Henderson, NV; Austin, TX; Seattle, WA; and Fort Worth, TX.

25. New York City is the most expensive U.S. city to live in.

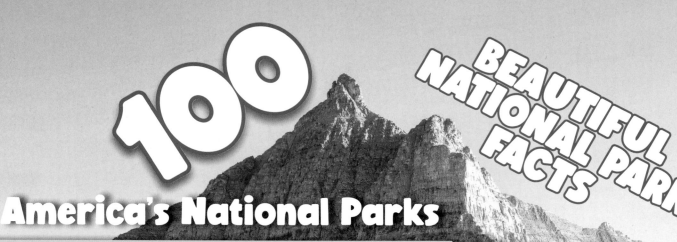

100

America's National Parks

	National Park	Location
1.	Acadia	Maine
2.	American Samoa	American Samoa
3.	Arches	Utah
4.	Badlands	South Dakota
5.	Big Bend	Texas
6.	Biscayne	Florida
7.	Black Canyon of the Gunnison	Colorado
8.	Bryce Canyons	Utah
9.	Canyonlands	Utah
10.	Capitol Reef	Utah
11.	Carlsbad Caverns	New Mexico
12.	Channel Islands	California
13.	Congaree	South Carolina
14.	Crater Lake	Oregon
15.	Cuyahoga Valley	Ohio
16.	Death Valley	California
17.	Denali	Alaska
18.	Dry Tortugas	Florida
19.	Everglades	Florida
20.	Gates of the Arctic	Alaska
21.	Gateway Arch	Missouri
22.	Glacier	Montana
23.	Glacier Bay	Alaska
24.	Grand Canyon	Arizona
25.	Grand Teton	Wyoming
26.	Great Basin	Nevada
27.	Great Sand Dunes	Colorado

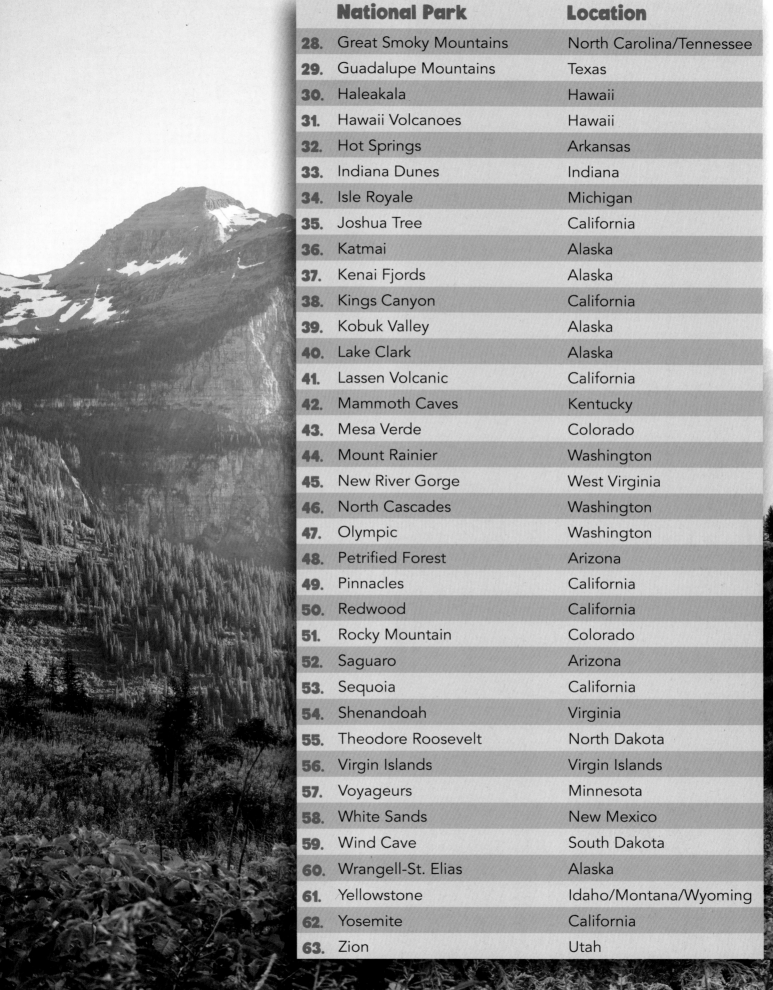

National Park	Location
28. Great Smoky Mountains	North Carolina/Tennessee
29. Guadalupe Mountains	Texas
30. Haleakala	Hawaii
31. Hawaii Volcanoes	Hawaii
32. Hot Springs	Arkansas
33. Indiana Dunes	Indiana
34. Isle Royale	Michigan
35. Joshua Tree	California
36. Katmai	Alaska
37. Kenai Fjords	Alaska
38. Kings Canyon	California
39. Kobuk Valley	Alaska
40. Lake Clark	Alaska
41. Lassen Volcanic	California
42. Mammoth Caves	Kentucky
43. Mesa Verde	Colorado
44. Mount Rainier	Washington
45. New River Gorge	West Virginia
46. North Cascades	Washington
47. Olympic	Washington
48. Petrified Forest	Arizona
49. Pinnacles	California
50. Redwood	California
51. Rocky Mountain	Colorado
52. Saguaro	Arizona
53. Sequoia	California
54. Shenandoah	Virginia
55. Theodore Roosevelt	North Dakota
56. Virgin Islands	Virgin Islands
57. Voyageurs	Minnesota
58. White Sands	New Mexico
59. Wind Cave	South Dakota
60. Wrangell-St. Elias	Alaska
61. Yellowstone	Idaho/Montana/Wyoming
62. Yosemite	California
63. Zion	Utah

1. The National Park Service was created in 1916 by President Woodrow Wilson.

2. Yellowstone National Park is the oldest U.S. national park. It was founded in 1872.

3. Wrangell-St. Elias National Park in Alaska is the largest national park, covering 13,005 square miles (33,683 sq km).

4. Death Valley National Park in California is the largest national park in the lower 48 states at 5,325 sq miles (13,793 sq km).

5. Gateway Arch National Park in Missouri is the smallest at just 193 acres (78 hectares).

6. Great Smoky Mountains National Park is the most visited national park, welcoming more than 12 million guests per year.

7. Grand Canyon National Park is number two, with around 6 million visits per year.

8. The tallest point in a national park is Denali in Alaska, 20,310 feet (6,190 m) above sea level.

9. Grand Teton National Park and Yellowstone National Park are just 10 miles (16 km) away from each other.

10. California has the most national parks, with nine. Alaska has eight national parks.

11. Arches National Park has the largest concentration of naturally formed stone arches in the world.

12. Everglades National Park protects more than 25 percent of Florida's subtropical wetlands.

13. Kobuk Valley and Gates of the Arctic are the only parks north of the Arctic Circle.

14. Gates of the Arctic is the least-visited park, with just 10,518 visitors in 2019.

15. Trail Ridge Road in Rocky Mountain National Park is the highest continuously paved road in the U.S.

16. Abraham Lincoln and Teddy Roosevelt have the most National Parks Service-controlled sites named for them.

17. Both Lincoln and Teddy Roosevelt have four different sites in the National Parks Service.

18. National parks are home to more than 400 endangered or threatened animal and plant species.

19. Hawaii's Haleakala National Park, on the island of Maui, is home to more endangered species than any other park.

20. South Dakota's Wind Cave was the first cave to be named a national park.

21. Delaware is the only state that does not have a national park nor a national monument.

22. Dry Tortugas National Park, off the coast of Florida, can only be reached by boat or plane.

23. National parks contain more than 75,000 archeological sites, and nearly 27,000 historic and prehistoric structures.

24. About 20,000 people work for the National Park Service.

25. The NPS also relies on more than 246,000 volunteers.

26. Glacier National Park in Montana contains 25 active glaciers and more than 700 lakes.

27. Glacier National Park borders Waterton Lakes National Park in Canada.

28. The National Park system has been called "America's best idea."

29. Biscayne National Park in Florida is 95 percent underwater.

30. Biscayne is known for its coral reefs and also contains hundreds of shipwrecks.

31. Mesa Verde National Park includes the more than 4,000 sites of the Ancestral Puebloan people.

32. One of those sites is the 150-room Cliff Palace, where about 100 people probably once lived.

33. Acadia National Park in Maine is the oldest park east of the Mississippi River.

34. Yellowstone National Park is home to more than 500 active geysers.

35. Yellowstone contains more than half the geysers in the world.

36. Badlands National Park in South Dakota is known for having lots of early mammal fossils.

37. The National Park of American Samoa is the only U.S. national park south of the Equator.

50 MAGNIFICENT MUSEUM FACTS

1. There are more than 35,000 museums in the United States.

2. That's more than all the McDonald's and Starbucks restaurants combined.

3. More than 726,000 Americans work in museums.

4. Museum volunteers contribute a million hours of service a week.

5. Museums aren't just physical places. They receive millions of online visits every year.

6. About 55 million visitors from school groups go to museums every year.

7. About 26 percent of American museums are located outside of major cities.

8. California has almost 3,000 museums, the most of any state.

9. New York State has the second-most museums, with about 2,500.

10. Texas is third, with about 2,000 museums.

11. There are about 300 museums in Los Angeles.

12. New York has about 140 museums.

13. San Francisco has about 132 museums.

14. Historical museums and sites make up 48 percent of American museums.

15. To encourage crowds to keep moving through his museum in the 19th century, showman P.T. Barnum put up signs saying, "This Way to the Egress."

16. Not knowing that "Egress" was another word for "Exit," some people followed the signs and ended up outside of Barnum's museum before they meant to leave.

17. The largest art heist in history occurred at the Isabella Stewart Gardner Museum in Boston in 1990. Thirteen paintings worth $500 million were stolen.

18. All of the empty frames that used to feature the stolen paintings are still hanging at the Gardner Museum.

19. You can see old presidential limousines at the Henry Ford Museum in Dearborn, Michigan.

20. The Smithsonian Institution has about 154 million objects in its collections and is still growing.

21. The Smithsonian Institution was founded with money from James Smithson, a British scientist.

22. Smithson had never been to America, and historians still aren't sure why he left all his money to start the museum when he died in 1829.

23. The Smithsonian's National Museum of African American History and Culture first opened in 2016.

24. The American Museum of Natural History in New York City is the largest natural history museum in the world.

25. There are more than 33 million objects in the American Museum of Natural History's collection.

26. A 94-foot-long (29-m) replica of a blue whale hangs in the American Museum of Natural History.

27. It takes three days to clean that whale. Workers use long-handled brushes and vacuum cleaners.

28. The American Museum of Natural History has one of the greatest collections of dinosaur fossils in the world.

29. It also has one of the largest collections of mammal and bird specimens.

30. The American Museum of Natural History had to build special columns under the building to support the 34-ton Cape York meteorite, the largest meteorite on display at any museum in the world.

31. The National WWII Museum in New Orleans has more than 100,000 items donated by WWII veterans.

32. Washington, D.C.'s International Spy Museum features the world's largest collection of espionage artifacts.

33. The Mütter Museum in Philadelphia houses many unusual medical artifacts, including slides of Einstein's brain.

34. Offbeat U.S. museums include the Museum of Questionable Medical Devices (Minneapolis, MN), the International Cryptozoology Museum (Portland, ME), and the Toilet Seat Art Museum (San Antonio, TX).

35. Baltimore's Visionary Art Museum only includes work created by self-taught artists.

36. There are many U.S. museums that focus on food.

37. Potatoes, pizza, Spam, mustard, and Jell-O all have museums devoted to them.

38. Each department of New York City's Metropolitan Museum of Art has its own library.

39. The Los Angeles County Museum of Art (LACMA) has one of the largest collections of Latin American art outside Latin America.

40. LACMA also has many exhibits on the movie and television industries.

Top 10 Most-Visited Museums in the U.S.

1. Metropolitan Museum of Art, New York City

2. American Museum of Natural History, New York City

3. National Museum of Natural History, Washington, D.C.

4. National Gallery of Art, Washington, D.C.

5. National Air and Space Museum, Washington, D.C.

6. National Museum of American History, Washington, D.C.

7. California Science Center, Los Angeles

8. National Museum of African American History and Culture, Washington, D.C.

9. Smithsonian American Art Museum, Washington, D.C.

10. Museum of Modern Art, New York City

40 SCREAMING FACTS ABOUT AMUSEMENT PARKS

1. The first roller coaster in the United States opened at New York's Coney Island in 1884.

2. The roller coaster was called the "switchback railway." It traveled about 6 miles (9.6 km) an hour and cost a nickel to ride.

3. Roller coaster loops are not usually circles. They are ovals.

4. In 1884, Phillip Hinkle invented the chain that pulls roller-coaster cars up that big first hill.

5. Before Hinkle's invention, people had to climb stairs to board the roller coaster at the top of the hill.

6. The first hill on a roller coaster is the steepest because that's where all the energy is stored up to power the coaster on the rest of the ride.

7. Ron Toomer, who pioneered steel roller coasters and suspended tracks, gets such bad motion sickness that he is unable to ride his own creations.

8. Kingda Ka, a coaster in New Jersey, is the world's tallest at 456 feet (139 m).

9. Kingda Ka also has the largest drop at 418 feet (127 m).

10. The world's oldest still-operating roller coaster is Leap-the-Dips in Pennsylvania. It opened in 1902.

11. An engineer named George Washington Ferris invented the Ferris wheel.

12. The first patent for bumper cars was filed in 1920.

13. The original bumper cars were quite dangerous and sometimes fell apart during the ride.

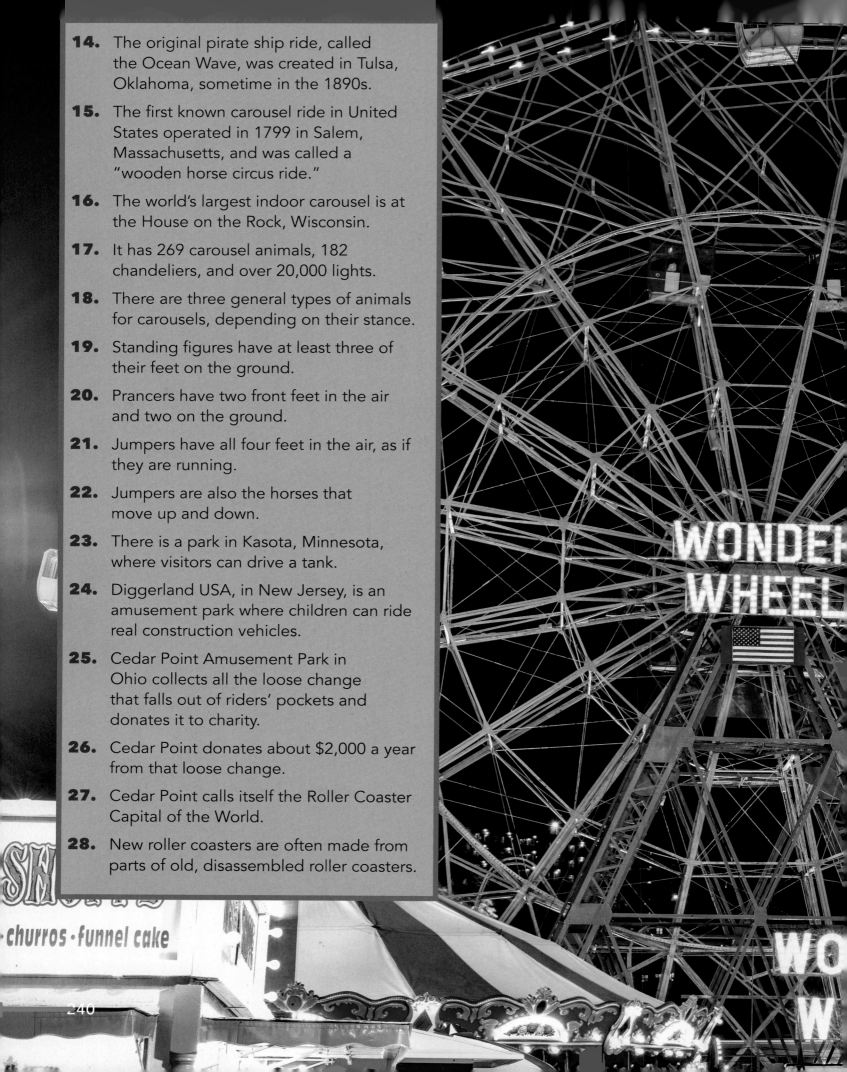

14. The original pirate ship ride, called the Ocean Wave, was created in Tulsa, Oklahoma, sometime in the 1890s.

15. The first known carousel ride in United States operated in 1799 in Salem, Massachusetts, and was called a "wooden horse circus ride."

16. The world's largest indoor carousel is at the House on the Rock, Wisconsin.

17. It has 269 carousel animals, 182 chandeliers, and over 20,000 lights.

18. There are three general types of animals for carousels, depending on their stance.

19. Standing figures have at least three of their feet on the ground.

20. Prancers have two front feet in the air and two on the ground.

21. Jumpers have all four feet in the air, as if they are running.

22. Jumpers are also the horses that move up and down.

23. There is a park in Kasota, Minnesota, where visitors can drive a tank.

24. Diggerland USA, in New Jersey, is an amusement park where children can ride real construction vehicles.

25. Cedar Point Amusement Park in Ohio collects all the loose change that falls out of riders' pockets and donates it to charity.

26. Cedar Point donates about $2,000 a year from that loose change.

27. Cedar Point calls itself the Roller Coaster Capital of the World.

28. New roller coasters are often made from parts of old, disassembled roller coasters.

churros · funnel cake

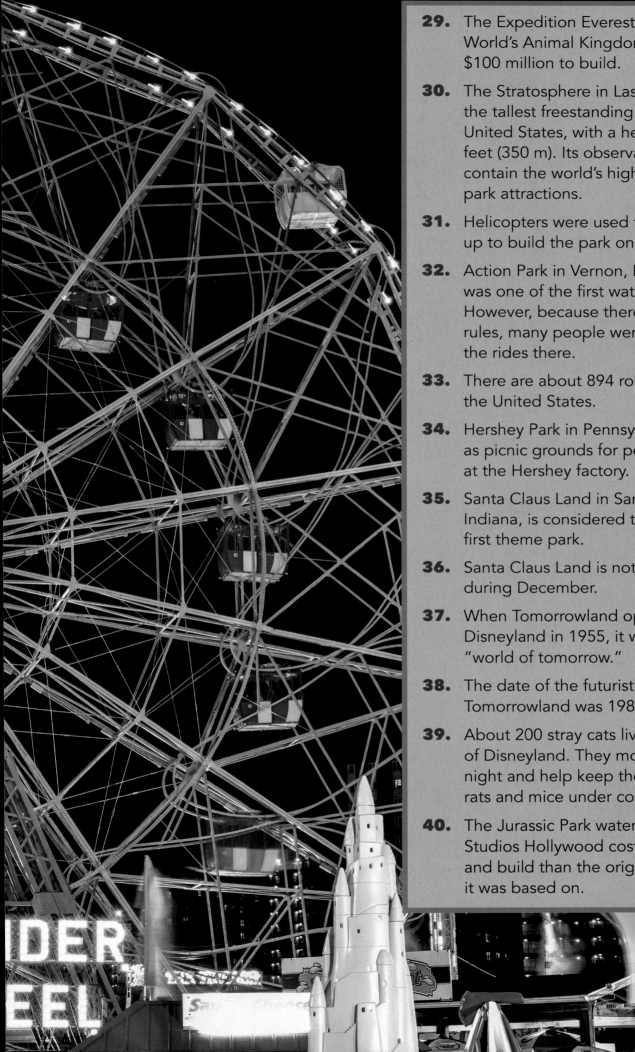

29. The Expedition Everest ride at Disney World's Animal Kingdom in Florida cost $100 million to build.

30. The Stratosphere in Las Vegas is the tallest freestanding tower in the United States, with a height of 1,149 feet (350 m). Its observation decks contain the world's highest amusement park attractions.

31. Helicopters were used to bring materials up to build the park on the Stratosphere.

32. Action Park in Vernon, New Jersey, was one of the first water parks. However, because there were few safety rules, many people were injured on the rides there.

33. There are about 894 roller coasters in the United States.

34. Hershey Park in Pennsylvania started out as picnic grounds for people who worked at the Hershey factory.

35. Santa Claus Land in Santa Claus, Indiana, is considered to be the world's first theme park.

36. Santa Claus Land is not open during December.

37. When Tomorrowland opened at Disneyland in 1955, it was set in the "world of tomorrow."

38. The date of the futuristic world in Tomorrowland was 1986.

39. About 200 stray cats live on the grounds of Disneyland. They mostly come out at night and help keep the population of rats and mice under control.

40. The Jurassic Park water ride at Universal Studios Hollywood cost more to design and build than the original movie it was based on.

30
SPOOKY FACTS ABOUT "HAUNTED" PLACES

1. The Sorrel-Weed House in Savannah, Georgia, is said to be haunted by two vengeful ghosts.

2. The Whaley House in San Diego, California, was built on the site of a graveyard and gallows.

3. The Whaley House is said to be haunted by "Yankee Jim" Robinson, who was executed on the site in 1852.

4. There have been more than 100 reported sightings of ghosts at Bachelor's Grove Cemetery in Chicago, Illinois.

5. People claim to have seen ghosts of people and animals, ghostly old cars, and even an entire phantom farmhouse at Bachelor's Grove.

6. One of New Orleans's most infamous haunted houses is the LaLaurie Mansion in the French Quarter. In 1834, Madame LaLaurie's house caught fire and people responding to the fire found evidence she had been abusing and torturing enslaved servants. The house is said to be haunted by the ghosts of LaLaurie's victims.

7. Marie Laveau, New Orleans's "Queen of Voodoo" died in 1851 but according to legend appears above the crypt where she is buried every June 23.

8. Many ghost stories are linked to the site of the Battle of Gettysburg in Pennsylvania.

9. People have reported hearing unexplained girls' laughter at St. Augustine's Light Station in Florida. Two teenage girls drowned there in 1874.

Local legends also say that St. Augustine's Light Station is haunted by the ghost of its builder, at least two lighthouse keepers, and 13 pirates.

The Winchester Mystery House in San Jose, California, has more than 160 rooms, 2,000 doors, and several secret staircases.

According to legend, Sarah Winchester, the widow of the man who invented the Winchester rifle, kept building onto the house to escape the ghosts of all the people killed by the rifle.

Waverly Hills Sanatorium in Louisville, Kentucky, was once a hospital for tuberculosis patients. Today, the building hosts ghost tours and a seasonal haunted house.

Fort East Martello Museum in Key West, Florida, features Robert the Doll, a supposedly haunted handmade doll.

Brave visitors can spend the night at the Trans-Allegheny Lunatic Asylum in West Virginia during ghost tours of the abandoned hospital.

Zak Bagans's The Haunted Museum in Las Vegas, Nevada, has a collection of artifacts from haunted places around the world.

The Haunted Museum itself is said to be haunted.

Forbes magazine called Texas "the most haunted state in America" in 2020.

Many people have reported seeing ghosts at the Alamo in San Antonio, Texas.

The ocean liner the *Queen Mary*, which is docked in Long Beach, California, is a popular place for ghost tours.

Travel + Leisure's Top 10 Most Haunted Cities

1. New Orleans, Louisiana
2. Chicago, Illinois
3. Savannah, Georgia
4. St. Augustine, Florida
5. Portland, Oregon
6. Gettysburg, Pennsylvania
7. Washington, D.C.
8. San Francisco, California
9. Salem, Massachusetts
10. San Antonio, Texas

35 FACTS ABOUT LIBRARIES

1. There are almost 117,000 libraries in the United States.

2. Philanthropist Andrew Carnegie donated $55 million between 1886 and 1919 to build 2,509 libraries around the world.

3. 1,679 of those libraries are in the United States.

4. The Library of Congress is the largest library in the world.

5. It contains more than 170 million items.

6. About half of the Library of Congress's book and serial collections are in languages other than English.

7. The collections contain materials in about 470 languages.

8. Anyone can visit the Library of Congress or do research there, but only members of Congress, the Supreme Court, and other government officials can check out books.

9. The Haskell Free Library and Opera House sits directly on the border between the Vermont, United States, and Quebec, Canada.

10. A black line on the floor of the Haskell Free Library marks the international boundary, but visitors are free to move from one side to the other without a passport.

11. In 2016, patrons at the San Jose Public Library in California owed $6.8 million in overdue fines.

12. The New York Public Library includes 87 libraries in New York City.

13. Two stone lions stand outside the main branch of the New York Public Library (NYPL) in New York City.

14. The NYPL stone lions are named Patience and Fortitude.

15. The NYPL main branch includes 125 miles (201 km) of shelves.

16. The NYPL's collection also includes pieces of Percy Bysshe Shelley's skull and locks of hair from several famous writers.

17. As of 2019, there were 146,500 librarians and 184,600 library technicians/assistants working in the United States.

18. Before typewriters and computers were common, librarians had to learn a specific kind of handwriting to fill out the catalog cards that tracked each book.

19. This style of writing was called "library hand."

20. Today's libraries lend out many different items besides books.

21. Some libraries lend tools, baking supplies, telescopes, taxidermy samples, and more.

22. An abandoned Walmart in McAllen, Texas, was turned into the largest single-floor public library in the United States.

23. The McAllen library measures 124,500 square feet (11,567 sq m).

24. There were more than 1.35 billion visits to public libraries in the U.S. in 2016.

25. 98 percent of libraries provide public computers and Wi-Fi for public use.

26. A 2019 survey showed that people go to the library three times more often than they go to the movies.

27. The Yale University Beinecke Rare Book and Manuscript Library is the largest building in the world for preserving rare books and manuscripts.

28. Beinecke's central shelving area includes glass walls and soft lighting to protect the works from direct light.

29. Reference librarians in U.S. public and academic libraries answer 6.6 million questions every week.

30. Academic libraries hold approximately 252.6 million ebooks.

31. Public libraries hold more than 87.2 million ebooks.

32. Academic librarians provide information services for almost 38 million people each year.

33. Students around the nation make more than one billion visits to school libraries every year.

34. A devastating fire at Los Angeles's Central Library in 1986 damaged or destroyed thousands of books.

35. After the Central Library fire, 1,700 volunteers sorted through the books that were left to figure out how many could be saved.

35 FUN FACTORIES

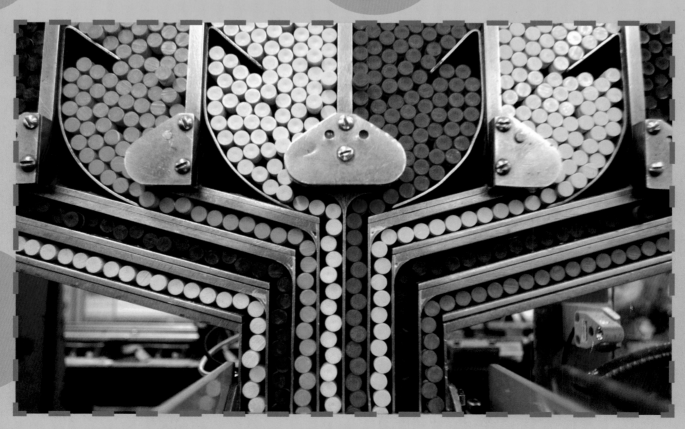

50 TOP TOURIST SITES
(ONE FOR EACH STATE)

1. Alabama—U.S. Space and Rocket Center
2. Alaska—Kenai Fjords
3. Arizona—Grand Canyon
4. Arkansas—Hot Springs National Park
5. California—Golden Gate Bridge
6. Colorado—Rocky Mountain National Park
7. Connecticut—Mystic Seaport
8. Delaware—Rehoboth Beach
9. Florida—Walt Disney World
10. Georgia—Georgia Aquarium
11. Hawaii—Pearl Harbor and USS *Arizona* Memorial
12. Idaho—Craters of the Moon National Monument
13. Illinois—Millennium Park
14. Indiana—Indianapolis Motor Speedway
15. Iowa—Field of Dreams
16. Kansas—*Brown v. Board of Education* National Historic Site
17. Kentucky—Cumberland Falls State Park
18. Louisiana—New Orleans's French Quarter
19. Maine—Acadia National Park
20. Maryland—Annapolis/ U.S. Naval Academy
21. Massachusetts—Faneuil Hall
22. Michigan—Henry Ford Museum
23. Minnesota—Mall of America
24. Mississippi—Vicksburg National Military Park
25. Missouri—Gateway Arch
26. Montana—Glacier National Park

35
TALL SKYSCRAPER FACTS

1. The word "skyscraper" originally described a top sail on a ship.

2. New York City has eight of the ten tallest buildings in the U.S.

3. Chicago has the other two of the ten tallest buildings in the U.S.

4. The first skyscraper was the Home Insurance Building in Chicago, built in 1885.

5. The Home Insurance Building was 138 feet (42 m) tall and was the first building to use a steel frame.

6. Famous architect Frank Lloyd Wright once designed a mile-high skyscraper. It would have been 5,280 feet (1,609 m) tall! But it was never built.

7. The Empire State Building was supposed to have a mooring mast for dirigibles (blimps) on top.

8. The Flatiron Building in New York City has a unique wedge shape.

9. In the late 1920s, Walter Chrysler and his architect arranged for the secret construction of a spire that added 125 feet (38 m) to New York City's Chrysler Building, making it 1,046 feet (319 m) tall, the tallest building in the world at that time.

10. The spire had been hidden inside the roof and was raised at the very end of construction.

11. Chrysler was an automaker, and he decorated the Chrysler Building with hubcaps, mudguards, and hood ornaments.

12. Less than a year later, the Empire State Building became the tallest building.

13. The Empire State was the first building to have more than 100 floors.

14. The Empire State Building is struck by lightning about 100 times a year.

15. It took only 410 days to build the Empire State Building.

16. On a foggy day in 1945, a plane crashed into the Empire State Building, killing 14 people.

17. In 2017, the 1,100-foot (335-m) Wilshire Grand Center in Los Angeles became the tallest building west of the Mississippi.

18. Before the Wilshire Grand Center was built, Los Angeles required tall buildings to have a helipad on top, creating lots of skyscrapers with flat roofs.

19. Skyscrapers are designed to sway in the wind.

20. During high winds, Chicago's Willis Tower can sway more than three feet (1 m).

21. The Willis Tower has six robotic window-washing machines mounted on the roof.

22. On a clear day, viewers can see four states from the Skydeck near the top of the Willis Tower: Illinois, Indiana, Wisconsin, and Michigan.

23. New observation balconies were built on the Willis Tower's 104th floor Skydeck in 2009. They have glass floors that jut out over the streets below.

24. Some tall buildings are big enough to have their own zip code.

25. The First Interstate World Center (Library Tower) in Los Angeles is located just 26 miles (42 km) from the earthquake-prone San Andreas Fault and has been designed to withstand an earthquake of 8.3 or more on the Richter scale.

Tallest Buildings in U.S. (2021)

#	Building	City	Height
1.	One World Trade Center	New York, NY	1,776 feet (541 m)
2.	Central Park Tower	New York, NY	1,550 feet (471 m)
3.	Willis Tower (former Sears Tower)	Chicago, IL	1,451 feet (442 m)
4.	Steinway Tower	New York, NY	1,428 feet (435 m)
5.	One Vanderbilt Place	New York, NY	1,401 feet (427 m)
6.	432 Park Avenue	New York, NY	1,396 feet (426 m)
7.	Trump International Hotel and Tower	Chicago, IL	1,389 feet (423 m)
8.	30 Hudson Yards	New York, NY	1,268 feet (386 m)
9.	Empire State Building	New York, NY	1,250 feet (381 m)
10.	Bank of America Tower	New York, NY	1,200 feet (366 m)

40 WILD WHITE HOUSE FACTS

1. George Washington never lived in the White House.

2. Even though he didn't live there, Washington helped to choose the site and approved the building's design.

3. French architect Pierre Charles L'Enfant, who designed the basic plan for Washington, D.C., suggested building a great palace for the president, similar to those in Europe.

4. Washington disagreed, saying that Americans had just won their freedom from a monarchy and didn't want their new leader living in a palace.

5. George Washington and Thomas Jefferson held a competition to see who would design the White House and the Capitol Building.

6. Rumor has it Jefferson anonymously submitted his own designs for both buildings.

7. James Hoban won the contest and designed the White House.

8. The cornerstone was laid on October 13, 1792.

9. John Adams was the first president to live in the White House.

10. Adams and his wife did not like living there. The rooms were cold and poorly furnished, servants had to walk a long way to get water, and swampy grounds attracted mosquitoes.

11. Very little of the original White House remains.

12. British forces burned the White House in 1814, leaving only the walls standing.

13. After the fire, President James Madison brought Hoban back to restore the mansion.

14. The restoration took three years, and Madison wasn't president by the time it was finished.

15. Another fire gutted parts of the West Wing on Christmas Eve in 1929.

16. The 1929 fire was caused by a blocked fireplace flue.

17. President Herbert Hoover left a Christmas party to direct the firefighting efforts.

18. The White House has been known as the "President's Palace," the "President's House," and the "Executive Mansion."

19. President Theodore Roosevelt officially gave the White House its current name in 1901.

20. President Theodore Roosevelt created the West Wing to separate the business areas from the residence.

21. President William Howard Taft created the Oval Office.

22. The president's and vice president's offices are in the West Wing.

23. The first lady's offices are usually in the East Wing.

24. In 1948, President Harry Truman and his family moved out of the White House after engineers found the building was unsafe.

25. Truman started an extensive renovation of the White House, which was completed in 1952.

26. The White House has 132 rooms, 35 bathrooms, and six levels.

27. There are also 412 doors, 147 windows, 28 fireplaces, 8 staircases, and 3 elevators.

28. Five full-time chefs work at the White House, and they can serve a full dinner to as many as 140 guests and just appetizers (hors d'oeuvres) to up to 1,000 guests.

29. It takes 570 gallons of paint to cover the outside of the White House.

30. The White House has many different recreation facilities, including a tennis court, track, swimming pool, movie theater, and bowling alley.

31. The White House address is 1600 Pennsylvania Avenue.

32. The White House is a national heritage site.

33. The building is owned by the National Park Service.

34. The East Room is the largest room in the White House. That's where dances and large gatherings take place.

35. The East Room hosted the high school prom of Susan Ford, daughter of President Gerald Ford, in 1975.

36. The second and third floors contain private living space for the president, the president's family, and the president's guests.

37. Many presidents' children grew up in the White House.

38. First lady Jacqueline Kennedy organized a school, held in the White House solarium, for Caroline Kennedy and 20 other pupils.

39. The White House has hosted at least 18 weddings.

40. The first White House wedding was for first lady Dolley Madison's sister in 1812.

Transportation

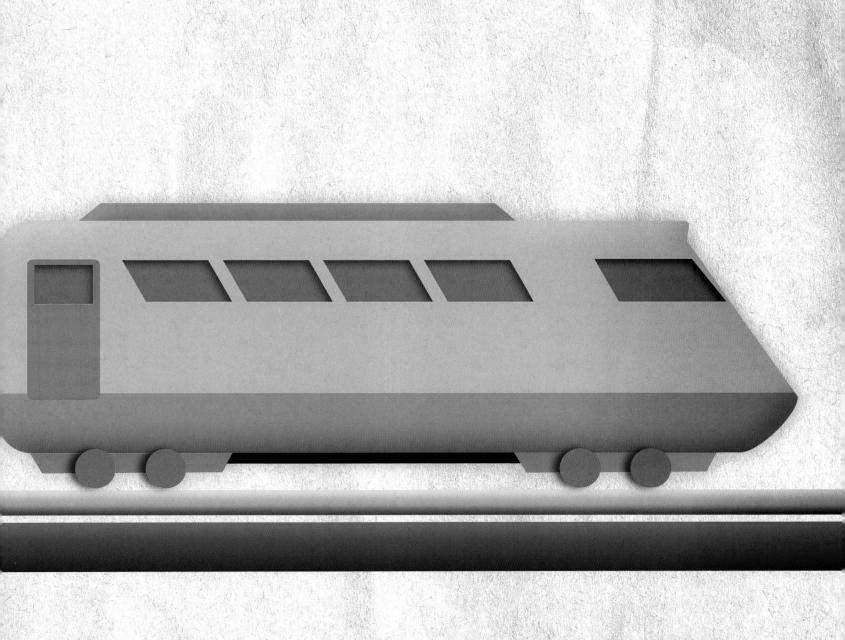

30
GROUNDBREAKING FACTS ABOUT THE TRANSCONTINENTAL RAILROAD

1. The idea for a transcontinental railroad that would link the United States from east to west was first presented to Congress in 1845.

2. As more people traveled west, the need for a better way to cross the country became more urgent.

3. In 1862, the Pacific Railroad Act tasked the Central Pacific and the Union Pacific Railroad Companies to build a transcontinental railroad.

4. Before the railroad was complete, it cost about $1,000 to cross the country. After the railroad was finished, the cost dropped to $150.

5. The building of the railroad was set up as a competition between the two railroads.

6. Each company would receive 6,400 acres of land (2,590 ha), later doubled to 12,800 acres (5,180 ha) and up to $48,000 in government bonds for every mile of track built.

7. Both companies set their first spikes in 1863.

8. The Union Pacific did not make much progress on building new track until May 1866 because of the Civil War.

9. The Union Pacific made progress across the Great Plains, while the Central Pacific struggled to build tunnels and track through the Sierra Nevada Mountains.

10. Workers on the railroad faced many dangers and many were injured or even killed.

11. The Central Pacific hired about 14,000 Chinese workers to build the railroad.

12. Chinese workers were paid about half as much as white workers, even though they worked 12 hours a day, 6 days a week.

13. Chinese railroad workers organized and went on strike in 1867 to protest the unfair treatment and improve their conditions.

14. Most of the workers for the Union Pacific were Irish immigrants and Civil War veterans.

15. The railroad included 19 tunnels.

16. Fifteen of these tunnels were built by the Central Pacific.

17. The company used gunpowder and nitroglycerine to blast tunnels through the mountains.

18. By the summer of 1867, the Union Pacific reached Wyoming.

19. They had covered nearly four times as much ground as the Central Pacific due to easier terrain.

20. The Central Pacific broke through the mountains in late June.

21. As the companies raced toward Salt Lake City, they cut corners, building unsafe bridges and sections of track that would have to be rebuilt later.

22. Charles Crocker, the construction supervisor for the Central Pacific, bet Thomas Durant at the Union Pacific $10,000 that his crew could lay the most track in a single day.

23. Crocker won the bet by laying 10 miles (16 km) of track to Durant's 7 miles (11 km).

24. Early in 1869, the two companies agreed to meet at Promontory Point in Utah.

25. On May 10, 1869, a crowd gathered to watch the driving of the ceremonial final spike that would link the tracks.

26. The ceremony used a spike made of 17.6-karat gold.

27. The heads of both the Central Pacific and Union Pacific missed when they tried to hit the spike.

28. The spike was finally driven in by a railroad worker.

29. The golden spike was removed after the ceremony and replaced with a traditional iron spike.

30. The transcontinental railroad cut travel time across the U.S. from several months to under a week.

25 BICYCLE FACTS

1. During the 1890s, bicycling became a huge craze in the U.S.

2. Orville and Wilbur Wright owned several bicycle shops in Dayton, Ohio, in the 1890s.

3. Not all early bikes looked like the ones we're used to today.

4. Cycling is one of the oldest competitive sports in the United States.

5. America's first organized bike race took place in Boston in 1878.

6. A bicycle club called the League of American Wheelmen was founded in 1880.

7. In 1884, Thomas Stevens became the first person to ride a bike across the U.S.

8. Three years later, Stevens became the first person to cycle around the world.

9. By the 1890s, more than 600 pro cyclists competed on a coast-to-coast national circuit race from San Francisco to Boston and in every major city in between.

10. The U.S. was once home to more than 100 cycling tracks.

11. New York City's Madison Square Garden was the home of the first velodrome, a bike-racing track with steeply banked curves.

12. Cycling races got their start in the 1890s as endurance events in which cyclists pedaled for six days straight without food or sleep.

13. After New York and Chicago passed laws prohibiting these cycling races in 1898, cyclists started racing in pairs that switched off every few hours.

14. These partnered bike races often lasted for six days.

15. At their peak popularity in the 1920s, the six-day bike races at Madison Square Garden and Chicago Stadium could draw tens of thousands of fans.

16. Between 1955 and 1958, the Huffy Radio Bicycle included a built-in radio.

17. Ten-speed bikes became popular in the 1970s, starting a racing fad called the Bike Boom.

18. The first mountain bikes were made in the U.S. in 1977.

19. BMX racing became popular after kids in California modified their bikes to be more like motorcycles and raced them off-road and on dirt tracks.

20. There are about 100 million bikes in America.

21. America ranks #2 in the world, behind China, for having the greatest number of bikes.

22. About 870,000 Americans commute to work on bicycles.

23. One car-sized parking space can hold between 6 and 20 bicycles.

24. The first U.S. bike-sharing program launched in Portland, Oregon, in 1994. It closed in 2001.

25. Dozens of cities now have their own bike-sharing programs, with riders logging millions of trips every year.

40 FACTS ABOUT THE HISTORY OF FLIGHT

1. Airplanes can fly because air moves faster over the top of the airplane wing than it does underneath. This creates lift.

2. The Wright Brothers achieved the first airplane flight in 1903.

3. The first flight lasted just 12 seconds. The plane traveled 120 feet (37 m). Orville Wright was the pilot.

4. Orville's brother Wilbur flew 852 feet (260 m) in 59 seconds later the same day.

5. The Wright brothers established the world's first test flight facility near Dayton, Ohio.

6. That test flight facility is now called Wright Patterson Air Force Base.

7. The first woman in the U.S. who was licensed to fly a plane was Harriet Quimby in 1911.

8. Quimby became the first woman to fly across the English Channel.

9. In 1927, Charles Lindbergh became the first person to fly solo across the Atlantic Ocean.

10. The transatlantic trip took Lindbergh 33.5 hours to fly from New York to Paris.

11. Amelia Earhart was the first woman to fly solo across the Atlantic Ocean.

12. Earhart, her navigator, and their plane disappeared in 1937 while trying to fly around the world.

13. World War I was the first major war to use airplanes in battle.

14. After the war, some military pilots became barnstormers.

15. Barnstormers were flying entertainers who traveled around, delighting crowds by performing dives and spins in the air.

16. Barnstorming shows often included performers who walked on the wings of the airplane while in flight.

17. Early airplanes had open cockpits. Pilots were exposed to rain, wind, ice, and freezing temperatures.

18. Pilot Chuck Yeager broke the sound barrier in 1947. He was the first person to fly faster than the speed of sound.

19. A Boeing 747 jet has 6 million parts.

20. Each engine on a Boeing 747 weighs almost 9,500 pounds (4,300 kg).

21. A 747's fuel tank holds almost 48,445 gallons.

22. The "black boxes" that record every flight's data are actually orange. The bright color makes them easy to find in the event of a crash.

23. There are 5,000 planes flying over the United States at a typical moment.

24. Pilots and co-pilots choose different meals when they have to eat while flying. If one of them gets food poisoning, the other one can still fly the plane.

25. Some airplanes used for long flights have secret bedrooms so the crew can nap in flight.

26. The longest military plane is the U.S. C-5 cargo plane. At almost 223 feet (68 m) long, it can carry large military equipment, such as tanks and trucks.

27. Airplanes usually fly about 35,000 feet (10,668 m), or 6½ miles (11 km) above the Earth.

28. A commercial jet can fly at speeds of up to 550–580 miles (885–933 km) per hour.

29. The Lockheed SR-71 Blackbird is the fastest plane on Earth. In 1976, this military plane flew 2,193 miles (3,529 km) per hour.

30. The Blackbird is so fast, it can outfly surface-to-air missiles.

31. Most commercial planes use autopilot during flight, but pilots control the plane during takeoffs and landings.

32. In 1986, a plane called the Rutan Voyager flew around the world without stopping or refueling.

33. It took nine days for pilots Dick Rutan and Jeana Yeager to complete the flight.

34. The Voyager carried 17 fuel tanks.

35. To increase fuel efficiency, Voyager weighed only 939 pounds (425 kg) and had no metal parts.

36. U.S. commercial airlines make about 5,670 flights per day.

37. In August 2020, U.S. airlines carried 23.7 million passengers on domestic and international flights.

38. In 1987, American Airlines saved $40,000 by removing one olive from each salad served to first-class passengers.

39. Online flight check-ins were first used by Alaska Airlines in 1999.

40. In a given hour, there can be 61,000 people in the air over the U.S.

40 FACTS ABOUT THE HISTORY OF AUTOMOBILES

1. Although early automobiles were invented and perfected in Germany and France, the U.S. soon became the center of the automobile industry.

2. In 1893, two bicycle mechanics named Charles Duryea and J. Frank designed the first successful American gasoline automobile.

3. Designed in Springfield, Massachusetts, their automobile would later be sold as the first American-made gas-powered car in 1896.

4. About 485 companies entered the U.S. automobile market between 1899 and 1909.

5. At the start of the 20th century, there were fewer than 8,000 cars in the US.

6. Many of them were powered by steam or electricity.

7. William Morrison, a chemist who lived in Des Moines, Iowa, introduced the first successful electric car in 1890.

8. In 1913, the U.S. produced more than three-quarters of the world's automobiles.

9. The Model T, sold by the Ford Motor Company from 1908 to 1927, was the earliest effort to make a car that average people could afford to buy.

10. In 1913, Ford introduced the assembly line, which sped up the mass production of automobiles.

11. In six months, the labor-time to build a Ford Model T was reduced from 9 hours and 54 minutes to 5 hours, 56 minutes.

12. Between 1913 and 1927, Ford produced more than 15 million Model Ts.

13. The Ford Model T was a self-starting vehicle with a left-sided steering wheel and an enclosed four-cylinder engine.

14. The Model T rode high above the ground, which meant it could handle rough dirt roads, making it popular among rural drivers.

15. Paved roads were not nearly as common before automobiles were common.

16. The Model T was the first Ford with all its parts built by the company itself.

17. The Model T cost $850 when it was first produced.

18. By 1927, the price of a Model T had dropped to $290.

19. Ford Motor Company founder Henry Ford said, "Any customer can have a car painted any color that he wants so long as it is black."

20. Ford replaced the Model T with the Model A.

21. William Durant, who had started out as a manufacturer of horse-drawn vehicles, founded General Motors in 1908.

22. In 1914, Horace and John Dodge started their own car company.

23. Before that, the Dodge brothers had supplied parts to the Ford Motor Company.

24. Dodge was the second-biggest car company in America until 1920, when both brothers died.

25. In 1925, Walter Chrysler started the Chrysler Corporation.

26. Ford, General Motors, and Chrysler emerged as the "Big Three" auto companies by the 1920s.

27. Manufacturing cars for the civilian market stopped in 1942, as automakers changed to producing vehicles for the military during World War II.

28. After the war ended, there was a huge demand for new cars.

29. The 1950s have been called the Golden Age of car design.

30. Cars in the 1950s had features like huge tail fins, big bumpers, whitewall tires, and large, bright lights.

31. Until the 1960s, most cars had poor gas mileage and created a lot of air pollution.

32. New safety and environmental protection rules changed the way cars were made.

33. After peaking at a record 12.87 million cars in 1978, sales of American-made cars fell to 6.95 million in 1982.

34. During the 1980s, cars became smaller, safer, and more fuel-efficient.

35. The U.S. consumes about half of the world's gasoline.

36. Tesla, founded in 2003, emerged as a significant player in the U.S. auto industry by making electric cars.

37. Tesla manufactured its 1 millionth car in 2020.

38. By 2018, 1 million electric cars were on U.S. roads.

39. By 2030, experts predicted there would be about 19 million electric vehicles on U.S. roads.

40. White is the most popular car color.

30 HIGH-FLYING FACTS ABOUT AIRPORTS

1. Hartsfield-Jackson Atlanta International Airport is the busiest airport in the world.

2. More than 110 million passengers traveled through Hartsfield-Jackson in 2019.

3. Most of those passengers were traveling on domestic flights.

4. More than 60,000 people work at Hartsfield-Jackson Airport.

5. When three-letter airport identification codes became standard, airports that had been using two letters added an X to the end of their codes.

6. Los Angeles International Airport is also known as LAX.

7. Los Angeles International's Theme Building was built in 1961. It looks like a giant steel and concrete spider.

8. The Theme Building once housed a restaurant and an observation deck.

9. Members can pay $4,500 a year, plus $2,700 extra per flight, to join a special private club at LAX called PS LAX.

10. Members of PS LAX get to use a separate VIP terminal with luxury extras and conveniences.

11. The highest commercial airport in the U.S. is Telluride Regional Airport in Colorado. At 9,070 feet (2,765 m) above sea level, the runway is often covered in snow.

12. Nashville International Airport in Tennessee features six concert stages.

13. General Mitchell International Airport in Milwaukee, Wisconsin, installed ping pong tables for people to play while they wait for their flights to board.

14. Tijuana International Airport, on the border between Mexico and the U.S., is the only airport to have terminals in two countries.

15. The world's oldest continuously operated airport is College Park Airport in Maryland.

16. It was established in 1909 by Wilbur Wright, one of the Wright brothers.

17. In 2019, more than $926,030.44 in loose change was left at security checkpoints in the U.S.

18. Unclaimed money is deposited in a special account to fund security at airports.

19. Items seized by U.S. airport security are often sold at auctions.

20. Miami International Airport has trained therapy dogs available for hugs and snuggles.

21. San Francisco International Airport has a therapy pig who wears costumes and performs tricks.

22. Indianapolis, Orlando, Chicago O'Hare, Portland, Pittsburgh, and St. Louis airports all have honeybee colonies on their grounds.

23. JFK International Airport in New York has an ARK Pet Oasis. It is the only facility of its kind in North America.

24. The Pet Oasis includes kennels, animal medical personnel, exercise areas, and more.

25. JFK also has virtual reality stations with games to entertain passengers.

26. Hungry? JFK has 150 restaurants.

27. JFK used to be named Idlewild Airport, but the name was to honor President John F. Kennedy after his assassination.

28. Airports make about 41 percent of their income from parking fees.

29. Denver International Airport covers 53 sq miles (137 sq km).

30. The Dallas-Fort Worth Airport has the longest average commute time from the city center, at 56 minutes.

25 HIT-THE-ROAD FACTS ABOUT HIGHWAYS

1. The first major highway in the U.S. was the "National Road."

2. The National Road was built between 1811 and 1834.

3. It traveled through six states: Illinois, Indiana, Ohio, Pennsylvania, Maryland, and West Virginia.

4. It was the first highway funded by the federal government.

5. The National Road was supposed to extend to St. Louis, Missouri, but the government stopped funding it before the last link could be built.

6. The Lincoln Highway was the first transcontinental highway in the U.S.

7. Built in 1913, the Lincoln Highway stretched for almost 3,400 miles (5,472 km) from New York to San Francisco.

8. Route 66 opened in 1926. This highway ran from Chicago to Los Angeles.

9. Route 66 was called "the Mother Road" and "Main Street of America."

10. Route 66 was the subject of a popular song and TV show.

11. President Dwight D. Eisenhower established the Interstate Highway System in 1956.

12. Eisenhower was inspired by the network of roads he saw in Germany during World War II.

13. Eisenhower also wanted a system of highways to move military equipment and evacuate citizens in case of a nuclear attack.

14. The U.S. Interstate Highway System covers 46,876 miles (75,440 km) and runs through all fifty states.

15. During the 1960s, activists stopped construction on parts of highways in New York, Baltimore, Washington, D.C., and New Orleans.

16. Each state is responsible for speed limits and other laws on the portion of an interstate highway that travels through it.

17. The red, white, and blue shields that show interstate numbers are trademarks of the American Association of State Highway Officials.

18. The design of the shields was chosen in a contest in 1957.

19. New York has the most interstates pass through it, with 29.

20. Hawaii has the fewest interstates with just three.

21. The interstate route numbers that run East-West end in an even number, while the North-South interstate route numbers end in an odd number.

22. The shortest interstate route is the 0.11-mile (0.18-km) segment of I-95 that runs through the District of Columbia.

23. The longest interstate route is I-90, which runs more than 3,020 miles (4,860 km) between Seattle, Washington, to Boston, Massachusetts.

24. At a cost of $8 billion, I-95 was the most expensive interstate to build.

25. I-95 is the longest north-south interstate route, running 1,908 miles (3,071 km) from Miami to the Canadian border in Maine.

101
AMAZING ATHLETES

1. **Hank Aaron:** Aaron broke Babe Ruth's career home run record when he hit his 715th homer in 1974. He went on to tally 755 home runs in his career.

2. **Kareem Abdul-Jabbar:** This NBA center helped his teams win six championships and was the league's all-time leading scorer with 38,387 points when he retired in 1989.

3. **Muhammad Ali:** This boxer called himself "The Greatest," and many people agreed with him.

4. **Mario Andretti:** Whether the track was paved, dirt, or a road race, auto racing legend Andretti won them all.

5. **Bob Beamon:** It took Beamon just six seconds to set a long jump world record at the 1968 Olympic Games, beating the previous record by almost two feet.

6. **Joan Benoit Samuelson:** This American runner won the first Olympic women's marathon in 1984.

7. **Simone Biles:** The most decorated American gymnast, Biles has achieved moves that no one else has even attempted.

8. **Larry Bird:** Along with Magic Johnson and Michael Jordan, Bird transformed the NBA of that era and later became successful as an NBA coach.

9. **Bonnie Blair:** Speed skater Blair dominated the sport and won six Olympic medals between 1988–1994.

10. **Tom Brady:** The star quarterback won six Super Bowls in 20 seasons with the New England Patriots before winning his seventh with the Tampa Bay Buccaneers in 2021.

11. **Jim Brown:** Brown ran for at least 100 yards in 58 of his 118 regular-season games, making him one of the best and toughest NFL running backs.

12. **Kobe Bryant:** Fiercely competitive, Bryant's 20-year career with the Los Angeles Lakers made him an NBA legend.

13. **Susan Butcher:** This American sled-dog racer dominated the sport in the 1980s and became the first woman to win three consecutive Iditarod races.

14. **Tracy Caulkins:** One of the best competitive swimmers of all time, Caulkins won 48 women's national championships and set records in all four swimming strokes.

15. **Wilt Chamberlain:** The only NBA player to score 100 points in a game, Chamberlain was a four-time MVP and one of the best to ever play.

16. **Roberto Clemente:** Before his tragic death in a plane crash while bringing supplies to earthquake victims in Nicaragua, outfielder Clemente had 3,000 hits.

17. **Babe Didrikson Zaharias:** Considered the best woman athlete at a time when sports opportunities for women and girls were scarce, Babe excelled in a number of track and field events, winning three Olympic medals, and in golf.

18. **Joe DiMaggio:** DiMaggio eventually won nine World Series with the stacked New York Yankees, but his 56-game hitting streak in 1941 made him a legend.

19. **Gertrude Ederle:** An Olympic medalist, Ederle became the first woman to swim across the English Channel in 1926.

20. **John Elway:** The quarterback for the Denver Broncos for 15 years, Elway has been called the best quarterback ever drafted.

21. **Chris Evert:** One of the most dominant women in tennis during the 1970s, Evert achieved records that have yet to be broken.

22. **Jennie Finch:** Pitcher who led the U.S. softball team to a gold medal at the 2004 Olympics and silver at the 2008 Games.

23. **Missy Franklin:** This swimmer was the first American woman to win four gold medals in a single Olympics.

24. **Lou Gehrig:** "The Iron Horse" played 2,130 straight baseball games until a fatal disease ended his career.

25. **Mia Hamm:** This soccer star led the U.S. team to victory in the 1999 World Cup.

26. **Ben Hogan:** Hogan won 13 tournaments even after a devastating car accident sidelined him for a year at the height of his golf career.

27. **Flo Hyman:** A groundbreaking volleyball player, Hyman was a star at the Olympics and the World Championships in the 1970s and 1980s.

28. **Bo Jackson:** A star in both football and baseball, Jackson was the first athlete named to play in the All-Star game in two sports.

29. **LeBron James:** "King James" rules the basketball court and is considered one of the greatest basketball players of all time.

30. **Michael Jordan:** Jordan led the Chicago Bulls to an astonishing six NBA championships between 1991 and 1998.

31. **Earvin "Magic" Johnson:** Johnson's play dazzled the NBA and made him one of the most popular and dominant stars of the 1980s.

32. **Florence Griffith Joyner:** This American track-and-field star was called the fastest woman in the world.

33. **Jackie Joyner-Kersee:** Possibly America's greatest track-and-field athlete, Joyner-Kersee won six Olympic medals in the heptathlon and long jump.

34. **Billie Jean King:** A winner of 39 Grand Slam tennis titles, King was also known for coming out on top in the "Battle of the Sexes" match and fighting for women's equality.

35. **Julie Krone:** American jockey who was the first woman to win a Triple Crown race at the Belmont Stakes in 1993.

36. **Michelle Kwan:** Kwan is the most decorated American figure skater in history.

37. **Katie Ledecky:** This swimmer won her first Olympic medal when she was 15 and went on to win five Olympic gold medals and 14 world championship gold medals.

38. **Lisa Leslie:** This WNBA star also led the U.S. team to four Olympic gold medals between 1996–2008.

39. **Nancy Lopez:** This golf legend won 48 LPGA Tour events and was the youngest woman to qualify for the LPGA Hall of Fame.

40. **Rocky Marciano:** The only heavyweight champion to retire undefeated, Marciano scored 43 knockouts in 49 fights.

41. **Bob Mathias:** In 1948, teenage Mathias won the Olympic gold medal in the decathlon, a grueling 10-event contest he had only started competing in that same year.

42. **Willie Mays:** This center fielder's 660 career home runs were just icing on the cake for the man many consider the best all-around baseball player of all time.

43. **Tamara McKinney:** The first American skier to win the alpine World Cup overall title.

44. **Ann Meyers:** Meyers was the first (and still the only) woman player to sign with an NBA team.

45. **Shannon Miller:** Gymnast who won seven Olympic medals, including with the "Magnificent 7," the first U.S. team to win gold in the women's team event.

46. **Joe Montana:** Playing best under pressure, this quarterback led the San Francisco 49ers to four Super Bowl wins.

47. **Jack Nicklaus:** "The Golden Bear" is one of the top golfers of all time and the only player until Tiger Woods to win three career grand slams.

48. **Diana Nyad:** Distance swimmer who holds many records in open-water swims, including between Cuba and Florida and around the island of Manhattan.

49. **Jesse Owens:** In just 45 minutes in 1935, Owens broke three track-and-field world records and tied another. In 1936, the Black athlete was the star of the Berlin Olympic Games, in defiance of Adolf Hitler's racist theories.

50. **Leroy "Satchel" Paige:** This star pitcher spent most of his career dominating in the Negro Leagues.

51. **Danica Patrick:** Patrick broke through barriers in both NASCAR and Indy racing to become the most successful woman driver yet.

52. **Walter Payton:** During Payton's 13 seasons with the Chicago Bears, he rushed for 16,726 yards, an NFL record at the time.

53. **Richard Petty:** Petty built stock-car racing into a hugely popular sport, winning a record number of championships along the way.

54. **Michael Phelps:** Swimmer Phelps is the most decorated Olympic athlete of all time, winning 28 medals.

55. **Megan Rapinoe:** This outspoken soccer star helped lead the U.S. women's team to victory in the 2019 World Cup.

56. **Mary Lou Retton:** In 1984, Retton became the first American woman to win the all-around gold medal in gymnastics.

57. **Jerry Rice:** A NFL wide receiver for 20 seasons, Rice won three Super Bowls with the 49ers and is considered one of the greatest football players of all time.

58. **Jackie Robinson:** Robinson took on an enormous spotlight as the first Black player in baseball's major leagues in 1947. He won rookie of the year and then MVP two years later.

59. **Sugar Ray Robinson:** This boxing champion had an amazing 128–1–2 record; Muhammad Ali called him "the king, the master, my idol."

60. **Ronda Rousey:** Considered one of the greatest female fighters ever, Rousey is the only woman to win both a UFC and WWE championship.

61. **Wilma Rudolph:** This track-and-field star was the first American woman to win three gold medals in a single Olympics.

62. **Babe Ruth:** Widely considered the best baseball player of all time, Ruth could hit more home runs than entire teams and held the records for most home runs in a season and most home runs in a career for more than 40 years.

63. **Pete Sampras:** Sampras won 14 Grand Slam tennis titles during his career, making him one of the top American tennis players of all time.

64. **Claressa Shields:** Shields was the first American boxer to win back-to-back Olympic gold medals in 2012 and 2016,

65. **Willie Shoemaker:** In his 42-year career as a jockey, Shoemaker won 11 Triple Crown races and was racing's biggest money winner between 1958 and 1964.

66. **Toni Stone:** Stone became the first woman to play professional baseball when she joined the Indianapolis Clowns of the Negro Leagues.

67. **Diana Taurasi:** Taurasi is one of the few women to win an Olympic gold medal (she won four), a WNBA championship (three), and an NCAA championship (three).

68. Misty May–Treanor and

69. Kerri Walsh Jennings: The greatest beach volleyball team of all time, May-Treanor and Jennings won three consecutive Olympic gold medals between 2004-2012.

70. Mike Tyson: One of the toughest heavyweight champions of all time, Tyson was called "Iron Mike" for his take-no-prisoners style of fighting.

71. Lindsey Vonn: One of the greatest alpine skiers of all time, Vonn won four World Cups as well as a gold medal in the 2010 Winter Olympics.

72. Abby Wambach: This soccer star scored more goals than any other American player—184 goals—in international competition.

73. Serena Williams: Serena dominated the tennis courts of the 21st century, winning 23 Grand Slam singles titles (and counting).

74. Ted Williams: Considered one of baseball's greatest hitters, Williams holds the record for the highest season batting average with a scorching .406.

75. Venus Williams: Serena's older sister and frequent doubles partner who was also a dominant singles player, winning 10 Grand Slam titles.

76. Tiger Woods: Woods turned pro by the age of 20 and has won more PGA Tour events than any other golfer.

25 Star Athletes With Disabilities

1. Jim Abbott: Born without a right hand, Abbott became a star pitcher in college and the major leagues.

2. Rocky Bleier: After losing part of his foot during the Vietnam War, Bleier won four Super Bowl rings with the Pittsburgh Steelers.

3. Steve Cash: Cash, who lost his right leg to cancer at age 3, was a goaltender with the U.S. Sledge Hockey National Team and won numerous Paralympic medals.

4. Tamika Catchings: Hearing impaired from birth, this 10-time WNBA All-Star also won four Olympic gold medals.

5. Tom Dempsey broke an NFL record when he kicked a game-winning field goal for 63 yards despite missing part of his right foot.

6. Jean Driscoll won the Boston Marathon's wheelchair division seven consecutive times in the 1990s.

7. George Eyser competed as a gymnast in the 1904 Olympics, despite having a wooden left leg. He earned six medals in one day, including three gold and two silver medals.

8. Jeff Float: U.S. swimmer Jeff Float became Deaf in infancy. At the 1984 Olympics, he helped the U.S. team win a gold medal in freestyle relay.

9. Zack Gowen: Although he lost a leg when he was young, Gowen became a professional wrestler in the WWE.

10. Pete Gray lost an arm in an accident when he was young but played major league baseball.

11. **Bethany Hamilton:** This surfer lost her left arm in a shark attack when she was 13 but went on to win many championships.

12. **Jason Lester:** Lester was the first athlete with a disability to complete the Ultraman World Championship, a three-day, multi-sport challenge.

13. **Jessica Long:** This swimmer won 23 Paralympic medals, making her one of the most successful Paralympians of all time.

14. **Kyle Maynard:** Born without hands or feet, Maynard won 36 wrestling matches in high school, became an MMA fighter, and climbed Africa's Mount Kilimanjaro.

15. **Tatyana McFadden:** McFadden won medals at both the Summer and Winter Paralympic Games in track-and-field and cross-country skiing.

16. **Alana Nichols:** Paralyzed from the waist down in a snowboarding accident, Nichols has competed in Paralympic basketball and skiing and won two gold medals.

17. **Erin Popovich:** Born with dwarfism, Popovich is a champion swimmer with 14 gold medals at Paralympic Games.

18. **Anthony Robles:** Born with one leg, Robles won the NCAA individual wrestling championship in 2010–2011.

19. **Oz Sanchez:** Sanchez medaled in handcycling at the 2008 and 2012 Paralympic Games.

20. **Sarah Reinertsen:** A runner and triathlete, Reinertsen was the first woman leg amputee to compete in the Ironman World Championship in Kona, Hawaii.

21. **Marla Runyan:** Legally blind since childhood, Runyan became an Olympic athlete and marathon runner, while also winning medals in the Paralympic Games.

22. **Melissa Stockwell:** Having lost one of her legs while serving in the Iraq War, Stockwell was the first Iraq veteran to make the U.S. Paralympic team.

23. **Kayleigh Williamson:** A runner born with Down Syndrome, Williamson has competed in many half marathons.

24. **Erik Weihenmayer:** This born adventurer became the first blind athlete to climb Mount Everest in 2001.

25. **Trischa Zorn:** Swimmer Zorn won 55 medals, including 41 golds, and was elected to the International Paralympic Hall of Fame.

50 U.S. OLYMPICS FACTS

1. The first Olympics shown by U.S. television was the 1960 Summer Games in Rome, Italy.

2. No country in the Southern Hemisphere has ever hosted a Winter Olympics.

3. The official languages of the Olympics are English and French.

4. From 1912–1948, artists participated in the Olympics: painters, sculptors, architects, writers, and musicians competed for medals.

5. The first modern Olympic Games took place in 1896.

6. The first women's sports, in 1900, were tennis, sailing, croquet, horseback riding, and golf.

7. Swimmer Michael Phelps has won 28 medals, more than any other athlete.

8. 23 of Phelps's Olympic medals were gold.

9. Phelps's nicknames included "the Flying Fish."

10. Swimmer Jenny Thompson won eight golds, three silvers, and a bronze across four different Games between 1992 and 2004.

11. Swimmer Dara Torres won four gold medals, four silver medals and four bronze medals.

12. Torres competed in 1984, 1988, and 1992, then came back to compete in 2000.

13. After retiring for the second time, Torres also came back to compete in the 2008 Games.

14. Only men compete in the ten-event decathlon.

15. Only women compete is the seven-event heptathlon.

16. The 2012 Summer Games were the first where all participating countries sent women athletes.

17. Only two American athletes have won medals in both the Olympic Summer and Winter Games.

18. In the Opening Ceremonies, Greece leads the athletes' procession.

19. The last team in the procession is the host country's.

20. Other teams march in alphabetical order in the host country's language.

21. At the Opening Ceremonies, athletes march in representing their countries.

22. At the Closing Ceremonies, the athletes march in as one big group.

23. The U.S. and 65 other nations boycotted the 1980 Olympic Games in Moscow.

24. The boycott was caused by the Soviet Union's invasion of Afghanistan.

25. The Olympic flag was first flown at the 1920 Games.

26. The Olympic mottos is "Citius, Altius, Fortius."

27. That's Latin for "Swifter, Higher, Stronger."

28. Tug-of-war was an Olympic event between 1900 and 1920.

29. The 1900 Olympics featured a swimming obstacle race.

30. Other events that are no longer in the Olympics are club swinging, pistol dueling, live pigeon shooting, rope climbing, and a diving event called the plunge for distance.

31. At the 1968 Winter Olympics, three American women tied for second place in the 500-meter speed-skating event. All three stood on the podium and received silver medals.

32. As of 2021, before the Summer Olympic Games, the United States had won the most medals in the history of the Olympics.

33. American athletes have won a total of 2,524 medals (1,022 of them gold) at the Summer Olympics.

34. American athletes have won another 305 medals (105 of them gold) at the Winter Games.

35. The U.S. Olympic team does not receive any government funding.

36. Many U.S. Olympians work other jobs while doing their strenuous Olympic training.

37. The 1992 U.S. Olympics men's basketball team was the first to include professional athletes.

38. The 1992 U.S. men's basketball team was nicknamed the Dream Team.

39. Some of the stars who played on the Dream Team were Michael Jordan, Magic Johnson, Larry Bird, David Robinson, and Patrick Ewing.

40. The United States women's basketball team won every gold medal between 1984 and 2016.

41. More than 600 athletes are expected to compete for the U.S. at the 2021 Summer Games in Tokyo.

42. Tarzan competed in the Olympics: Johnny Weissmuller, an athlete-turned-actor who played Tarzan in 12 movies, won five gold medals in swimming in the 1920s.

43. Twenty of Team USA's athletes at the 2018 Winter Games were dads.

44. One athlete was a mom.

45. That mom was cross-country skier Kikkan Randall.

46. 76 percent of the 2018 Olympic team had attended college.

47. At the 2018 Games, Maame Biney became the first Black woman on Team USA to compete in short-track speed skating.

48. In 2018, Erin Jackson became the first Black woman on Team USA to compete in Olympic long-track speed skating. She qualified after just four months of training.

49. 140 members of the 2018 Team USA were competing in their first Olympics.

50. Thirty-six members of the team had family members who also competed in the Olympics.

277

75 SUPER SPORTS CHAMPIONSHIP FACTS

1. The first major league baseball World Series was played between the Pittsburgh Pirates and the Boston Americans in 1903.

2. That contest was a nine-game series, not the seven games played today.

3. Nine-game series were also played from 1919 to 1921.

4. Boston won the first World Series, five games to three.

5. There have been 116 World Series as of 2020.

6. The American League has won 66, and the National League has won 50.

7. The New York Yankees have won the most World Series titles with 27.

8. The St. Louis Cardinals are a distant second with 11 wins.

9. The 2016 World Series featured the Chicago Cubs and the Cleveland Indians, the two teams with the longest championship gap in history.

10. The Cubs hadn't won the Series since 1908, and the Indians hadn't won since 1948.

11. The Cubs won the 2016 World Series.

12. Some fans blame the Cubs failure to win a World Series in so long on a curse placed on the team by William Sianis before Game 4 of the 1945 World Series at Wrigley Field, when Sianis's pet goat was not allowed entry.

13. In 1904, the National League champions, the New York Giants, refused to play against the American League champs, the Boston Americans, because the Giants' manager didn't like the American League president. So there was no World Series that year.

14. There was no World Series in 1994 because the players were on strike.

15. The longest World Series game in both time and innings was Game 3 of the 2018 matchup between the Boston Red Sox and the Los Angeles Dodgers. The Dodgers won 3–2 after 7 hours, 20 minutes and 18 innings.

16. As of 2020, six teams have never won a World Series.

17. Those teams are the Tampa Bay Rays, the Colorado Rockies, the Seattle Mariners, the Texas Rangers, the Milwaukee Brewers, and the San Diego Padres.

18. The Seattle Mariners have never even appeared in a World Series.

19. The Yankees have won back-to-back World Series six times, more than any other team.

20. The team that wins the World Series receives the Commissioner's Trophy, which is made of sterling silver and features flags of all the major-league teams.

21. Don Larsen pitched the only perfect game in World Series history in 1956.

22. In 1919, the Cincinnati Reds beat the Chicago White Sox in the Series. A year later, eight White Sox players were accused of accepting money from gamblers to lose on purpose. The story became known as the Black Sox Scandal.

23. The players in the Black Sox Scandal were found not guilty but banned from pro baseball for life.

24. The first Super Bowl was played on January 15, 1967.

25. The game was originally called the AFL-NFL Championship Game.

26. The Green Bay Packers defeated the Kansas City Chiefs 35–10 in that first game.

27. The name "Super Bowl" was first used in 1969.

28. Using Roman numerals to number the Super Bowls also began in 1969.

29. As of 2021, the Pittsburgh Steelers and the New England Patriots are tied for the most Super Bowl wins with six each.

30. As of 2021, the New England Patriots and the Denver Broncos have the most Super Bowl losses, with five each.

31. Miami has hosted the Super Bowl 11 times as of 2021, more than any other city.

32. 2017's Super Bowl LI was the only game to go into overtime, with the New England Patriots beating the Atlanta Falcons.

33. Peyton Manning and Tom Brady are the only quarterbacks to win Super Bowls with two different teams.

34. Tom Brady has won seven Super Bowls, more than any other quarterback.

35. Brady was also the oldest quarterback to win a Super Bowl. He was 41 when he won the 2021 contest.

36. In 1980, the Pittsburgh Steelers became the first Super Bowl winners to visit the White House.

37. Five Hall of Fame quarterbacks from western Pennsylvania have played in the Super Bowl.

38. Those five are Johnny Unitas, Joe Namath, Joe Montana, Dan Marino, and Jim Kelly.

39. In odd-numbered Super Bowls, the NFC team is the "home" team. AFC teams are the "home" team at even-numbered Super Bowls.

40. Although the Baltimore Colts beat the Dallas Cowboys in Super Bowl V in 1971, Cowboys linebacker Chuck Howley was named the game's MVP. He's the only player to earn the honor as a member of the losing team.

41. A power outage at New Orleans's Superdome stopped 2013's Super Bowl XLVII for 34 minutes.

42. There has never been a shutout in the Super Bowl.

43. The Miami Dolphins hold the record for fewest points scored in a Super Bowl. In 1972, they lost to Dallas, 24–3.

44. The Cleveland Browns, Detroit Lions, Houston Texans, and Jacksonville Jaguars have never played in the Super Bowl.

45. From 1985 to 1997, the NFC team won 13 straight Super Bowls.

46. The Packers, Dolphins, 49ers, Cowboys, Broncos, Patriots, and Steelers have all won back-to-back Super Bowls.

47. Pittsburgh is the only team to have won back-to-back Super Bowls on two separate occasions.

48. Joe Montana not only won all four of his Super Bowl appearances, he did it without throwing a single interception in any of the games.

49. In 1973, the Miami Dolphins won every regular-season game and the Super Bowl. They are the only team to ever have a perfect record.

50. The Chicago Bulls won all six NBA Finals in which they appeared.

51. The Boston Celtics have won the most NBA championships, with 17 wins.

52. The Celtics won seven straight titles between 1960 and 1966.

53. Magic Johnson averaged 12+ assists per game in the NBA Finals six times. No other player has accomplished that even once.

54. Elgin Baylor scored an NBA Finals-record 61 points over the Boston Celtics in Game 5 in 1962.

55. Baylor also holds the record for the most NBA Finals appearances without a title, appearing in eight Finals without winning any of them.

56. Darko Milicic is the youngest player to win an NBA championship. He was just 18 years and 361 days old when he won an NBA title with the Detroit Pistons in 2004.

57. Robert Parish is the oldest player to win an NBA title. He was 43 years old when he won with the Chicago Bulls in 1997.

58. During the 2016 NBA Finals, LeBron James led all players on both teams in points, rebounds, assists, steals, and blocks in series. He is the only player in NBA history to lead all five categories for an entire playoff series.

59. Robert Horry is the only player in NBA history to win multiple championships with three different teams. He won two with the Houston Rockets, three with the Los Angeles Lakers, and two with the San Antonio Spurs.

60. Michael Jordan scored at least 20 points in every Finals game in which he played, a total of 35 games.

61. Every member of the team that wins the NHL's Stanley Cup gets the cup for one day to do whatever he likes with it.

62. Many players have eaten food out of the Cup, including cereal, meatballs, and ice cream.

63. The U.S. has won more Women's World Cup soccer titles than any other country.

64. But the U.S. men have never won a World Cup soccer title.

65. The "500" in Indy 500 stands for 500 miles (805 km), the length of the race.

66. It takes 200 laps to complete the Indy 500.

67. The first Indy 500 took place in 1911.

68. The first Indy 500 winner, Ray Harroun, drove at an average speed under 75 miles (121 km) per hour.

69. Today's Indy winners average between 140 miles (225 km) and 186 miles (299 km) per hour.

70. The first Masters golf championship was played in 1934.

71. Today, Masters winners receive more than $2 million, a gold coin, a trophy, and a coveted green jacket.

72. Masters winners only keep the green jacket for one year.

73. The U.S. Open is the last tennis Grand Slam tournament of the year.

74. Althea Gibson, one of the first Black tennis players, won the U.S. Open in back-to-back years, 1957 and 1958.

75. When Arthur Ashe won the 1968 U.S. Open, he was the first Black man to win a Grand Slam event.

55 CHAMPION COLLEGE SPORTS FACTS

1. More college baseball players go pro than players of any other sport.

2. A 2008 study of 400,000 college students who participated in athletics showed that only 1 of every 25 of those students went on to compete professionally.

3. The NCAA reported that 10.5 percent of baseball players will go from college to pro.

4. 4.1 percent of ice hockey players and 2 percent of football players turn pro.

5. Men's soccer and women's basketball have the lowest percentage of playing at a professional level after college.

6. In the 2017–18 academic year, a record 494,992 students competed in NCAA sports in the United States.

7. Male NCAA athletes made up approximately 56 percent of the athlete population.

8. 278,614 male athletes competed in 2018.

9. 216,378 female athletes competed in 2018.

10. In 2020, 61.3 percent of male college student athletes in United States were white, and 18 percent were Black.

11. For women, those numbers were 70 percent white and 9.2 percent Black.

12. Football was a major sport on a college level long before the NFL.

13. For many years, there was no college football championship game. Instead, polls declared a champion.

14. Kentucky is the all-time winningest NCAA men's basketball team, with a 2,318–712 win-loss record.

15. The National Invitation Tournament (NIT) is the oldest U.S. basketball tournament. It was first played in 1938.

16. The Temple Owls won the first NIT, beating the Colorado Buffaloes 60–36.

17. Only six teams played in the first NIT.

18. The first NCAA basketball tournament was played in 1939.

19. Pete Maravich of LSU holds the records for most points in a season and most points in a college career.

20. Maravich scored 3,667 points between 1968 and 1970.

21. Mike Krzyzewski coached Duke to a record 97 tournament wins and five NCAA titles between 1984 and 2021.

22. Kelsey Plum of the University of Washington holds the record for the most points in an NCAA Division I women's basketball season with 1,109 points.

23. Plum also holds the record for most career points with 3,527 points scored between 2014 and 2017.

24. USC has won the College World Series a record 12 times.

25. UCLA has won the NCAA softball title a record 12 times.

26. The University of Oklahoma has the longest winning streak in college football. They won 47 games in a row from 1953 to 1957.

27. Future NFL star Drew Brees holds the record for the most attempted passes in a college football game (83).

28. The maximum number of overtimes in a college football game is seven.

29. A seven-overtime game happened twice. Each game was played in 2001 and each time, the Arkansas Razorbacks was one of the teams.

30. In 1976, Ove Johannson of Abilene Christian kicked a 69-yard field goal, the longest on NCAA record books.

31. In 2014, Florida State scored a record 723 points in its football season.

32. The Heisman Trophy is given to college football's most outstanding player.

33. Notre Dame, Ohio State, and Oklahoma have each produced seven Heisman Trophy winners.

34. Archie Griffin of Ohio State is the only person to win the Heisman Trophy twice.

35. 115,109 fans attended the 2013 Michigan-Notre Dame game, setting the all-time attendance record for a college football game.

36. The bulldog and the eagle are tied as the most common mascots in college football. Fifteen Division I schools have one of these mascots.

37. The most lopsided game in college football history occurred in 1916 when Georgia Tech beat Cumberland 222–0.

38. The Rose Bowl is the oldest college football bowl game. It was first played in 1902.

39. UCLA has won the most NCAA basketball tournaments.

40. North Carolina has made the most Final Four appearances.

41. 2008 is the only year all four Number 1 seeds made it to the NCAA Final Four.

42. The first College World Series was played in Kalamazoo, Michigan, in 1947.

43. In 1950, the College World Series moved to Omaha, Nebraska, where it is still played today.

44. Future president George H.W. Bush was the captain of the Yale team that played in the 1949 College World Series.

45. The first College World Series featured only eight teams.

46. Today's College World Series includes 64 teams.

47. The first NCAA men's hockey championships was played in 1948.

48. The University of Michigan holds the record of most NCAA men's hockey championships with nine wins.

49. The first NCAA women's hockey championships weren't played until 2001.

50. The University of Minnesota has won six women's hockey titles, including the two highest-scoring title games in the history of the sport.

Five Winningest NCAA Colleges

School	Championships
1. Stanford	123 titles in 20 sports
2. UCLA	118 titles in 20 sports
3. Southern California	107 titles in 17 sports
4. Oklahoma State	52 titles in 5 sports
5. Penn State	51 titles in 10 sports

Captain of championship college baseball team, while completing college in 2½ years after war service. Phi Beta Kappa— Economics

20 STRIKING FACTS ABOUT YOUTH SPORTS

1. About 35 million boys and girls play organized youth sports each season.

2. Up to 70 percent of players stop playing youth sports after the age of 13.

3. About 85 percent of coaches are parents coaching their own kids' teams.

4. Soccer is the fastest-growing youth sport.

5. Concern about concussions and long-term damage has reduced the number of children playing tackle football.

6. In 2014, Mo'ne Davis was the first female pitcher to win a Little League World Series game.

7. Davis was also the first girl to pitch a shutout in post-season Little League play.

8. Major youth sports organizations include Little League Baseball and Softball, Pop Warner Football, CYO Basketball, American Youth Soccer, and Girls on the Run.

9. Many youth sports were canceled in 2020 because of the COVID-19 pandemic.

10. More kids living in suburbs play youth sports than children in cities or rural communities.

TOP 10 YOUTH SPORTS IN THE U.S.

1. Basketball
2. Soccer (outdoor)
3. Baseball
4. Football (tackle)
5. Gymnastics
6. Volleyball
7. Track and Field
8. Soccer (indoor)
9. Football (touch)
10. Softball

535
INCREDIBLE
FINAL FACTS

25 MEGA FACTS ABOUT DINOSAURS

1. More dinosaurs have been found in the United States than in any other country.

2. The first discovery of dinosaur remains in North America was made in 1854 by Ferdinand Vandiveer Hayden in the upper Missouri River.

3. Hayden discovered a collection of dinosaur teeth.

4. In 1856, William Parker Foulke discovered the first reasonably complete dinosaur skeleton, *Hadrosaurus foulkii*.

5. Hadrosaurus was found in a sand pit in Haddonfield, New Jersey.

6. For many years, Hadrosaurus was the only dinosaur on public display. Copies of the skeleton were made for other museums in the United States and Europe.

7. Hadrosaurus fossils have also been found in Minnesota, Missouri, Montana, Oregon, and California.

8. Dinosaur skeletons were found for the first time in large numbers in the Garden Park area of Colorado and Como Bluff, Wyoming, in the late 1870s.

9. Paleontologists rushed to discover dinosaur fossils in Colorado and Wyoming, setting off a fierce and bitter rivalry.

10. The Dinosaur Trail is a series of preserved dinosaur footprints in Colorado.

11. A T. Rex named Sue is the largest and most complete T. Rex skeleton every found.

12. You can visit Sue at Chicago's Field Museum.

13. The first stegosaurus skeleton was found in Colorado.

14. Dinosaur fossils have been found in 35 of the 50 U.S. states.

15. Massachusetts and Connecticut are the only states in New England where dinosaur fossils have been found.

16. Nevada is the only Western mountainous state that does not have any dinosaur fossils.

17. A new species of the meat-eating dinosaur Allosaurus was discovered in Utah in 1996.

18. That new species went on display at Utah's Natural History Museum in 2020.

19. Kentucky, Iowa, Minnesota, New Hampshire, Rhode Island, Vermont, and Wisconsin have no dinosaur fossils.

20. Scientists believe that because those states were mostly below sea level during the time dinosaurs roamed the Earth, there was little soil to preserve fossils.

Top 5 States Where Dinosaur Fossils Have Been Found

1. California
2. Wyoming
3. Montana
4. New Mexico
5. Utah

287

30 AMAZING HISTORICAL WOMEN

1. **Jane Addams:** Addams founded Hull House to provide job training, education, and opportunities for America's newest arrivals.

2. **Susan B. Anthony:** One of the most important leaders of the women's suffrage movement, Anthony fought to give women the right to vote.

3. **Alice Ball:** This young Black scientist discovered a treatment for leprosy, but was not given credit for many years.

4. **Clara Barton:** Barton founded the American Red Cross and cared for wounded troops during the Civil War.

5. **Nellie Bly:** A reporter who would do anything to track a story, Bly became famous for her investigative reporting and amazing adventures.

6. **Margaret Bourke-White:** Bourke-White's searing photos of families during the Great Depression and the Dust Bowl captured a moment in time.

7. **Amelia Earhart:** The first woman to fly solo across the Atlantic Ocean, Earhart became one of history's greatest mysteries when she disappeared in 1937.

8. **Gertrude Elion:** Elion won a Nobel Prize for her work in developing drugs used to treat leukemia, organ transplants, and AIDS.

9. **Louise Erdrich:** This Chippewa author's work explores Native American culture and traditions.

10. **Zora Neale Hurston:** This writer of the Harlem Renaissance explored Black storytelling and inspired future generations of authors.

11. **Jovita Idar:** A journalist and activist, Idar campaigned for fair treatment of Mexican Americans.

12. **Laura Cornelius Kellogg:** An Oneida activist and author, Kellogg fought the destruction of Native American culture and was a founding member of the Society of American Indians.

13. **Harper Lee:** Lee's classic novel *To Kill a Mockingbird* explores segregation and racial tension in the deep South.

14. **Barbara McClintock:** McClintock's work with the genetics of corn led to important discoveries about DNA.

15. **Patsy Mink:** The first woman of color to serve in Congress, Mink was also a lawyer and activist.

16. **Toni Morrison:** Morrison won the Nobel Prize for Literature in 1993 for work exploring memorable Black characters and themes.

17. Sandra Day O'Connor: The first female Supreme Court justice, O'Connor served on the highest court in the U.S. for 25 years.

18. Georgia O'Keeffe: Known for her paintings of flowers and the desert, O'Keeffe was one of the most influential modern artists.

19. Rosa Parks: When Parks refused to give up her seat on a segregated bus, she kick-started a major milestone in the civil-rights movement.

20. Sally Ride: Ride became the first U.S. woman in space in 1983.

21. Eleanor Roosevelt: As first lady, Roosevelt became a tireless crusader for the poor at the height of the Great Depression.

22. Vera Rubin: This American astronomer discovered dark matter, which makes up 84 percent of the universe.

23. Sacagawea: This Shoshone woman explorer guided Lewis and Clark's "Corps of Discovery" during their exploration of the Louisiana Purchase territory.

24. Margaret Chase Smith: This Maine politician was the first woman to serve in both chambers of Congress.

25. Helen Taussig: Taussig pioneered an operation that saved thousands of babies with heart problems.

26. Marie Tharp: Tharp created a map of the ocean floors and discovered important clues about continental drift.

27. Alma Thomas: The first Black woman artist to hold a solo exhibit at the Whitney Museum, Thomas's brightly colored paintings became a beacon during the civil rights movement.

28. Sojourner Truth: An abolitionist and human-rights activist, Truth's powerful "Ain't I a Woman" speech was a highlight of the women's rights movement.

29. Harriet Tubman: Having herself escaped from enslavement, Tubman went back into the South and led hundreds into freedom.

30. Chien-Shiung Wu: A Chinese American scientist, Wu made huge contributions to the study of nuclear and particle physics.

40
COOL FACTS
ABOUT CURRENCY

1. One U.S. bill weighs a gram.

2. 454 U.S. bills weigh a pound.

3. The most counterfeited denomination is the $20 bill.

4. The $100 bill is the second-most counterfeited.

5. The typical lifespan of a $1 bill is just 18 months.

6. Paper money can be exposed to more viruses and bacteria than a toilet seat.

7. Worn-out bills are shredded and recycled as building material.

8. Worn-out coins are melted down and made into new coins.

9. The Massachusetts Bay Colony was the first colony to make coins in 1652.

10. The Department of the Treasury issued the first paper money in the U.S. in 1862.

11. That money came in denominations of one cent, five cents, 25 cents, and 50 cents.

12. The U.S. Secret Service was founded in 1865 to fight counterfeiting, not to protect the president.

13. The Federal Reserve Act of 1913 created 12 Federal Reserve Banks.

14. Those banks are located in Boston, New York City, Philadelphia, Cleveland, Richmond, Atlanta, Chicago, St. Louis, Minneapolis, Kansas City, Dallas, and San Francisco.

15. The letter inside the seal on a bill shows which Federal Reserve banks issued it.

16. Before the Federal Reserve was founded in 1913, each bank made its own money.

17. Mint marks "S," "D," "P," or "W," designate which U.S. Mint produced the coin.

18. U.S. bills contain many features to prevent counterfeiting, including color-changing ink.

19. There are many representations of the number 13 on a dollar bill. These refer to the 13 colonies.

20. It takes 15 years of training for a person to become an engraver, those who illustrate bills.

21. Money engravers illustrate backward. The design is flipped to print bills.

22. Quarters and dimes have ridges because people used to shave off the edges of these coins when they were made of more valuable metals.

23. Coins also have ridges to help the visually impaired identify them.

24. There are 119 ridges on a quarter.

25. It costs two cents to manufacture a penny.

26. It is against the law for a living U.S. president to appear on a coin.

27. In 1909, Abraham Lincoln became the first American pictured on an American coin.

28. In 2021, quarters featuring Black poet Maya Angelou and astronaut Sally Ride were first announced.

29. The largest denomination ever printed in the U.S. was a $100,000 gold certificate.

30. It was issued in 1934 and was only used for transactions between banks.

31. The largest denomination ever circulated was the $10,000 bill.

32. Today, the $100 bill is the highest publicly circulated denomination.

33. U.S. paper money is actually made of cloth: a blend of cotton and linen.

34. Some people once mended torn bills with a needle and thread.

35. The eagle pictured on the American silver dollar was a bird named Peter who lived at the U.S. Mint in Philadelphia from 1830 to 1836.

36. After he died, Peter was preserved and can still be seen at the Mint today.

37. The first chartered bank in the United States was the First Bank of the United States.

38. It was founded by the U.S. Congress in Philadelphia in 1791.

39. The first bank-issued credit card appeared in Brooklyn in 1946.

40. The first credit card that could be used in many different places was the Diners Club card in 1950.

40 SUPER STAMP FACTS

1. Prepaid postage stamps were introduced in 1847.

2. Before that, sometimes the person who received a letter had to pay for it, not the person who sent it.

3. The first U.S. general-issue stamps were a five-cent stamp picturing Benjamin Franklin and a ten-cent stamp picturing President George Washington.

4. In 1940, Booker T. Washington became the first Black man to appear on a U.S. stamp.

5. Pocahontas was the first famous Native American person to be portrayed on a stamp, in 1907.

6. In 1903, Admiral David Farragut became the first Hispanic American person on a U.S. stamp.

7. Martha Washington was the first American woman on a U.S. stamp. She received the honor in 1902.

8. The first woman on a U.S. stamp was Queen Isabella of Spain, in 1893.

9. The first commemorative U.S. stamps were issued in 1893 to celebrate the 400th anniversary of Christopher Columbus's voyages to the New World.

10. The Stamp Fulfillment Service facility in Kansas City, Missouri, is located in an underground limestone cave.

11. The facility's year-round temperature and humidity level allow stamps to be maintained in mint condition, and being underground keeps stamps and employees safe from dangerous weather.

12. Self-adhesive stamps were introduced in 1992.

13. By 2005, 98 percent of stamps were self-adhesive.

14. The first Forever Stamp was issued in 2007.

15. That first Forever Stamp featured an image of the Liberty Bell.

16. Forever Stamps do not have a set value and can be used no matter what the current price of stamps is.

17. Some stamps, called semi-postal stamps, are priced higher than standard stamps, with the extra money going to charity.

18. Semi-postal stamps have raised millions of dollars for good causes.

19. The U.S. printed 13.7 billion stamps in 2020.

20. The Postal Service has printed more than 140 stamps honoring different veterans and military history.

21. The most popular U.S. postage stamp ever sold was one of rock singer Elvis Presley, issued in 1993.

22. More than 124 million Elvis Presley stamps have been sold.

23. Americans were asked to vote on what image of Elvis they wanted to appear on the stamp.

24. In 1918 about 100 stamps showing an airplane were accidentally printed upside down. These stamps, called the Inverted Jenny, are very valuable.

25. About 20 million people collect stamps in the United States.

26. People who collect stamps are called philatelists.

27. A set of 10 Marvel character stamps was released in 2006. They are among the bestselling stamps of all time.

28. President Franklin D. Roosevelt was an avid stamp collector.

29. There is usually a ten-year waiting period between when a person dies and when they can appear on a stamp.

30. The main exception to this rule is dead presidents.

31. Stamps commemorating presidents can be released on the president's first birthday following their death.

32. The first animal to appear on a U.S. stamp was a bear.

33. In 1845, the St. Louis Post Office issued a set of stamps featuring two bears.

34. The largest collection of stamps in the United States is housed at the William H. Gross Stamp Gallery in Washington, D.C.

35. In the United States, stamps are placed in the upper-right corner of the envelope.

36. This rule started in the 1890s after machines began to sort mail.

37. The first perforated stamp issued in the U.S. was printed in 1857.

38. That stamp featured a picture of George Washington and was worth three cents.

39. Before perforations, people had to cut or tear individual stamps from a sheet of paper.

40. The first triangular postage stamp was issued in 1997 and the first round stamp in 2000.

50 AWFUL DISASTER FACTS

1. 1865—*Sultana* Explosion: A ship's boiler exploded, killing 1,800, most of them former Union prisoners returning home after the Civil War.

2. 1871—Great Chicago Fire: A fire that burned for three days killed about 300 people, left more than 100,000 residents homeless, and destroyed much of the city.

3. 1871—Peshtigo Fire: On the same day as the Great Chicago Fire, another fire in Wisconsin killed about 1,200 people and destroyed 1.2 million acres (485,623 ha).

4. 1876—Ashtabula Railroad Disaster: As a train traveled over a bridge over the Ashtabula River in Ohio, the bridge collapsed and the train crashed into the river, killing 98 of the 159 people on board.

5. 1889—Johnstown Flood: Bad construction and heavy rains led to a dam break and a flood that killed more than 2,200 people.

6. 1903 —Iroquois Theatre Fire: A fire in a Chicago theater killed 602 people.

7. 1904—*General Slocum* Fire: A ship carrying people on a fun day trip caught fire and sank in New York City's East River, killing 1,021 people. It was the city's worst disaster until the terrorist attacks of September 11 almost 100 years later.

8. 1906—San Francisco Earthquake: A massive quake followed by a huge fire killed at least 3,000 people and left 200,000 homeless.

9. 1911—Triangle Shirtwaist Factory Fire: A fire in a factory killed 146 workers, who were mostly young women. The tragedy led to labor reforms.

10. 1918—Great Train Wreck: Two trains collided head-on at high speed in Nashville, killing 101 people, because one of the trains failed to pull onto a siding to let the other train pass.

11. 1918—Cloquet Fire: A fire that started when sparks from a train ignited scrap wood wiped out 40 towns, destroyed 4,000 houses, and killed more than 450 people in Minnesota.

12. 1918—Malbone Street Wreck: A train speeding through a tunnel in New York City took a curve at a high speed, causing the train to derail and killing almost 100 people.

13. 1919—Boston Molasses Flood: A storage tank burst and flooded the city with a 40-foot (12-m) wave of sticky molasses. Twenty-one people died.

14. 1928—St. Francis Dam Collapse: A poorly built dam in California collapsed, killing between 400 and 600 people.

15. 1933—Long Beach Earthquake: A magnitude 6.3 quake killed 115 people and led to rules for building safer schools and other public buildings.

16. 1934—*Morro Castle* Fire: This ship caught fire at sea and ran aground near Asbury Park, NJ. The crew abandoned ship, leaving 135 passengers to die.

17. 1937—*Hindenburg* Explosion: The German airship caught fire while landing at Lakehurst, NJ, killing 36 people.

18. 1937—New London, TX, School Explosion: A gas explosion at a school killed more than 295 people.

19. 1942—Cocoanut Grove Fire: A fire at a crowded Boston nightclub killed 492 people who were trapped inside.

20. 1944—Hartford Circus Fire: During a performance in Hartford, CT, a circus tent caught fire, killing 167 people.

21. 1944—Port Chicago Explosion. A munitions explosion at a naval facility in Los Angeles killed 320 soldiers and sailors, most of whom were Black, and injured 390 more.

22. 1944—Cleveland Gas Explosions: A pair of explosions caused by a leaking storage tank of gas killed 130 people, destroyed 79 homes, and more than 200 vehicles.

23. 1947—Texas City Disaster: A fire onboard a ship carrying chemicals set off a chain reaction of fires and explosions that killed at least 581 people in America's worst industrial accident.

24. 1956—Grand Canyon Midair Collision: Two commercial planes collided over the Grand Canyon, killing 128 people and leading to new laws to make air travel safer.

25. 1958—Our Lady of the Angels Fire: A fire at a Catholic school in Chicago killed 92 children and three nuns.

26. 1960—Park Slope/Miller Field Plane Crash: 128 people on the planes and six on the ground were killed when two planes collided over New York City.

27. 1963—*Thresher* Submarine Sinking: A U.S. nuclear submarine sank off the coast of Massachusetts during diving tests, killing all 129 sailors on board.

28. 1971—Alaska Airlines Flight 1866: Navigational errors led the pilots of this flight to crash into a mountain near Juneau, Alaska, killing all 111 people on board.

29. 1975—Wreck of the *Edmund Fitzgerald*: All 29 crew members died when this cargo ship sank during a storm on Lake Superior. The wreck later became the subject of a popular song.

30. 1975—Eastern Airlines Flight 76: Despite a bad storm, Flight 76 was cleared to land at New York's La Guardia Airport. The plane crashed, killing 113 people.

31. 1976—*MV George Prince* Ferry Disaster: A ferry filled with workmen cut in front of a tanker on the Mississippi River outside St. Charles Parish, Louisiana. 78 of the 96 people on board the ferry were killed.

32. 1978—PSA Flight 182: 144 people were killed when a private plane and a commercial jet collided over San Diego, California.

33. 1979—American Airlines Flight 191 Crash: This plane crashed right after takeoff when one of its engines fell off, killing 273 people.

34. 1981—Hyatt Regency Walkway Collapse: Two walkways collapsed and crashed into a hotel lobby, where a dance was being held, killing 114 people.

35. 1982—Pan Am Flight 759 Crash: A thunderstorm caused this Pan Am flight to crash just outside of New Orleans, killing 153 people.

36. 1985—Delta Airlines Flight 191: High storm winds were blamed for the crash of this plane at Dallas-Fort Worth airport, killing 137 people.

37. 1986—*Challenger* Explosion: The space shuttle exploded 73 seconds after takeoff, killing all seven astronauts on board, including teacher Christa McAuliffe.

38. 1987—Northwest Airlines Flight 255 Crash: A four-year-old child was the only survivor when this plane crashed shortly after taking off from Detroit, killing 156 people.

39. 1988—Yellowstone Fires: A series of forest fires burned 36 percent of the National Park, making it the largest fire in Yellowstone's history.

40. 1989—*Exxon Valdez* Oil Spill: A massive oil spill in Alaska's Prince William Sound killed hundreds of thousands of birds and other animals and contaminated 1,300 miles (2,100 km) of coastline.

41. 1991—Oakland Hills Fire: In just two days, this firestorm burned 3,000 homes and apartment buildings and killed 25 people.

42. 1993—Amtrak Train 2 Crash: Traveling through fog, this train derailed in a swamp because of a damaged bridge, killing 47 people and injuring 103.

43. 1996—ValuJet Flight 592: Improperly stored cargo caused this plane to crash into the Florida Everglades, killing all 110 people on board.

44. 1996—TWA Flight 800 Explosion: 230 people died when the jet exploded over the Atlantic Ocean, shortly after taking off from New York.

45. 2001—American Airlines Flight 587 Crash: Just two months after the September 11 terror attacks, Flight 587 crashed into a residential neighborhood in New York City, killing all 260 on board and five people on the ground.

46. 2003—*Columbia* Destruction: The space shuttle broke apart during re-entry because of damaged heat tiles, killing all seven crew members.

47. 2008—Metrolink Train Crash: A commuter train struck a freight train on a sharp curve in Chatsworth, California, killing 25 people in one of the worst train crashes in California history.

48. 2010—*Deepwater Horizon* Oil Spill: The largest marine oil spill occurred in the Gulf of Mexico when a rig exploded, releasing almost 210 million gallons (795 million liters) of oil into the water.

49. 2013—Yarnell Hill Fire: A wildfire in Arizona killed 19 firefighters, making it the deadliest blaze in Arizona's history.

50. 2018—Camp Fire: Coming after years of drought, California's deadliest wildfire to date killed at least 85 people and destroyed 19,000 homes.

25 POPULAR PET FACTS

1. 38 percent of American households have at least one dog.

2. 25 percent have at least one cat.

3. Fish are the most popular exotic pet in the U.S.

4. Reptiles are the second-most-popular exotic pet.

5. 94 percent of pet owners say their pet makes them smile at least once a day.

6. Every dog has a unique nose print.

7. 9 percent of dog owners have birthday parties for their pet.

8. Cats have no collarbone, which is one reason why they are so flexible.

9. Cats have four rows of whiskers.

10. A cat's whiskers are sensitive to air currents.

11. Many Americans get their pet dogs and cats from shelters or rescue groups.

12. Less than 10 percent of small mammals are adopted from shelters.

13. Almost all small animals are bought from pet stores.

14. Spaying and neutering your pet is the best way to reduce overpopulation.

15. California has the largest number of pets.

Total Number of Pets in the U.S.

1.	Dogs	76.8 million
2.	Fish	76.3 million
3.	Cats	58.4 million
4.	Poultry	15.3 million
5.	Birds	7.5 million

Number of U.S. Households That Own a Pet

1.	Dogs	48.2 million
2.	Cats	31.9 million
3.	Fish	10.5 million
4.	Reptiles	3.7 million
5.	Birds	3.5 million

40 FACTS ABOUT THE FLAG

1. There have been 27 versions of the American flag.

2. The first flag had 13 stripes and 13 stars to represent the 13 colonies.

3. Each time a state was added to the nation, a star was added to the flag.

4. New stars were traditionally added on the July 4 after a new state was admitted.

5. The official names of the colors of the flag are Old Glory Red, Old Glory White, and Old Glory Blue.

6. An executive order in 1912 specified the order of the stars on the flag.

7. Before 1912, flags often showed odd arrangements of stars.

8. Between 1795 and 1818, the flag had 15 stripes for the 15 states that were part of the Union.

9. The 50-star flag design was chosen in a contest.

10. Seventeen-year-old Robert Heft submitted the winning design in 1958.

11. Heft's design was chosen out of 1,500 entries.

12. Heft created the flag as part of an art class assignment, and only received a grade of B-minus.

13. The 50-star flag is the longest-running design, since no new states have been admitted since 1959.

14. The flag that flew at Fort McHenry and inspired "The Star-Spangled Banner" is on display at Smithsonian's National Museum of American History.

15. A piece of the Fort McHenry flag sold at an auction in 2011 for $38,000.

16. The flag has its own holiday.

17. Flag Day celebrates the anniversary of the Flag Resolution of 1777.

18. In 1885, a Wisconsin teacher named Bernard Cigrand held what is believed to be the first recognized Flag Day.

19. Flag Day was established by President Woodrow Wilson in 1916.

20. Flag Day is celebrated on June 14, thanks to an Act of Congress signed by President Harry Truman in 1949.

21. Flag Day is not a federal holiday, and it is a state holiday only in Pennsylvania.

22. In 1969, Neil Armstrong placed a U.S. flag on the moon.

23. Five more American flags have gone to the moon.

24. The U.S. Flag Code created rules for how the flag should be treated and displayed.

25. One of the rules is that damaged flags should not be thrown away. They have to be burned in a respectful manner.

26. Some organizations and communities collect flags to be burned in ceremonies.

27. The code also says that the flag should not be used in advertising.

28. The flag should not be displayed at night unless it is properly lit.

29. The flag's "Old Glory" nickname comes from sea captain William Driver.

30. Driver named the flag on his ship "Old Glory" in 1831.

31. Despite the legend, Betsy Ross probably did not sew the first U.S. flag.

32. That legend started when Ross's grandson made the claim in 1870, but it has never been proven by historians.

33. During the 19th century, politicians tried to restrict using the flag's image for commercial purposes.

Seven Historic Places Where the Flag is Displayed 24/7

1. Fort McHenry, Baltimore, Maryland

2. Flag House Square, Baltimore, Maryland

3. U.S. Marine Corps Memorial, Arlington, Virginia

4. The Green of the Town of Lexington, Massachusetts

5. The White House, Washington, D.C.

6. U.S. Customs ports of entry

7. National Memorial Arch, Valley Forge State Park, Pennsylvania

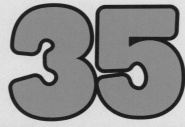

NECESSARY NATURAL RESOURCES FACTS

1. Many natural resources are mined to make energy, like coal, natural gas, and oil.

2. Other resources are used for manufacturing and construction, like timber and minerals.

3. The U.S. has the largest coal reserves in the world, about 491 billion tons.

4. Wind and solar resources are harder to measure but can still be used for energy.

5. The value of natural resources in the United States is about $45 trillion.

6. Mining and logging in order to get to resources can be dangerous.

7. Water is not only an important resource for drinking and irrigation, it also provides an easy way to transport goods.

8. Water can also be used to create power.

9. Hydroelectric plants harness the force of moving water to create electricity.

10. Grand Coulee Dam in Washington is the largest hydroelectric dam in the U.S.

11. Washington, California, Oregon, and New York create the most hydroelectric power.

12. Coal helped the U.S. become powerful during the Industrial Revolution.

13. Although its use has declined, coal still fuels some U.S. power plants today.

14. The first oil company in the U.S. was founded to remove oil floating in water in Titusville, Pennsylvania.

15. On August 21, 1859, William Smith struck oil in Titusville. This was the first time a drill was used to tap oil at its source.

16. Oil was once easily available on the West Coast, which helped the U.S. Navy fuel ships during wartime.

17. Edward L. Doheny drilled Los Angeles's first oil well in 1892.

18. By 1897, there were 2,500 wells and 200 oil companies in the Los Angeles area.

19. During the 1920s, hundreds of oil rigs crowded the beaches in California.

20. In the 1920s, the U.S. supplied two-thirds of the world's oil.

21. The United States is the world's largest producer of helium.

22. Small amounts of helium are recovered during natural gas production.

23. Since 1960, the U.S. government has stored the nation's supply of helium in the Bush Dome Reservoir in Amarillo, Texas.

24. Bauxite is an important ore that is used to create aluminum.

25. Copper is used to make pipes and electric cables.

10 Natural Resources Found in the U.S.

1. Water
2. Soil
3. Timber
4. Oil
5. Natural gas
6. Coal
7. Iron
8. Bauxite
9. Copper
10. Helium

100 U.S. POPULATION FACTS

Here are the 50 U.S. states in order of population as of April 2020:

#	State	Population	#	State	Population
1.	California	39.53 million	26.	Kentucky	4.50 million
2.	Texas	29.14 million	27.	Oregon	4.23 million
3.	Florida	21.53 million	28.	Oklahoma	3.95 million
4.	New York	20.20 million	29.	Connecticut	3.60 million
5.	Pennsylvania	13.00 million	30.	Iowa	3.19 million
6.	Illinois	12.81 million	31.	Utah	3.27 million
7.	Ohio	11.79 million	32.	Nevada	3.10 million
8.	Georgia	10.71 million	33.	Arkansas	3.01 million
9.	North Carolina	10.43 million	34.	Mississippi	2.96 million
10.	Michigan	10.07 million	35.	Kansas	2.93 million
11.	New Jersey	9.28 million	36.	New Mexico	2.11 million
12.	Virginia	8.63 million	37.	Nebraska	1.96 million
13.	Washington	7.70 million	38.	Idaho	1.83 million
14.	Arizona	7.15 million	39.	West Virginia	1.79 million
15.	Massachusetts	7.02 million	40.	Hawaii	1.45 million
16.	Tennessee	6.91 million	41.	New Hampshire	1.37 million
17.	Indiana	6.78 million	42.	Maine	1.36 million
18.	Maryland	6.17 million	43.	Rhode Island	1.09 million
19.	Missouri	6.15 million	44.	Montana	1.08 million
20.	Wisconsin	5.89 million	45.	Delaware	989,948
21.	Colorado	5.77 million	46.	South Dakota	886,667
22.	Minnesota	5.70 million	47.	North Dakota	779,094
23.	South Carolina	5.11 million	48.	Alaska	733,391
24.	Alabama	5.02 million	49.	Vermont	643,077
25.	Louisiana	4.65 million	50.	Wyoming	576,851

Population density of U.S. states in 2020
(number of people per square mile)

#	State	Density	#	State	Density
1.	New Jersey	1,263.0	26.	Louisiana	107.8
2.	Rhode Island	1,061.4	27.	Alabama	99.2
3.	Massachusetts	901.2	28.	Missouri	89.5
4.	Connecticut	744.7	29.	West Virginia	74.6
5.	Maryland	636.1	30.	Minnesota	71.7
6.	Delaware	508.0	31.	Vermont	69.8
7.	New York	428.7	32.	Mississippi	63.1
8.	Florida	401.4	33.	Arizona	62.9
9.	Pennsylvania	290.6	34.	Arkansas	57.9
10.	Ohio	288.8	35.	Oklahoma	57.7
11.	California	253.7	36.	Iowa	57.1
12.	Illinois	230.8	37.	Colorado	55.7
13.	Hawaii	226.6	38.	Maine	44.2
14.	Virginia	218.6	39.	Oregon	44.1
15.	North Carolina	214.7	40.	Utah	39.7
16.	Indiana	189.4	41.	Kansas	35.9
17.	Georgia	185.6	42.	Nevada	28.3
18.	Michigan	178.0	43.	Nebraska	25.5
19.	South Carolina	170.2	44.	Idaho	22.3
20.	Tennessee	167.6	45.	New Mexico	17.5
21.	New Hampshire	153.8	46.	South Dakota	11.7
22.	Washington	115.9	47.	North Dakota	11.3
23.	Kentucky	114.1	48.	Montana	7.4
24.	Texas	111.6	49.	Wyoming	5.9
25.	Wisconsin	108.8	50.	Alaska	1.3

50 WILD FACTS ABOUT WEATHER AND STORMS

1. In the U.S., lightning strikes the ground 25 million times a year.

2. The largest hailstone in the U.S. was the size of a volleyball.

3. Baseball-sized hail can hit the ground at 100 miles (161 km) per hour.

4. In 1995, a hailstorm in Fort Worth, Texas, buried roads under two feet of hail.

5. The deadliest winter storm in the U.S. was the "Blizzard of '88."

6. From March 11–14, 1888, up to 4 feet (1.2 m) of snow fell in the northeast. More than 400 people died, 200 in New York alone.

7. On March 12, 1993, the "Storm of the Century" paralyzed the eastern half of the United States. The storm included tornadoes, high winds, floods, ice, and heavy snow.

8. The "Children's Blizzard" hit the Great Plains on January 12, 1888, during a school day. 235 people died. 213 of them were children.

9. In 1998, an ice storm in New York and New England damaged millions of trees and caused $1.4 billion in damages.

10. The United States has more tornadoes every year than any other country.

11. The U.S. averages 1,274 tornadoes per year. Most do not do much damage.

12. May is the most active month for tornadoes.

13. The most common region for tornadoes is the Midwest. This area is called Tornado Alley.

14. In 1925, a tornado traveled 218 miles (352 km) across three U.S. states.

15. Texas has the most tornadoes per year.

16. Oklahoma City has been hit by more tornadoes than any other major city.

17. Hurricanes usually strike the southern and eastern coasts of the United States.

18. Florida has the most hurricanes per year.

19. September is the most active month for hurricanes.

20. The largest number of hurricanes active at once is six. This has happened several times.

21. Cape Hatteras has been hit by the most hurricanes.

22. In 2015, a milky rain fell on parts of Washington, Oregon, and Idaho.

23. The strange rain in the Northwest was caused by chemicals in a dust storm.

24. Eight alligators fell from the sky over South Carolina in 1887.

25. In 1932, it was so cold that Niagara Falls froze solid.

26. In 1899, the Mississippi River froze down its entire length and chunks of ice were seen in the Gulf of Mexico.

27. The 1899 cold spell has been called the greatest cold snap in American history.

28. The windiest place in the United States is Mount Washington, New Hampshire, with an average wind speed of 35 miles (56 km) per hour.

29. The least windy city is Oak Ridge, Tennessee, with an average wind speed of 4 miles (6 km) per hour.

30. The U.S. National Weather Service sends up weather balloons from more than 90 weather stations across the country.

31. In the United States, the Citizen Weather Observer Program uses amateur meteorologists with homemade weather stations to provide forecasts.

32. The first weather satellite was launched on April 1, 1960.

33. The heaviest snowfall ever recorded in Los Angeles occurred on January 10–11, 1949, when 0.3 inch (0.8 cm) fell.

34. Scientists used to think no two snowflakes were alike.

35. However, in 1988, a research center identified a set of twin crystals from a Wisconsin storm.

36. An estimated 1.23 inches (3 cm) of rain fell in just one minute on July 4, 1956, in Unionville, Maryland.

37. In 1925, the "Tri-State Tornado" traveled 219 miles (352 km) from Ellington, Missouri, to Princeton, Indiana, over 3.5 hours.

38. In April 1991, a tornado carried a personal check for 223 miles (359 km) from Stockton, Kansas, to Winnetoon, Nebraska.

39. Miami, Florida, is the rainiest city in the mainland United States, with an average total of 62 inches (158 cm) per year.

40. Phoenix, Arizona, receives 211 days of sunshine a year.

41. The deadliest storm to strike the United States was the "Great Galveston Hurricane," which hit Galveston, Texas, in 1900.

42. Between 8,000 and 12,000 people died in the Galveston storm and flooding.

43. The deadliest tornado outbreak was the Tri-State Tornado which traveled through Missouri, Illinois, and Indiana in 1925, killing 695 people.

44. The Okeechobee Hurricane hit Florida in 1928, killing between 2,500 and 3,000 people.

45. Hurricane Maria in 2017 destroyed much of Puerto Rico and killed 3,000 to 5,000 people.

46. In July 1995, Chicago was hit by a week-long heat wave that sent temperatures as high as 115 degrees Fahrenheit (46 degrees Celsius). Over 700 people, most of them elderly and poor, died.

47. Four years later, another heat wave in Chicago killed 114 people.

48. Mount Rainier in Washington receives more than 56 feet (17 m) of snow per year.

49. Alta, Utah, is one of the highest towns in the U.S., and it's also one of the snowiest. The town receives more than 48 feet (14.6 m) of snow a year.

50. The last of Alta's snow usually melts by the Fourth of July.

50 FAVORITE FOOD FACTS

1. Ketchup used to be sold to people as medicine.

2. Most major fast-food chains started as local restaurants.

3. McDonald's sells 2.5 billion hamburgers a year.

4. Chipotle once estimated it uses at least 97,000 avocadoes every day.

5. Boston cream pie has been the Massachusetts state dessert since 1996.

6. More than 46 million turkeys are eaten on Thanksgiving.

7. President George H.W. Bush once announced, "I'm President of the United States and I'm not going to eat any more broccoli!"

8. About 3.5 tons of red, white, and blue jelly beans were sent to the White House for President Ronald Reagan's inauguration.

9. Pepperoni is the most popular pizza topping in the U.S.

10. The average American eats 2,000 pounds (907 kg) of food a year.

11. Froot Loops are all the same flavor.

12. The chimichanga was invented in the U.S.

13. The egg roll and fortune cookies were also invented in America.

14. Machine-sliced bread first appeared in 1928.

15. In colonial times, lobster was so cheap, it was fed to people being held in prisons and jails.

16. Raw pistachios can spontaneously catch fire.

17. Astronaut John Young smuggled a corned beef sandwich into space.

18. Ripe cranberries bounce.

19. Bad eggs float.

20. Many packages of shredded cheese contain wood pulp to keep the cheese from sticking together.

21. An ear of corn almost always has an even number of rows. That number is usually 16.

22. One hamburger patty can contain meat from hundreds of cows because of the way meat is processed.

23. The Popsicle was created in 1905 when an 11-year-old boy left a cup of soda and water outside overnight and the mixture froze.

24. There is a famous saying, "as American as apple pie," but apple pie was not invented in America.

25. Bananas and watermelon are technically berries, but strawberries are not.

26. Honey never goes bad.

27. Almost all of the wasabi in the United States isn't wasabi at all. It's horseradish dyed green.

28. Ruth Wakefield invented the chocolate chip cookie in the 1930s at her restaurant, the Toll House Inn in Massachusetts.

29. People in Hawaii eat more Spam than any other state.

30. Thomas Jefferson's cook introduced macaroni and cheese to the U.S.

31. The U.S. government sets limits on the small amounts of insects allowed to be present in packaged foods.

32. Chocolate can have up to 60 insect fragments per 100 grams.

33. Pizza Hut used to be the nation's biggest buyer of kale.

34. All the kale that Pizza Hut was buying wasn't eaten—it was used for decoration on the restaurants' salad bars.

35. 49 percent of American adults eat a sandwich every day.

36. German chocolate cake was invented in Texas, not Germany.

37. In 2015, astronauts ate food grown in space for the first time.

38. Americans eat 500 million pounds (227 million kg) of peanut butter a year.

39. Americans consume about 130 pounds (59 kg) of sugar every year.

40. Coca-Cola was originally sold in drugstores as a medical drink.

Top 5 Fast Food Restaurants in the U.S.

1. McDonald's
2. Starbucks
3. Chick-fil-A
4. Taco Bell
5. Burger King

Top 5 Most Popular Foods in the U.S.

In a 2020 poll, Americans were asked what they would pick if they could only eat one food for the rest of their lives. Here are the results:

1. 21 percent chose pizza
2. 16 percent chose steak
3. 13 percent chose hamburgers
4. 11 percent chose tacos
5. 11 percent chose pasta

50 HOLIDAY FACTS TO CELEBRATE

1. Turkey was not on the menu at the first Thanksgiving.

2. Instead, the Pilgrims and Native Americans probably ate venison, duck, goose, oysters, lobster, eel, fish, pumpkins, and cranberries.

3. The first Thanksgiving celebration lasted for three days.

4. Abraham Lincoln proclaimed Thanksgiving as a national holiday in 1863.

5. Sarah Josepha Hale, who also wrote "Mary Had a Little Lamb," wrote letters to presidents for 17 years to argue for Thanksgiving as a national holiday.

6. The tradition of football on Thanksgiving began with a college game in 1876.

7. The first NFL game on Thanksgiving was played in 1920.

8. The first Macy's Thanksgiving Day Parade did not feature any balloons.

9. In 1924, the Macy's parade featured live animals from the Central Park Zoo.

10. The Rockefeller Center Christmas tree has more than 250,000 lights.

11. Christmas is the biggest commercial holiday.

12. Halloween is the second largest commercial holiday in the United States.

13. In 2018, Americans spent more than $9 billion on Halloween candy, costumes, and decorations.

14. Jack o'lanterns have sometimes been carved out of turnips, potatoes, and beets.

15. When the tradition came to America, people began using pumpkins.

16. New York City throws the biggest Halloween parade every year.

17. Princesses and superheroes are the most popular Halloween costumes.

18. An old superstition says that wearing new clothes on Easter will bring good luck.

19. The idea of an Easter Bunny who gives out candy started in Germany during the Middle Ages.

20. Immigrants brought the Easter Bunny tradition to the United States.

21. Americans eat more than 16 million jellybeans every year.

22. President Ronald Reagan was a famous fan of jellybeans and always kept a stash.

23. Around 90 million chocolate bunnies are sold for Easter.

24. The White House Easter Egg Roll has been celebrated since 1878.

25. The tradition started when some children asked President Rutherford B. Hayes to let them roll eggs on the White House lawn.

26. Irish immigrants began observing St. Patrick's Day in Boston in 1737.

27. The first St. Patrick's Day parade in America was held in New York City in 1766.

28. Chicago dyes the Chicago River green every St. Patrick's Day.

29. The date for Lunar New Year (often celebrated as Chinese New Year) changes every year.

30. It is celebrated during the second new moon after the Winter Solstice and can fall any time between January 21 and February 20.

31. Chinese tradition says that Buddha asked all of the animals to meet him on New Year's Day and named a year after each of the twelve animals that showed up.

32. The animals in the Chinese calendar are the dog, boar, rat, ox, tiger, rabbit, dragon, snake, horse, sheep, monkey, and rooster.

33. Juneteenth, celebrated on June 19, is also known as Freedom Day, Jubilee Day, Liberation Day, and Emancipation Day.

34. Juneteenth marks the day in 1865 that a Union general announced to Texas that all formerly enslaved people were free.

35. Rosh Hashanah is the Jewish New Year celebration, traditionally marked by eating sweet or round foods, such as apples and honey.

36. Yom Kippur, the Jewish Day of Atonement, comes ten days after Rosh Hashanah.

37. Yom Kippur is a solemn day when Jews fast and pray.

38. During Sukkot, some Jewish families eat meals outside in a shelter called a sukkah.

39. The eight-day festival of Hanukkah is also called the Festival of Lights.

40. Fried foods such as potato latkes and jelly doughnuts are traditionally eaten during Hanukkah.

41. Another festival of lights is Diwali, the celebration of "victory of light over darkness, good over evil, and knowledge over ignorance."

42. Diwali is celebrated by Hindus, Sikhs, Jains, and some Buddhists.

43. Passover is a week-long celebration of the deliverance of the Jewish people from slavery in Egypt.

44. Many families have a special meal called a Seder during Passover with traditional foods, prayers, stories, and songs.

45. During the month of Ramadan, many Muslims fast from sunrise to sunset.

46. Eid al-Fitr celebrates the end of Ramadan.

47. The Fourth of July celebrates the signing of the Declaration of Independence.

48. Popular Fourth of July celebrations include fireworks, parades, and barbecues.

49. The tradition of Fourth of July fireworks started in Philadelphia in 1777.

50. On November 11 every year, Veterans Day honors people who served in the military.

index

Note: Page numbers in italics indicate photo or illustration.